DISCONNECTED
deceit and betrayal at
WorldCom

Lynne W. Jeter

WILEY

John Wiley & Sons, Inc.

Published by John Wiley & Sons, Inc., Hoboken, New Jersey.
Published simultaneously in Canada.

For general information on our other products and services, or technical support,
please contact our Customer Care Department within the United States at
800-762-2974, outside the United States at 317-572-3993 or fax 317-572-4002.

Wiley also publishes its books in a variety of electronic formats. Some content that
appears in print may not be available in electronic books. For more information
about Wiley products, visit our Web site at www.wiley.com.

Library of Congress Cataloging-in-Publication Data:

Jeter, Lynne, 1960–
    Disconnected : deceit and betrayal at WorldCom / Lynne Jeter.
        p. cm.
    ISBN 0-471-42997-X (cloth : alk. paper)
    1. WorldCom (Firm)—Corrupt practices.   2. Telecommunication—Corrupt
practices—United States.   3. Business failures—United States.   I.
Title.
    HE7797.W67   2003
    384'.065'73—dc21

                                                                    2002155496

Printed in the United States of America.

10   9   8   7   6   5   4   3   2   1

CONNECTING THE PIPES: A WORLDCOM TIME LINE

1899	Cleyson L. Brown founds Brown Telephone Company, a predecessor of Sprint, in Abilene, Texas.
1941	On August 27, future WorldCom CEO Bernard J. "Bernie" Ebbers is born in Edmonton, Alberta, Canada.
1963	John D. "Jack" Goeken, a General Electric (GE) manufacturer's representative selling two-way radios from Springfield, Illinois, creates Microwave Communications Incorporated to build a communications system for truck drivers and dispatchers along Route 66 between St. Louis and Chicago. Soon after, AT&T, Illinois Bell, Southwestern Bell, General Electric, and Western Union file petitions to shut down the company. Future WorldCom CFO Scott Sullivan prepares for grade school.
1967	Ebbers graduates from Mississippi College with a degree in physical education, moves 55 miles south to Brookhaven, Mississippi, and begins coaching basketball at Hazlehurst High School.

1969	MCI becomes title sponsor of the prestigious PGA tour event Heritage Classic, held annually at the Harbour Town Golf Links in the Sea Pines Resort of Hilton Head Island, South Carolina. Ebbers is now working in distribution for Stahl-Urban Company, a family-owned garment manufacturing plant in Brookhaven.
1972	Brown Telephone Company, now located in Westwood, Kansas, is reorganized as United Telecommunications, another predecessor company of Sprint. By the end of the 1950s, it had become the second-largest non-Bell telephone company in the United States.
1973	Future WorldCom CEO John Sidgmore graduates from the State University of New York (SUNY) at Oneonta and begins selling computers, then known as "bulky, programmable calculators."
1974	In March, Goeken files a lawsuit against AT&T, citing violation of the Sherman Antitrust Act.
1983	In January, Murray Waldron begins selling long-distance service for The Phone Company (TPC) in Jackson, Tennessee, one of hundreds of new start-up long-distance resellers in the United States. On August 5, Judge Harold H. Greene gives the final approval to a consent decree breaking up AT&T, the world's largest corporation. Later that month, after successfully selling long-distance service in three midsize markets, Waldron and fellow Tennessean William "Bear" Rector travel to Hattiesburg, Mississippi, to assess the market potential. Dealmaker Bill Fields of Tupelo, Mississippi, connects Waldron with David Singleton of Brookhaven, Mississippi, who introduces him to hotelier Bernard J. "Bernie" Ebbers. In September, they meet for the first time in a Hattiesburg coffeehouse. On October 12, Ebbers, Murray Waldron, Bill Fields, Carl Aycock, Max Thornhill, Danny Dunnaway, David Singleton, Charles Vickery, and

	Jerry and Margaret Loden divvy up 1,000 shares of Long Distance Discount Services, Inc. (FIN #64-0681440). Future WorldCom CFO Scott Sullivan graduates from the State University of New York (SUNY) at Oswego.
1984	On January 1, Judge Greene's ordered breakup of AT&T's Bell System is effective. On January 14, the switch is flipped and the first LDDS long-distance phone call is made. On May 9, the Mississippi Public Service Commission officially approves LDDS's application to operate as a long distance reseller.
1985	With the long-distance reseller heavily in debt, Ebbers takes over as head of LDDS in April and sets in motion a plan to grow the company by acquisitions. Some of the first purchases are ReTel Communications in Franklin, Tennessee, and TPC in Jackson, Tennessee. Around the same time, Ebbers also shakes up the management team, hiring 24-year-old Chris Eddy to supervise Waldron and others.
1986	Future WorldCom CFO Charles T. Cannada meets Ebbers when Ebbers hires him for accounting work on a personal investment—a pineapple farm in Costa Rica. In June, Eddy lands the University of Southern Mississippi account, the biggest money-maker to date for the company. At year-end, annual revenues total $8.6 million. United Telecommunications launches domestic long-distance service under the Sprint brand name.
1987	LDDS acquires Southland Systems of Mississippi.
1988	LDDS acquires Comlink 21 and Telephone Management Corporation (TMC).
1989	On August 14, LDDS becomes a public company when it acquires Advantage Companies, Inc., whose board chairman is future WorldCom compensation and stock option committee chairman Stiles A. Kellett, Jr. LDDS stock is approximately 84 cents. In

	October, Cannada joins LDDS as CFO. LDDS hires Arthur Andersen as its independent auditor.
1990	Ebbers meets future Salomon Smith Barney telecom analyst Jack B. Grubman.
1991	On January 1, LDDS stock is $1.32. The company acquires National Telecommunications and Mid-American Communications. Customers are billed 3.6 billion minutes and annual revenues top $700 million.
1992	LDDS acquires Prime Telecommunications and TeleMarketing Investments. The company partners with Bell Canada. Ebbers meets Sullivan when LDDS buys Advanced Telecommunications Corporation in December. LDDS reports annual revenues of approximately $948 million.
1993	In March, LDDS acquires Dial-Net Inc. In a three-way merger deal on September 13, LDDS acquires Metromedia Communications Corporation and Resurgens Communications Group. British Telecom acquires a 20 percent stake in MCI; BT and MCI form Concert Communications.
1994	Cannada steps down as CFO; Ebbers names Sullivan to the company's top financial post. Grubman joins Salomon Smith Barney. On December 30, LDDS completes the IDB WorldCom acquisition.
1995	LDDS swallows its first big fish—its key supplier, WilTel. In May, Ebbers renames the company WorldCom. In August, WorldCom hires future controller David F. Myers. Basketball superstar Michael Jordan joins the WorldCom team as spokesperson. WorldCom pleads guilty in U.S. district court for donating money to Public Service Commission candidates. WorldCom bills 19.4 billion minutes and reports annual revenues of approximately $3.9 billion. More than 7,000 employees work in 160 offices worldwide.
1996	In February, President Bill Clinton signs into law the Telecommunications Act of 1996. Grubman is

a bright young talent on Wall Street. On April 22, Salomon begins allocating millions of dollars in IPOs to Ebbers and other WorldCom executives, who will sell them for $18 million profit in a practice called "spinning." WorldCom inks deals with GTE Long Distance, Ameritech Communications, Southwestern Bell Mobile Systems, and Electronic Data Systems (EDS). WorldCom acquires stake in Irish Telecommunications and buys Choice Cellular. On August 26, WorldCom lands MFS Communications, new owner of Internet giant UUNET and home of John Sidgmore. A two-for-one stock split is announced. Sullivan is elected to the WorldCom board. *Wall Street Journal* ranks WorldCom No. 1 in shareholder return for the previous decade. Standard & Poor's 500 index adds WorldCom to the list. *Fortune* magazine names Ebbers a rising star.

1997   WorldCom acquires BLT Technologies and America Online's ANS Communications. Sullivan comes up with a plan for WorldCom to outbid British Telecom and acquire MCI even though both long-distance resellers are three times the size of WorldCom. On November 10, Sullivan successfully pulls off the largest merger in history when WorldCom's $42 billion unsolicited takeover bid for MCI is made public. Investors since 1990 enjoyed an unheard of 225-to-1 return.

1998   WorldCom acquires stake in Brazil's Embratel Participacoes and soon after, a stake in Mexico's Avantel. WorldCom completes acquisitions of three rival companies—MCI, Brooks Fiber, and CompuServe. Sullivan receives the *CFO* Excellence Award for M&A (mergers and acquisitions), and the magazine names him a "compensation champ" for earning $19.25 million for the year. On July 31, Ebbers buys Douglas Lake Ranch in British Columbia for an estimated $66 million. Year-end revenues total approximately $17.6 billion.

1999   MCI WorldCom purchases remaining interest in Brazil's Proceda Technology and acquires SkyTel Communications and Wireless One. On May 6, Ebbers nixes the Nextel deal. On June 21, World-Com stock price peaks at $64.50. On August 6, MCI WorldCom's network goes haywire for 10 days, shutting down more than 3,000 ISPs, banks, and corporations, including the Chicago Board of Trade. In September, *Forbes* names Ebbers the 174th richest American and the 376th richest man in the world with a $1.4 billion net worth. MCI WorldCom outbids BellSouth to make a play for Sprint. Ebbers drops MCI from the company name. Key executives continue exiting WorldCom; Sidgmore becomes less active in daily operations. Financial entries are manipulated to offset declining revenues.

2000   On April 28, WorldCom shareholders bless the WorldCom-Sprint merger. On July 13, after learning that the U.S. Department of Justice and the European Union would challenge the WorldCom-Sprint merger, Ebbers calls off the deal. World-Com stock price slips to $46.07. Ebbers' numbered spot on the Forbes 400 wealthiest American list falls to 368. On September 6, the WorldCom compensation committee authorizes the first loan of $50 million to Ebbers. The day after Sullivan produces a third-quarter report glossing over a few "challenges," the committee authorizes an additional $25 million loan to Ebbers. On December 27, Ebbers receives another $25 million company loan.

2001   In January, WorldCom stock closes below $10. On February 28, WorldCom gives 6,000 employees the pink slip as the company continues streamlining operations. In May, WorldCom COO Ron Beaumont is faxed an anonymous note pointing out improper billings. On June 8, Ebbers introduces two tracking stocks, WorldCom Group (Nasdaq: WCOM) and MCI Group (Nasdaq: MCIT). That same month, former WorldCom employees joined a shareholder lawsuit against the company in federal court, with allegations representing a scandalous laundry list of accounting errors. In July, Ebbers gains control of Digex by acquiring Intermedia. The company reports annual revenues of $35.2 billion and total debt of $30.2 billion. The book cooking continues.

March 7, 2002   The SEC questions WorldCom on a sweeping list of topics, including accounting practices.

April 2, 2002   With an additional $65 million loan, Ebbers signs an agreement pledging stocks and assets as collateral for the total $408.2 million company loan.

April 3, 2002   WorldCom reduces its U.S.-based staff by 3,700 jobs.

April 29, 2002   After 17 years at the helm, Ebbers resigns as WorldCom CEO.

April 30, 2002   Sidgmore is named WorldCom CEO and devises a turnaround plan. Soon after, he orders a complete assessment of WorldCom's myriad divisions and subsidiaries and a thorough examination of the company's books as part of a 30-day plan to reboot WorldCom and reassure investors and analysts.

May 9, 2002   WorldCom's bond rating is lowered to junk status.

May 14, 2002   A world-record number of WorldCom shares—670 million—are traded and AXA Financial of France ends up with nearly 11 percent of the company. KPMG replaces Arthur Andersen as the company's independent auditor and accountant.

May 16, 2002   *Fort Worth Weekly* publishes "Accounting for Anguish," an investigative piece about former WorldCom employee and whistleblower Kim Emigh.

May 28, 2002   Internal auditor Gene Morse discovers $500 million in fraudulent computer expenses.

June 11, 2002   Sullivan is dismissive when WorldCom internal audit team leader Cynthia Cooper questions him about the company's record keeping of assets and expenses.

June 13, 2002	Cooper reports findings to WorldCom audit committee chairman Max Bobbitt.
June 15, 2002	Arthur Andersen is convicted of obstruction of justice for shredding documents in the Enron case.
June 17, 2002	Standard & Poor's lowers WorldCom's corporate credit rating.
June 19, 2002	Sullivan is asked to submit a written explanation overnight.
June 20, 2002	Sullivan submits White Paper to WorldCom board members.
June 21, 2002	Faced with intense market pressure, Grubman downgrades WorldCom stock to "underperform speculative."
June 24, 2002	WorldCom shares fall below $1.
June 25, 2002	WorldCom discloses $3.8 billion accounting fraud. WorldCom stock plunges to 20 cents in after-hours trading. Myers resigns; Sullivan is fired. Soon after, the company lays off the first wave of 17,000 employees even as its top salespeople are being treated to a paid vacation at a posh Hawaiian resort.
July 1, 2002	WorldCom files key events summary with the SEC; state and federal officials launch investigations into possible corporate criminal misdeeds.
July 8, 2002	The U.S. House Financial Services Committee interrogates Ebbers, Sullivan, Grubman, Arthur Andersen senior partner Melvin Dick, Sidgmore, and WorldCom Chairman Bert Roberts.
July 12, 2002	The tracking stock structure is officially eliminated. Twenty-five banks file lawsuit to request an immediate freeze of $2.65 billion of WorldCom assets.
July 19, 2002	Heritage Classic Foundation terminates contract with WorldCom as title sponsor of the Heritage Classic PGA Tour event.
July 21, 2002	WorldCom files the largest bankruptcy in the world.
July 28, 2002	Sidgmore appoints restructuring experts Gregory F. Rayburn as CRO and John S. Dubel as CFO.

July 30, 2002	President George W. Bush signs into law the Sarbanes-Oxley Act of 2002, a sweeping corporate reform bill.
August 1, 2002	Sullivan and Myers are arrested and charged with securities fraud, conspiracy to commit securities fraud, and filing false statements with the SEC.
August 8, 2002	WorldCom discloses additional $3.3 billion accounting fraud. With other disclosures, the total to date is approximately $7.68 billion.
August 13, 2002	The House Financial Services Committee issues subpoena to Salomon Smith Barney seeking details of the firm's allocation of shares in IPOs to WorldCom executives during the technology stock boom days.
August 28, 2002	A seven-count indictment is filed in federal court charging Sullivan with a long-running conspiracy to artificially boost earnings reports by hiding operating expenses. Myers is named an unindicted co-conspirator.
September 11, 2002	Sidgmore resigns as WorldCom CEO.
September 26, 2002	Myers pleads guilty to one count each of securities fraud, conspiracy to commit securities fraud, and filing false statements with the SEC.
September 30, 2002	New York Attorney General Eliot Spitzer files complaint against Ebbers that he participated in "spinning," in violation of New York's Martin Act.
October 7, 2002	Former WorldCom accounting director Buford "Buddy" Yates Jr. pleads guilty to charges of conspiracy and securities fraud.
October 10, 2002	Former WorldCom accountants Betty Vinson and Troy Normand plead guilty to charges of conspiracy and securities fraud.
November 4, 2002	Bankruptcy court examiner Dick Thornburgh unveils first interim report on WorldCom, which reflects another $3 billion in accounting irregularities that could be added to the tally.

November 5, 2002	After a series of political missteps that embarrassed the Bush White House, SEC Chairman Harvey Pitt resigns under pressure on Election Day 2002, when Republicans regain control of the Senate and retain control of the House. The SEC files additional fraud charges against WorldCom, saying that the company inflated earnings by almost $2 billion more than it had previously disclosed, and permanently bans Myers and Yates from acting as officers or directors of a public company.
November 12, 2002	William Webster, chairman of SEC's new accounting oversight board, resigns under pressure following Pitt's resignation.
November 15, 2002	WorldCom names former Hewlett-Packard president and Compaq Computer turnaround wizard Michael D. Capellas as chairman, CEO and president.
November 26, 2002	WorldCom strikes a deal with the SEC to settle the civil fraud suit against the company.
December 2, 2002	Capellas begins official first day on the job defending his $50 million pay package.
December 6, 2002	WorldCom lays off 3,000 workers.
December 10, 2002	President Bush selects investment banker William H. Donaldson, former chairman of the New York Stock Exchange, as the new SEC chairman.
December 17, 2002	Six WorldCom board members resign, a day after two judges approve Capellas' pay package, and Capellas' turnaround plan begins in earnest.

CONTENTS

If you are not all-distance in this business, you won't go the distance.

Former WorldCom CEO Bernie Ebbers

We all got along famously at the beginning.

WorldCom CEO John Sidgmore

It floors me sometimes that none of us knew. Just like any company, they kept us worker bees in the dark.

Former WorldCom associate, August 2002

On a cool, sunny morning in mid-May 2002, a former WorldCom associate crawled out of her new blue metallic Ford Explorer, opened the rear door, and plucked a gift from behind the back seat. She expertly fluffed the shiny red bow, using a well-manicured fingernail to curl the loose tendrils of ribbon, and smoothed the white wrapping paper while checking the taped edges. After tucking a card under the trimmings, she looked up at the massive structure that housed the headquarters of one of the largest conglomerates in the world. She noticed that the vast American flag draped across the façade was billowing in the wind. This time, she hoped her mission would be successful. She was determined to see company controller David F. Myers.

As she walked briskly across the visitor's parking lot and past the fountain to the main lobby, with a breeze slightly lifting her short skirt and her high heels clicking on the pavement, she recalled the daily trek to work every morning, when she had occasionally passed Myers driving a BMW 7-Series from Madison, a yuppie suburb north of Jackson. She used to tease him for driving like a grandpa—slow and overly cautious. "You're always in my way," she'd joke when she would see him later in the hallway. When they arrived at corporate headquarters in Clinton, Mississippi, she would head to the employee parking lot on the far side of the campus while Myers steered to the covered parking garage that housed executives' luxury cars—Jaguars, Volvos, Mercedes, Lincolns, and Infinitis—including Bernie Ebbers' white Land Cruiser. Like most lower-level employees, the associate had opted not to pay the $500 annual fee for the privilege of parking in the shade, which still required a brief jaunt outdoors. Instead, she had trekked to the main building with numerous other employees who, from time to time, especially in inclement weather, would grumble about the "peon parking lot" being located so far away.

In the six months since she resigned from WorldCom, she had dropped by corporate offices several times to visit coworkers and friends, including Myers. Before she left, Myers and his workout buddies, or "spotters," including Quincy Burton, a handsome well-built black man with impeccably low body fat, had routinely worked out around the same time every day in the company gym and had become chummy with the associate. But then, Myers, a down-to-earth kind of guy with an open-door policy, had been friendly with everyone. He was constantly asking folks about their families, hobbies, and friends. When the associate gave notice, Myers had teasingly asked why she would possibly want to leave.

When coworkers threw the associate a going-away party, Myers sent comfort food. Everyone laughed. "It was *so* David," they said. Some employees, however, cautioned the associate about being too friendly with Tier 2s, like Myers. "That's taboo," they'd say, referring to the inverted pyramid that employees knew well: supervisors, managers, senior managers, directors, vice presidents, Tiers 3, 2, 1, and then WorldCom CEO Bernie Ebbers at the top. "As with all big bosses at all jobs, we as employees were made to fear David because of his clout," she said. But that didn't faze the associate.

On the past several trips, gaining entry to corporate offices had become increasingly difficult. In addition to upgrades implemented after the September 11, 2001, terrorist attacks in New York City and Washington, DC, higher-level security measures had been put in place since her last visit in early spring, when she had attended an associate's wedding shower. Myers had been unavailable then, too. A senior manager had walked her to his office, but returned, saying he was on a conference call. The associate remembered thinking, "This is weird. I'm sure he'd like to say hello."

On that May morning, the associate signed the guest log in the lobby and was waiting to be escorted upstairs by a WorldCom employee when she noticed men in black suits milling around the atrium. When she asked a fellow employee who "those grim-looking guys" were, she was told, "That's those people looking into our stuff . . . yeah, girl . . . they're looking into everything." Despite the heightened security, no one asked what was inside the box.

By the time the associate arrived on the fourth floor of the second building, where Myers' office was located, the mood was ominous. Susan Eady, Myers' administrative assistant, seemed frazzled and was uncharacteristically abrupt as she explained that Myers was in a meeting, not to be disturbed. The associate asked Susan, "Is he even here?" and was told, "Oh, yeah, he's here." Myers had become untouchable.

Later, the associate learned that Myers and WorldCom CFO Scott Sullivan had been meeting behind closed doors, scrambling to justify improper journal entries that totaled nearly $4 billion. Cynthia Cooper, head of the company's internal audit team, had been questioning the duo about discrepancies on the books that had artificially boosted earnings in 2001 and early 2002 to impress shareholders and Wall Street. At the time, the ploy had worked, but WorldCom's board was not impressed when they discovered the chicanery and asked Sullivan and Myers to resign. Myers immediately quit. When Sullivan refused, he was fired. And on June 26, the public became aware of the world's largest-ever corporate accounting scandal.

The financial death knell continued for WorldCom, the nation's second largest long-distance provider, the largest competitive provider of local telephone services, the largest carrier of international traffic, and the world's largest Internet carrier with operations to some 100 countries on six continents. A month later, WorldCom would file the world's largest bankruptcy filing in corporate history. Before the long, hot summer was over, WorldCom would more than double the amount of its accounting discrepancies to $7.3 billion, the House Financial Services Committee would subpoena and then grill the major players in the alleged conspiracy, and Sullivan and Myers would be handcuffed and indicted. Myers would later plead guilty. Three other WorldCom accounting executives would be indicted and also plead guilty, and the company would be the focus of state, national, and international investigations. "It's all very sad," said the associate. "Just awful. It floors me sometimes that none of us knew. Just like any company, they kept us worker bees in the dark."

Millions of people around the world were riveted by WorldCom's economic collapse. They wondered how another

American-based conglomerate, a pioneer of the telecom boom, whose value had skyrocketed 7,000 percent in the 1990s, could fall so hard and so fast. It drew even more attention because it happened so soon after the implosion of Enron, which had culminated in the world's largest bankruptcy in corporate history in December 2001. WorldCom would soon capture that distinction.

People from all walks of life watched as WorldCom's betrayal devastated their investments and retirement nest eggs; they wanted to know what went wrong—when, why, and how. Who was to blame? Was Ebbers' heavy-handed management style a factor in WorldCom's demise? Was the board of directors so closely aligned with Ebbers that he was given carte blanche to do as he pleased with no oversight? Was it Sullivan's cavalier can-do-anything attitude? Was it pressure from unrealistic stockholder expectations? Or was it the influence of the European and U.S. regulators who denied their blessing on the WorldCom/Sprint blockbuster marriage in June 2000? Was this tiny company from rural Mississippi, the poorest state in the nation, a fluke from the start? News organizations from around the globe set up camp near corporate headquarters in Clinton, Mississippi, and its Internet offices in Virginia, searching for answers. There were few.

At the time WorldCom collapsed, the global juggernaut served more than 20 million customers, with its residential arm handling 70 million phone calls every weekend. The company's contracts with the government of the United States affected 80 million Social Security beneficiaries, air traffic control applications for the Federal Aviation Administration, network management for the Department of Defense, and critical data network services for the United States Postal Service. The conglomerate provided long-distance voice and data communications services for the House, the Senate, and the General Accounting Office, and similar services for nearly every government agency under its FTS2001 contract.

WorldCom also provided support for law enforcement and homeland security agencies as well as agencies connected with national security. Its annual revenues totaled more than $30 billion, and even after midyear layoffs, WorldCom employed more than 60,000 people worldwide. Its blue-chip customers included RJ Reynolds Tobacco, Federal Express, Nasdaq, and AOL Time Warner.

WorldCom—and the entire telecommunications industry— had come a long way from Route 66, where the long-distance wars began. Telecommunications pioneer John D. "Jack" Goeken, a high school graduate who became known as "the phone world's most prolific inventor," was a General Electric (GE) manufacturer's representative. He was selling two-way radios from Springfield, Illinois, in the early 1960s when the idea occurred to him to build microwave towers along Route 66 between St. Louis and Chicago and to sell radios to truck drivers and dispatchers.

When Goeken created Microwave Communications Incorporated in 1963 to bring the revolutionary idea to fruition, American Telephone & Telegraph (AT&T), Illinois Bell, Southwestern Bell, and Western Union immediately filed petitions to shut down the company. In the complaint, AT&T predicted: "There is no need for this type of service and the company is going to go bankrupt."

In 1968, William G. "Bill" McGowan stepped in to help Goeken raise money and to expand the network coast to coast. They acquired land leases on which to build the towers and "built (MCI) from a firm grown out of dissatisfaction with AT&T's long distance service between Chicago and St. Louis into today's multibillion international long distance telephone corporation wrote the Associated Press.

MCI's challenge to AT&T's monopoly in a March 1974 lawsuit citing violation of the Sherman Antitrust Act ultimately led to the breakup of AT&T, when Ma Bell, as everyone knew her, was laid to rest. "The seedlings of WorldCom were planted on January 8, 1982, when Charles Brown, last chairman of legendary Ma Bell, capitulated to antitrust chief William Baxter," wrote Discovery Institute's John C. Wohlstetter. "Facing imminent defeat in the government's antitrust suit, Brown elected to end his company's litigation nightmare and accept Baxter's vision of juridicially separate long-distance and local markets." The landmark breakup resulted in AT&T's agreement to divest itself of its 22 wholly owned Bell operating companies that provided local telephone service and the formation of a new AT&T and seven regional telephone holding companies, known as the regional Bell operating companies. Many Baby Bells were simply renamed—Qwest and Verizon were later versions—but the long-distance landscape had irreversibly changed.

The divestiture forced AT&T to lease long-distance phone lines at a 40 to 70 percent discount to small, regional companies, who would then resell the lines' data-carrying capacity, or bandwidth. MCI, GTE, Sprint, Western Union, and Allnet offered long-distance service even before the ordered breakup, though not at deeply discounted rates. Before Judge Harold Greene's ordered breakup became effective, hundreds of start-up phone companies began popping up all over the United States, and in January 1984, many were established seemingly overnight.

Melvin C. Davis Sr. of Seminary, Mississippi, a Southern Bell (now BellSouth) communications consultant who joined the AT&T affiliate in 1955 and retired in 1983, realized immediately that Judge Greene's order would transform the telecommunications industry. "When the order came down, I saw the handwriting on the wall and decided I'd better get out of there and do something I could make a living at, so I switched to the insurance industry," said Davis, who retired in 2002 from a second successful career. "When I bowed out of the situation, AT&T was still the big dog on the street, and nobody else was even close, but I knew it was a matter of time before the marketplace was flooded with competitors."

Murray Waldron, a native of Dyersburg, Tennessee, had been watching the events unfold and saw the potential to make big bucks. If, for example, a customer could be charged $1 for a 50-cent phone call, and a simple piece of switching equipment required for routing the calls could handle 40 calls at once, the potential to make $20 a minute was extremely alluring. Using that example, if the switcher was maxed out around the clock, a phone company could make $28,800 a day, just for starters. To Waldron, the long-distance business "seemed like a gold mine waiting to be found."

1

Migrating South

These checks addressed to Bernie started arriving at the house, so my wife and I put them in a box. People had sent money to help pay for his tuition, books and supplies. I thought, "Geez, this is pretty kind of fabulous."

> Brent Foster, former high school and college classmate of former WorldCom CEO Bernie Ebbers.

The WorldCom sales executive was crouched over his desk, fingering his forehead and sweating at the thought of CEO Bernie Ebbers finding out he had sold company stock earlier in the week. It was Friday and he was hopeful that Ebbers hadn't noticed. He knew that Ebbers, a telecom mogul who rarely used e-mail or a cell phone and responded primarily via handwritten faxes and landline phones, requested daily printouts of stock activity and spent hours scouring the names of shareholders who exercised options or sold shares. He had heard stories of Ebbers' wrath descending on disloyal employees, and everyone knew that selling company stock was a capital offense. Nobody wanted to be on "Bernie's List." But he and Ebbers were "best buds," as others described them, often dining out with their significant others, so he was hopeful that he would be spared.

Shortly before lunchtime on that crisp October day in 2000, Ebbers, a rugged-looking cowpoke with a neat, white beard and piercing blue eyes, dressed in a leather vest and faded Levis and chewing a cigar, knocked on the executive's door and invited him to lunch. Though startled, he readily agreed. He was relieved as he climbed into Ebbers' SUV, convinced he was still in the CEO's good graces. While they gnawed on barbequed ribs at one of Ebbers' favorite nearby haunts, not a word was mentioned about the stock transaction. They talked weather. They talked business. They talked sports, mostly discussing the Jackson Bandits, Ebbers' minor-league hockey team, and the Major League Baseball playoffs. They wondered, would the Atlanta Braves win the division title this year? (The executive recalled that the New York Yankees would later win their twenty-sixth world championship title after beating the crosstown rival Mets 4–2 in Game 5 of the World Series at Shea Stadium.)

Arriving at the executive's office door following lunch, Ebbers slapped him on the back with his turquoise-jewelry clad hand before swaggering down the hall. For a split second, the executive fixated on the Cuban heels of Ebbers' trademark alligator boots. Without going in, he knew. Inside, his computer had been removed, his personal belongings had been stuffed in boxes, and a security guard was waiting to escort him to his car. He had been fired.

Ebbers was an unlikely choice to run a company that many people say never should have happened. But oddities defined the sinewy CEO who had been a milkman, bartender, bar bouncer, car salesman, truck driver, motel manager, garment factory foreman, and high school basketball coach before heading what would become the most feared telecom company in the world.

Born Bernard J. Ebbers on August 27, 1941, he was the second of five children in a working-class, devotedly religious family in Edmonton, Alberta. He grew up in relative poverty, where assuming debt often was the only way to acquire creature comforts. His dad, John Ebbers, a traveling salesman, mostly peddled hardware and tires. "Our work ethic came from our father," said his brother, Jim Ebbers. "Dad was always a hard worker. Dad always provided for us very well . . . and gave us what we needed, like a million other people out there. We were an ordinary family." Brent Foster, a former classmate of Ebbers, described the family as "a class act." "Bernie's mom and dad are just kind, thoughtful people," said Foster. "They bank a lot on their religion. They're the kind of people you like to hang around."

After Ebbers completed the first grade, the family moved to California. Four years later, the family set up camp at a mission post on a Navajo Indian reservation just outside Gallup, New Mexico, where the elder Ebbers was a business manager and the Ebbers siblings amused themselves by playing cards. "We didn't have much," Ebbers told Thomas J. Neff and James M. Citrin in *Lessons from the Top.* "If my dad had a few dollars left in his pocket at the end of the month, we would go out and eat hamburgers as a family. I remember the most exciting Christmas for me was the year my sister received a deck of 'Old Maid' cards and I received a deck of 'Animal Rummy' cards. I don't know if that fueled a passion. My father and my brothers and I are fairly competitive, driven people. Maybe it's genetics."

Five years later, the Ebbers family returned to Edmonton, Alberta, an oil and gas town situated in the North Saskatchewan Valley and framed by the picture-perfect Canadian Rockies. Originally, the community had been populated by several Indian tribes—Blackfoot, Peigan, Blood, Sarcee, Slavey, Cree, Chipewyan, and Beaver. In the 1880s, Europeans migrated to the region, and French and English-speaking pioneers from Eastern Canada began to outnumber the Indians. Until settlers farmed wheat, the primary industry revolved around Hudson's Bay Company and North West Company trading posts, which competed for beaver pelts until the companies merged in 1821. By 1890, the railway defined Alberta.

A boomtown with plentiful opportunities, Edmonton evolved into a clean and cosmopolitan, yet unglamorous and cold, metropolis of about a million people. Known as the City of Champions, it was home to four-time Stanley Cup winner Wayne Gretzky's Oilers in the 1980s. Alberta's centerpiece and top tourist attraction is the West Edmonton Mall, the world's largest entertainment and shopping center—it spans the equivalent of 48 city blocks.

With a strong religious right-wing element permeating the free enterprise system, the work ethic in Edmonton was based on the oil patch creed: People who worked hard without complaint did not need higher education. In time, they could become wealthy. Ironically, Ebbers' home province became the first in Canada to convert to digital switching and to provide individual telephone line service to every resident. Alberta was also the first region in North America to integrate high-speed cable modem technology. David Staples, a business reporter for *Edmonton Journal* said, "To leave here at a time of such opportunity, Bernie must have really loved Mississippi, the religious feel down there."

At six-foot-four, Ebbers played basketball at Victoria Composite High School in downtown Edmonton, where he was a forward on a basketball team coached by John Baker. "If it wasn't for Bernie, I probably would've started," said Foster, a second-string forward who first met Ebbers during a snowstorm, when he stopped to give Ebbers and his sister a ride to school. "The reality is, his talent was far superior to mine. We had a pretty big team, including a six-foot-eight center, Doug Krentz, and we won a city championship during the late 1950s. No egos, good coaching. We were a tight-knit bunch of guys who had a good time."

After high school, Ebbers struggled for a while. He juggled part-time jobs during two brief college stints. Stringent science courses doomed him at the University of Alberta, where physical education was his chosen course of study. He had no better luck at Calvin College in Grand Rapids, Michigan, where some professors viewed him as a slacker. "Bernie was a bright light," said Foster. "There's no question about that. It's just that we weren't applying ourselves. Let's face it. He got into the University of Alberta, so he obviously had the marks . . . probably in the top 20 percent of his class." After the Calvin College debacle, Ebbers returned to Edmonton briefly, where he delivered bread and milk and worked as a bouncer.

Baker and Foster unwittingly played pivotal roles in Ebbers' next move. On a trip to Seattle, Foster tagged along with Baker, who was finishing up graduate work at the University of Washington. "Coach Baker told me I should be going to university . . . and that I should look around the campus, so I did," said Foster. To pass the time while waiting for Baker to exchange Canadian currency in a local bank, Foster picked up a brochure that had been left behind in the lobby. It featured Mississippi College, a small, private liberal arts college on a picturesque campus located about 2,700 miles away in the Deep South.

"It looked like the perfect place," said Foster. "If I could go someplace far away, I could concentrate on studying. If I stayed close to home and let my friends continue to influence me, I'd party all the time. The tuition was a lot less there than in northern states, with no out-of-state fees, and from a money point of view, it fit my budget. So away I went."

Foster took the train to Jackson, Mississippi, a sprawling metropolis that served as the state capital. "The train ride was an adventure in itself, seeing the different terrains and different ways people dressed and lived," he said. "When we crossed the Mississippi state line, I was overwhelmed by the huge black population. We hardly saw any in Edmonton."

From Jackson, Foster took a cab to Clinton, a lovely, historic bedroom community located about 10 miles west, and home of Mississippi College. He was immediately impressed. The oldest institute of higher learning in the state and the second oldest Baptist college in the nation, Mississippi College was the first university in the United States to graduate a woman. The landscape featured a unique blend of antebellum structures, Victorian-era homes, and historic red brick buildings perched on verdant rolling hills. Brick streets in downtown Clinton were lined with aged oaks and grand magnolia trees. An area steeped in history, city hall was located on the site of Union General William Tecumseh Sherman's headquarters during the siege of Jackson, and the grounds of China Hill, circa 1841, were used as a campsite for Union soldiers following the Battle of Champion Hill. The college was deeply traditional. No alcohol. No black students on campus. And mandatory chapel services three times a week. Foster enrolled for the fall semester.

Despite an affinity for his new home, living in the Deep South was "a huge adjustment," said Foster. "The heat was oppressive, but the cockroaches were worse. Up here, we have teeny little things. Down there, they're so big, they fly. That really caught me off guard. I remember one guy took me for a swim in a pond, and a head popped out of the water, and I said, 'What the heck is that?' He laughed and told me it was a water moccasin. He said, 'Ah, don't worry, they won't bite you in the water.' I found later that they would. By Christmas, I thought, 'I'm going home.' It was too much for me. Then I thought . . .

'I'll stick it out another semester' . . . and bingo, it all clicked. So that summer, Bernie asked me about it. I think he was kinda like me, wanting to get away. I was obviously pretty high on the college."

Ebbers and a mutual buddy, Dave Prins, enrolled that fall. Ebbers once told an acquaintance that one reason he decided to move to the subtropical climate was because "delivering milk in 30 degrees below zero isn't a real interesting thing to do with the rest of your life." Together with Foster and Foster's new bride, Peggy, the foursome headed south for the three-day trip in Foster's mother's white convertible Ford Galaxy. "It was going to be a honeymoon trip, but I kinda destroyed (that) by allowing those two idiots to get on board," said Foster, with a laugh. "Anyway, it worked out fine. It covered a bunch of expenses and we took turns driving." Over the years, they took many routes between Mississippi and Alberta, but the Canadians usually traveled through Saskatchewan, Montana, Colorado, Texas, Tennessee, and Louisiana.

Peggy landed a job in the registrar's office at Mississippi College working with assistant registrar Clarice Mooney, who became a key contact for enrolling Foster's Canadian pals. About half a dozen Edmontonians attended Mississippi College for at least a semester or two. "I'd give her a dingle and she'd set these guys up," said Foster. "She didn't do it for Bernie because Peggy wasn't in the office yet. I think Bernie and Dave just came down on a wing and prayer and got in." Looking back on that day in the Seattle bank, Foster remarked, "The odds of finding this pamphlet and ending up down there with Bernie, well, I guess it's just fate."

Ebbers arrived at Mississippi College with only two pairs of blue jeans, two short-sleeve shirts, one long-sleeve shirt, and a jacket. He roomed with fellow basketball player William Lewis, now president of Pearl River Community College in Poplarville, Mississippi, and as juniors, they plunged into a weight-training program to beef up. "[Bernie] almost played with reckless abandonment," said teammate Larry Hill, describing Ebbers' efforts on the basketball court. "He was full force."

Ebbers curried favor with James Allen, his coach and mentor, who arranged a basketball scholarship for him. A fun-loving and kind family man with two sons, Allen always looked after "all his boys." One day, Ebbers, who already had a strong religious background, expressed doubt about a sermon at the nearby First Baptist Church. "Allen told him, 'Boy, shut that door,'" said alumni dean Van D. Quick. "Coach Allen pulled out an old Bible and led him to a salvation experience."

Allen once told Ebbers, who could be painfully shy, that he needed to find a nice, good-looking girl to settle down with and even joked that he would pay for the marriage license. "Bernie *was* painfully shy, especially around girls," said Foster. "In high school, he would certainly not have been classified as a Casanova. He was probably like a lot of his compatriots. We were all painfully shy. Maybe because of the people you hang around, you reap those characteristics. Besides, we were more interested in playing sports. That was basically what our life was all about, to the detriment of all other things, including our social life." When Ebbers wed Linda Pigott, a devout Christian woman from Magnolia, Mississippi, in 1968, with Lewis acting as his best man, Allen paid the $5 license fee as promised.

A freak accident interrupted Ebbers' basketball career before his senior year at Mississippi College. While driving back to school from Canada, Ebbers was dropping off a pal near Grand Rapids, Michigan, when he had car trouble. "They ran out of gas in a tough part of town and walked up to a bar to ask where the nearest gas station was and things turned ugly. These guys chased them down the street and one guy threw a bottle at Bernie. It hit him on the Achilles heel and severed it completely, ending his basketball career, for that year anyway."

While laid up for two weeks with his foot in a cast, Ebbers came up with an ingenious plan to return to Mississippi College despite being unable to fulfill his scholarship requirements. A scholarship fund was created. "These checks addressed to Bernie started arriving at the house, so my wife and I put them in a box," said Foster. "He didn't phone me or anything. When he got down there, he asked if there was any mail. I said, 'Yeah, there's a ton of it.' People had sent money to help pay for his tuition, books and supplies. I thought, 'Geez, this is pretty kind of fabulous.' Bernie never said if it was 800 or 8,000 bucks. He just picked them up and left."

That fall, to help defray some of Ebbers' school expenses, Allen asked him to coach the college junior varsity team. Ebbers agreed and asked Foster to help run practices and drive the team bus. "We didn't have a very good basketball team, but we sure did have a good time," said Foster. "Bernie did a darn good job coaching that group of guys, too. And we got to see a lot of southern states—Texas, Louisiana, Alabama—that we normally would not have seen if we hadn't gotten involved."

Oddly, Ebbers, a devout Christian who was a nonconformist, felt comfortable in a state that simmered with racial strife in the 1960s and where outsiders were often eyed with suspicion. Mississippi had been in the national limelight many times, almost always unfavorably. In the fall of 1962, when James Meredith enrolled as the first African American student at the University of Mississippi, he was escorted to the administration office by out-of-state National Guard troops while protesters lined the sidewalk chanting obscenities. In 1963, NAACP field secretary Medger Evers was gunned down in the driveway of his Jackson home. The bullet-riddled walls of Alexander Hall on the campus of Jackson State University continue to serve as a reminder of a protest that got out of hand on May 14, 1970, resulting in the deaths of two students by local law enforcement.

Ebbers had attended grade school with Hispanics in California and had been a minority on the Indian reservation in New Mexico, but had not lived in a place with a significant African American population. Later, he would quietly take action to mend the racial rift in ways that would go largely unnoticed, even by the outspoken Reverend Jesse Jackson. "We were there during the most interesting time in Mississippi's history regarding segregation," said Foster. "It was a fabulous time to be there, at least from our point of view."

While Mississippi was a temporary home for his Canadian pals, Ebbers chose to stay. It was an unusual choice—in part because of the unique business climate in the Deep South, where good old boys have their own lingo and game rules, and deals are often made with a handshake, a wink, or a nod. Many times, negotiations went on over beef and drinks in places like The Room at Tico's Steak House in Ridgeland. Ebbers would later hold court there, and waitresses occasionally would brag about receiving $1,000 tips. Mississippi had long been one of the poorest states in the nation, often holding last place on vital issues of health care, education, and quality of life. Manufacturing and agriculture—mainly poultry, cotton, and forestry—remained the biggest moneymakers. Unpredictable weather that peppered the seemingly endless stretch of land (long-ago mudflats of the Mississippi River) had wreaked havoc with agricultural crops for centuries. For Mississippi farmers, life was wickedly difficult.

After graduating in 1967 with a bachelor's degree in physical education and a minor in secondary education, Ebbers moved 55 miles south to Brookhaven, an oil and timber town of 10,000, and a strong religious community. The majority Baptist population repeatedly voted down liquor sales. "If you go fishing with one Baptist, he'll drink all your beer," goes a local joke. "If you go fishing with two Baptists, you'll have all the beer to yourself."

Former AOL Time Warner COO Bob Pittman, a pioneer of the technology age, was the most famous Brookite other than Ebbers to later make global headlines. A former radio deejay, Pittman founded MTV at the age of 27 and went on to serve as CEO for Six Flags Entertainment and Century 21 Real Estate. Ironically, AOL Time Warner, the world's largest media company, was also under investigation for accounting problems when Pittman left the company on July 18, 2002. Located on Interstate 55, Brookhaven was an easy two-hour drive to New Orleans, an aged port city with a vastly different culture. "You can go from one world to another in practically no time," said a local resident, who frequented the Big Easy. "I do, often."

With his new bride, Ebbers bought a modest home and coached basketball at nearby Hazlehurst High School for a year. "He enjoyed being in charge," said Bobby West, a junior varsity player at Mississippi College. "He always had plenty of nerve (and) dared anybody not to like it. The night before cuts, I can remember going to his dorm room . . . to find out if I was going to make the team. I remember him enjoying that to the fullest. He got the most out of that, and then told me to get on out, knowing all the time I was going to make it."

The year Ebbers coached at Hazlehurst, Sells Newman was a tall, lanky senior basketball player at Crystal Springs High School, a rival school located about 10 miles away. "Bernie hasn't changed a bit," said Newman in 2002. "He was always very competitive, always a very nice happy-go-lucky guy. I ran into him recently at Schimmel's restaurant and told him anytime he wanted to hit a few hoops, I'd give him a $5 challenge. His wife said, 'Don't challenge him. That's what he always likes.'"

During the summer, Ebbers coached Little League baseball in Hazlehurst, a small railroad town that did not have enough teams for competition. He asked Lamar Bullard, a Little League coach in Brookhaven, if he could bring his

Hazlehurst players to Brookhaven for a few games. Bullard agreed, and the two coaches worked together all summer on the baseball field. Bullard, then senior vice president of Stahl-Urban Company, was impressed by Ebbers' character and asked him to consider working at the family-owned garment factory in Brookhaven, where men's sportswear and outerwear had been manufactured since 1935. Six weeks later, Ebbers joined the company. After four or five years, he had worked his way up to distribution manager, but quit to start his own business. "Bernie was a bright young man who had more potential than we were able to reward him with at that time," said Bullard. "I guess he felt it was time to be his own boss."

Ebbers purchased Sand's motel and restaurant for an undisclosed sum in nearby Columbia, the state's fourth oldest city and former state capital. Located in the bottomland of the Pearl River, next door to an auto salvage center, the 40-room motel often housed roughnecks who worked on oil wells in the area. "I've stayed in some dumps, but Sand's was the worst dump I'd ever stayed in," said a former WorldCom executive, referring to a night he spent in the motel with high school football teammates in the 1970s during a championship game road trip. "I don't know if it was Bernie's at the time. I hope not." To save money, the Ebbers moved on-site with their first child, Treasure. Later, the couple had two more daughters, Joy and Faith, one of whom they adopted. "We lived like a band of gypsies in a two-bedroom house trailer," said Ebbers. "My wife looked after the maids and I did the maintenance."

Through church connections, Ebbers met Danny M. Dunnaway and Carl J. Aycock, roommates and Sigma Alpha Epsilon fraternity brothers at the University of Southern Mississippi (USM). Later, they would be key players in the creation of LDDS, the forerunner to WorldCom. Originally from Georgia, Aycock married during his junior year of college, and after earning a math degree, settled in Columbia to work as an accountant for Dunnaway's dad, part owner of several Dollar General franchises, a five-and-dime type store. After graduating from USM with an accounting degree, Dunnaway headed to law school at Ole Miss, known formally as the University of Mississippi. The trio kept in touch, and soon after Dunnaway returned to the area with a law degree and joined his dad in business, Ebbers persuaded him to invest in motels.

After demonstrating how a motel could double in value in five years and also make a modest operating profit, Ebbers convinced Dunnaway and Jewel Felker to invest in the motel business. The trio purchased the Jones Motel in Collins, a 65-room property in a rural town driven by the poultry industry, where chicken entrails permeated the air. A local football hero, Tater Jones, and his wife, Bernice, had built the motel. In 1936, Jones kicked Seminary High School to a state championship. "It's been so far back, I can't remember which it was—a field goal or PAT—but it was good enough to win that game," said Jones. Even though the rate was never posted, locals speculated that motel rooms were sometimes rented by the hour, probably when the Joneses, highly regarded citizens of Covington County where the Jones Motel was located, were out of town.

Speck's, the restaurant adjacent to the motel, was equally famous. It was owned by Speck Graham and was a busy meeting place for local politicians and traveling preachers. Attracted perhaps by a wall-size wildlife photographic mural of two fawns in the woods, hunters and fishermen often gathered in the smoke-filled restaurant to chomp on fried chicken and green beans. Even though Speck's and the Jones Motel had different owners, many people thought of them as a single entity, and the restaurant was a great place to gossip.

Aycock joined the venture when the foursome purchased a third property, the Marshall Motel in West Point, Mississippi. Built in the 1950s by Barnes Marshall, the town's former multi-term mayor, the 43-room motel was clean but antiquated. After two days of training by Ebbers, Dunnaway took over as on-site manager. Ebbers returned to Sand's. Felker continued to manage the Jones Motel. By design, when the properties were consolidated, Ebbers, the sole owner of Sand's, owned the lion's share of the business. In 1977, when the group focused on additional hotel ventures, Dunnaway bought the others' interest in the Marshall Motel and exited the group. He sold the motel in early 1983.

Ebbers' motel chain, Master Corporation, continued adding properties, mostly in Mississippi, including a motel in Grenada and a Hampton Inn in Brookhaven. Ebbers upgraded the portfolio considerably when he built a comparatively upscale property, a 62-room Best Western motel in Brookhaven. At one point, Ebbers, who was dedicated to the hotel business, was the Best Western Governor of Mississippi, representing the state's franchise owners. By mid-1983, Master Corporation had seven properties and the base of operations had been moved from Columbia to Brookhaven. "I remember driving down to see Bernie . . . and he was telling me about slicing tomatoes for (the restaurant)," said Foster, who returned to Canada to pursue a teaching career after finishing graduate school at Mississippi College. "I remember him saying, 'You've got to slice tomatoes this thick because that's where a lot of your profit is.' From a business point of view, he really started to evolve from that kind of beginning."

Even though he no longer had an investment in Master Corporation, Dunnaway accepted Ebbers' job offer to direct operations for the motel group after he relocated to Brookhaven and found himself with idle time. "Mr. Ebbers told me, 'Hang on, Danny, there may be an opportunity for an investment,' and within 30 to 60 days, LDDS came along," said Dunnaway.

Spirituality was a bond for these men, who lived in the buckle of the Bible Belt. David Singleton and Max Thornhill, both Brookites who had raised money for various projects, knew Ebbers through a prayer group at First Baptist Church of Brookhaven. They would also figure largely in the formation of LDDS. When he relocated to Brookhaven in the late 1970s, Aycock became active in the Faith Presbyterian Church. When Dunnaway returned to Brookhaven, he became involved in Abundant Life Church, a charismatic nondenominational and multiracial church. Dunnaway said, "We all believed in our hearts this was what we were supposed to do."

Information, Please

Bernie Ebbers wasn't even there when we formed the company.
Murray Waldron, founder of LDDS,
forerunner of WorldCom

D espite corporate lore, the beginning of WorldCom did not occur with Ebbers holding court in a Hattiesburg coffeehouse in September 1983. Instead, the founding meeting occurred a month earlier, and only two men were present: Murray Waldron and William "Bear" Rector, both Tennesseans who met in an air-conditioned Hattiesburg diner to escape the oppressive summer heat. Hurricane Alicia was brewing in the Gulf, the temperature had soared into the mid-90s, and the humidity was almost unbearable.

Waldron's interest in the long-distance market began in January 1983, shortly after Judge Harold Greene ordered the breakup of AT&T's Bell System to open up competition in the long-distance market. The divestiture forced AT&T to lease long-distance phone lines at deeply discounted rates to small, regional companies, who would then resell the lines' data-carrying capacity, or bandwidth, to small businesses. Even before the ordered breakup, MCI, GTE, Sprint, Western Union, and Allnet offered long-distance service. "A lot of WATS (wide area telephone service) resellers were already doing business, but they weren't necessarily competing on the open market," said Mississippi Public Service Commissioner Nielsen Cochran. "They were buying many thousands of minutes from local carriers for say, three cents a minute, and reselling them for six. That was all perfectly legal, as long as they had a certificate from the commission."

The Dyersburg, Tennessee, native began researching the possibilities of reselling long-distance service in small towns, where MCI and Sprint did not offer service. A buddy told him about The Phone Company (TPC) in Jackson, Tennessee, a start-up reseller of long distance. The next day, Waldron dropped by TPC offices and met the owners. He reviewed the sales plan and offered to be the company's first salesperson. After taking a two-hour training program, Waldron spent two months in the western part of the state and sold 300 accounts. He focused on smaller towns surrounding the metropolitan area of nearly 400,000, located on Interstate 40 between Memphis and Nashville. Selling long-distance service was such a new concept that his wife, Alice, called the Tennessee Public Service Commission to make sure it was legal. It was.

When TPC opened an office in Clarksville, Tennessee, Waldron moved to the blue-collar manufacturing community and repeated the process. In May, the company opened Netcom, a TPC spin-off, in Tupelo, Mississippi, a city located in the northeast corner of the state and known for its furniture industry and as the birthplace of Elvis. There he met Bill Fields, a financial planner, venture capitalist, and self-proclaimed "deal doer" who would later play an important role in the formation of LDDS.

After a particularly exhausting day selling accounts, Waldron was back in a local motel room in Tupelo that night when he felt compelled to drop to his knees in prayer. "My life hadn't been what it should've been, and I told the Lord to take control of it," said Waldron. "When I got up, I felt the world had been lifted off my shoulders. The next day, I started putting some numbers together, not really thinking about it, but I knew I was onto something really big that could only happen with the Lord's blessing."

Back home that weekend, Waldron's wife received a phone call from Rector's wife, who had invested in a long-distance company in Clarksville, Tennessee. Waldron told his wife to pass the word that if she wanted to make more money, he could put together a similar deal. Half an hour later, "Bear" Rector was at Waldron's house to learn more about the plan. Cashing in on the federally mandated AT&T breakup by reselling WATS lines—buying bandwidth and selling minutes in an industry with regulated prices—seemed like a powerful idea with unlimited potential.

"Bear asked me, 'Where ya going to put the thing?' and I told him either Franklin or Columbia, Tennessee," said Waldron. "He said, 'Have you ever thought about Hattiesburg, Mississippi?' and I said that I hadn't. I'd been to Hattiesburg many times for National Guard training at Camp Shelby and liked it. We got out a map and saw that it was truly a 'Hub City,' just like they called it. By Monday morning, we were down here."

They picked up a 1983 Hattiesburg Ma Bell phone directory, which stated the AT&T rate to Seattle was 74 cents for the first minute and 49 cents for each additional minute. They headed to the local chamber of commerce to see how many long-distance companies were doing business in the area. "When the girl at the desk asked, 'What's that [long-distance companies]?' we looked at each other and said, 'sounds like a gold mine.'"

The sultry summer night that Hurricane Alicia was threatening to come ashore, Waldron and Rector were in a Hattiesburg diner hovered over a table littered with crumpled napkins and trying to drum up a name for their new company. After refilling their glasses with iced tea, a waitress asked what they were doing. They told her, and on a whim, asked her to suggest a name. She walked away and mulled it over for a moment, then whipped out an ink pen and scrawled LDDC for Long Distance Discount Company. The "C" was in the shape of a telephone receiver with microwave beams radiating from it on a now legendary white napkin that Waldron keeps in his home office. "We thought 'Services' sounded better than 'Company,' but that's the only change we made," said Waldron. At the time, Ebbers and Waldron had not even met.

On the way home to Tennessee, Waldron and Rector stopped in Tupelo to tell Fields about their progress. Fields began courting investors, including David Singleton of Brookhaven, who had worked with him on several projects but was initially reluctant to invest significant funds for a start-up in an industry dominated by AT&T. After Singleton caught a TV interview between *Today Show* cohost Jane Pauley and AT&T Chairman Charles L. Brown about changes in the long-distance market, he became enthusiastic about the idea.

"Fields . . . called me in September of '83 and asked if I could raise $650,000, to which I voiced my doubt," Singleton told the British Broadcasting Company (BBC). "There was not that kind of money around in my world, with people who could afford to take real risk. Venture risk . . . I'd never heard of divestiture. I didn't fully understand what (Bill) was saying, but I trusted him."

Singleton contacted Ebbers, whom he had known since 1979, and a meeting in Hattiesburg was arranged. Ebbers later told Singleton, "The business plan was lousy, but the idea was good."

Before Waldron and Rector drove the 400 miles south to Hattiesburg for the second time, Rector got cold feet. "He said his daddy was afraid he was going to lose all his money by putting it in one basket, so I told him to do what he needed to do, that everything would work out," said Waldron. "So I drove to Tupelo alone, met Bill, and we headed to Hattiesburg where we met up with David and Bernie."

On the day of the meeting, Singleton called Ebbers to offer him a ride, but Ebbers had decided not to go. "I asked why," said Singleton. "He said that he had read an article where AT&T was going to lowball everybody and run them out of business. And candidly, I said to him, 'Well, you owe it to me after the money I raised for your motels to get in the car, and at least let's go see what the guy's got to say. And let's penetrate the numbers. If we don't like it, or you don't like it after that, fine. But don't say no when you haven't even talked to the guy. And so he went."

In a booth at the Days Inn coffee shop in Hattiesburg, where Waldron, Fields, Singleton, and Ebbers met for the first time, Ebbers took charge. He reviewed Waldron's numbers and projections, which Ebbers would later describe as fictitious, but no deal was made. "When we got up and started out the door, Bill went out, David went out, and Bernie reached out and held the door," said Waldron. "He said, 'Wait, we can put this deal together.'"

Ebbers knew he could rally support from Aycock and Dunnaway, but was unhappy about paying 10 percent commission on $650,000 to Fields and Singleton. "He just had a hard time starting out $65,000 in the hole," said Singleton. "And I was not surprised to hear him say that. But in the moment he said it, I realized he's bought it. Or he's buying it." On the ride back to

Brookhaven, with Singleton driving, Ebbers in the passenger seat, and Fields in the back seat, they closed the deal. "I looked at Bill in the mirror and released him from his commitment to me, and said that I trusted the two of them, 'cause I did."

While LDDS was being created, future WorldCom CFO Scott D. Sullivan was fresh out of college with an accounting degree from the State University of New York (SUNY) at Oswego, a renowned party school. He lived in the bland, four-story Cayuga Hall along with 400 other students and was involved in Delta Mu Delta, a national honorary business society founded in 1913. A straight-A student, Sullivan had attended Bethlehem Central High School, where he was considered one of the cool guys. He excelled in sports as a wrestling standout, and in academics as a member of Sigma Kappa Delta, an honorary high school fraternity. Oswego professor William Lundy told the alumni magazine that his former student displayed a "unique ability to get along with others."

Before he finished college, Sullivan had job offers from six of the "Big Eight" accounting firms before signing with KPMG in Albany, New York. In a record four years, he would become an account manager, landing major clients such as General Electric. "Even back in 1983, Scott had executive presence and the tact and maturity that made him able to gain respect and confidence from others," said Lundy. "The characteristic that distinguished Scott was his communication prowess—speaking and writing clearly and listening attentively, understandingly and responsively."

Future WorldCom CEO John William Sidgmore, a native of Spring Valley, New York, had preceded Sullivan in the SUNY system a decade earlier, where he earned a bachelor of arts degree in economics from the Oneonta campus in 1973. "It's funny talking to all these Harvard and Stanford guys that go, 'Oh, that's good, a state college in New York,'" he later said. Other SUNY alumni included designer Calvin Klein, singer Natalie Merchant, and comedian Billy Crystal. Sidgmore had immediately gone to work selling computers, then described as "bulky, programmable calculators," a far better job than he had held delivering newspapers as a teenager or driving a beer truck while in college. By the time LDDS was formed, he was in the middle of a 14-year stint at General Electric Information Services (GEISCO).

When the first 1,000 shares of LDDS were tallied at a dollar apiece, Fields, who became the first chairman of the board, had the biggest portion of the upstart company with 170 shares, or 17 percent. Ebbers, Aycock, Dunnaway, and Thornhill each had 145 shares, or 14.5 percent. Waldron originally had 100 shares, but took a brief break from the meeting, during which Ebbers gave him 10 more, for a total of 11 percent. "I started to leave again," Waldron joked. Jerry and Margaret Loden, who owned Total Telephone Company, Inc., in Tupelo and were looking for another investment and knew Fields, had 70 shares for 7 percent; Singleton had 50 shares for 5 percent; and Charles Vickery of Jackson, Tennessee, a technical guru who was brought in to run the switch that became the heart of the LDDS network, ended up with 20 shares, or 2 percent.

Three days later, Ebbers called Waldron for reassurance. Could buying bandwidth and selling minutes in a regulated industry present an opportunity for unlimited profitability, and if well managed, provide cash flow to grow his motel business? "He asked me, 'Why do you think Bell is going to let you do this?' I told him it was already ruled on and Bell didn't have any choice," said Waldron.

In the spring of 1984, Fields, Singleton, Thornhill, and Waldron met in Jackson to answer routine questions from state public utility commissioners about their application to operate as a long-distance carrier. Immediately following the breakup of AT&T, the Mississippi Public Service Commission (PSC) had been inundated with certification applications and had allowed in-state facilities-based telecommunication companies to operate pending approval. Fields, a diabetic, was the designated spokesperson, but a few minutes before the meeting, he became ill and his speech began to slur. "Bill was such a good guy, but he couldn't get up there and talk because he sounded like he was drunk," said Waldron. "I thought, golly, someone else is going to have to answer those questions, so I got up there and Bill sat in the back of the room and watched." Aycock later told a reporter that it was an amazing feat because "we knew nothing about long distance." The Mississippi PSC officially approved the application on May 9, 1984, six months after LDDS began selling its services.

The first official company meeting took place in the fall of 1983 at Master Corporation headquarters in Brookhaven, a former Texaco service station owned by Thornhill, a Texaco distributor. The initial registered office for LDDS was 312 North Green Street in Tupelo, with reference to another office located at 2303-B West Main Street in Tupelo, inside the Total Telephone offices. However, the Mississippi PSC application listed 3418 Hardy Street, Suite C, in Hattiesburg. The tiny office suite in Piccadilly Plaza, a blond brick two-story building on the main artery of the city and across the street from the University of Southern Mississippi, housed the switch for the company. Ebbers led the inaugural meeting with a brief prayer, a gesture that would become customary. Board members often discussed important issues over steaks at Western Sizzlin restaurant in Hattiesburg.

Of the nine original investors, only four—Ebbers, Dunnaway, Aycock, and Thornhill—cosigned a joint and several liability note for $450,000 to buy the Honeywell Roadrunner Digital Edition System telephone switching equipment and $200,000 for working capital from State Bank & Trust Co. in downtown Brookhaven. The others were unwilling or unable to take the financial risk. At the time, Thornhill's and Ebbers' net worth totaled $2.9 million and $2.8 million, respectively. Even though Aycock and Dunnaway were worth less than a million each, the bank allowed them to equally share in the assets. Ebbers and Aycock co-owned Sand's, valued then at one million dollars, with reported equity of $326,000 and a mortgage of $674,000. Ebbers paid $98,000 for a home in Brookhaven that he had acquired June 1, 1983. The market value was $102,000, and he still owed $50,000. By choice, Ebbers wasn't on the original board of directors.

As soon as the equipment was ordered, Waldron went on a selling spree and presold 200 customers. "The biggest problem in the beginning was convincing people we could do what we said we could do," he said. Floyd Franks, who owned a commercial real estate office on Hardy Street and was Archie Manning's favorite receiver at Ole Miss, was the company's first client. Floyd Franks & Associates' four phone lines were assigned account number 00001.

Well-liked and widely admired, Franks was an excellent choice to kick off LDDS. Franks could rarely go anywhere without being reminded of the historic 1969 Ole Miss-Alabama football game, the first nationally televised prime-time college football game. ABC aired it on a Saturday night from Legion Field in Birmingham. Scott Hunter was the quarterback for Alabama. Manning was the arm of the Ole Miss Rebels. The game was an incredible display of offensive magic by both teams in which the last team to score would win. It was Alabama, 33–32. Decades later, Franks, now a managing partner for New York Life in Birmingham, said people in Alabama still talk in reverent tones about The Game.

"When Murray came in and told me he could guarantee 30 percent savings on my long-distance bill, I was skeptical, but I was in the mood to save money," said Franks, who remembered paying the required $50 sign-up fee. "I instinctively trusted him and made the decision based on my gut feeling, which is how I made most business decisions in those days. When the first phone bill came in, Murray's promise held true."

The switch was scheduled to be turned on in December, but unseasonably cold temperatures may have hampered its delivery and installation. As soon as Waldron realized that service would be delayed, he sent letters to everyone who had paid a sign-up fee and offered to return their money. Ironically, Franks was the only one who requested a refund. He signed up again a month or so later and retained the inaugural account number.

When the switch was flipped January 14, 1984, with 80 ports capable of handling 40 calls at once, LDDS had 200 customers. On the first day, 46 calls were completed, with the office making at least half of them, primarily to Brookhaven. The first full month's billing, from January 20 to February 20, was $6,996. At the end of the month, LDDS, Inc. listed total assets of $562,019.33, and listed total liabilities and equity as the same amount, $562,019.33. In February 1984, LDDS suffered a $24,032.70 net loss, and a year-to-date loss of $52,603.99. Notes payable included $143,169.87 to Action/Honeywell, $244,920 to Lincoln Lodging, and $10,000 to Master Corporation.

Despite landing impressive accounts like Forrest General Hospital, a 537-bed regional medical center serving a 16-county area of south Mississippi, LDDS was bleeding money for two primary reasons: exorbitant line costs and the inability to pursue sizable accounts with elaborate switching systems. Nobody knew how to configure the lines so that LDDS could make money, and Waldron sought help. "I was in a South Central Bell meeting in Atlanta that anyone connected with long distance could attend, and rode from the hotel to the airport with a guy from Jackson, Mississippi, who (handled) line costs," said Waldron. "I asked him what we were going to have to do to get our line costs down and he said, 'You've got to hire somebody and it's going to cost you about $60,000 a year for this person to show you how to put all the circuits together.' When I brought that up, Bernie's exact words were, 'Nobody's worth $60,000 a year.' So he contracted three technical guys from Jackson. I was told that one was hired because he had been a large account salesman and we needed big accounts, even though he had primarily been an order taker. I think the board came up with enough stock to give them 25 percent of the company. A year later, it cost us about $180,000 to buy them out."

By the end of 1984, LDDS was roughly $1.5 million in debt, and Fields, a brilliant strategist but a less effective manager, offered to step down as point man and lobbied Ebbers to take over the company. One day around noon, the two men hopped in Ebbers' gray Chevrolet station wagon and headed to a nearby restaurant while Fields pitched his case. "Bernie could tell you on a daily basis what he'd spent to have a single motel room available," said Fields, who had been involved in several of Ebbers' motel acquisitions. "We needed someone with that kind of analytical mind." Fields described Ebbers as an income operator, who "is only aware of expenses (and) doesn't care about building debt." He is the one that "grows a company," said Fields. After the meeting, Ebbers expressed interest but was noncommittal. He later joked that the board simply needed "the meanest SOB they could find."

No matter who was running the show, the fledgling company required additional working capital to survive and LDDS board members were in a dilemma. "I remember we met on a Sunday afternoon at the office on the bypass in Brookhaven and agreed that because we couldn't make any money, if somebody walked in right then and assumed the note, we'd let the company go," said Dunnaway. "It was unanimous. It was also disheartening."

Ebbers, Thornhill, Aycock, and Dunnaway reluctantly agreed to sign another note for an undisclosed sum. Around the same time, sources indicated, but no documented proof surfaced, that Ebbers became a U.S. citizen, perhaps because it was a requirement to obtain a liquor license for motel bars. The situation might not have come up earlier because some of the first motels Ebbers owned were located in dry counties, where alcohol was not legally allowed.

"We didn't know if we were going to sink or swim," said Dunnaway, "and Bernie looked at the group and said, 'Look, if we're going under, I at least want to pilot the ship.'"

3

The Spending Spree

I am not a technology dude.

Bernie Ebbers, Chief Executive Officer, LDDS

When Ebbers took the helm in April 1985, he admittedly lacked telecommunications experience. However, he was a cost-cutter and bargain hunter. He knew how to sell hotel rooms and figured the same marketing skills applied, plus he could buy the talents he needed. He surrounded himself with "good old Mississippi boys" and set a turnaround plan in motion.

He initiated a four-point growth strategy that called for internal growth, the selective acquisition of small long-distance companies with limited geographic service areas and market shares, the consolidation of certain third-tier long-distance carriers with larger market shares, and international expansion. Within six months, LDDS was in the black, in part because of Ebber's management approach, and in part because the line cost configuration problem had been resolved. In 1986, LDDS reported earnings of $644,000.

"In the earliest days of WorldCom, I was a passive investor and not involved in the company," said Ebbers. "It was only after the company was in desperate financial straits that I became involved. It was strictly a matter of survival. When I did, my vision was simple. I planned to get our profits up, hoping somebody would buy us. Obviously, that has not happened."

Ebbers quickly determined he could make more money by maintaining a small staff while boosting sales, snapping up more bandwidth, and selling it at a greater discount than his competitors. Economy of scale was critical to the success of the crowded long-distance reselling market. Because the market, and sometimes state public utilities commissions, set the rates that companies could charge, and the volume of bandwidth determined the costs, more money could be made by acquiring larger pipes, which lowered per unit costs. Buying up contiguous regional long-distance resellers and channeling them through the LDDS system was the key. As a formula emerged, the first of 75 acquisitions in 15 years began, with LDDS initially gobbling up small long-distance resellers to the south and west, such as ReTel Communications in Franklin, Tennessee, and The Phone Company in Jackson, Tennessee. "It's very interesting about that company in Jackson, Tennessee, (that Waldron initially worked for)," said Singleton. "That company went bankrupt and . . . it was the first company we ever bought. I remember being at the country club on a cold winter day with brown grass . . . and buying that company."

Ebbers made several personnel changes and on February 24, 1986, hired Chris Eddy, then 24, to manage the southern Mississippi operations. Ebbers had heard about Eddy through Diana Day, sales manager for TMC, a reseller in Jackson that he had his eye on acquiring. With that move, Waldron, who had been the company's first branch manager, began reporting to Eddy. At that time, LDDS had billings of approximately $300,000 a month.

Ebbers and Singleton, the self-described midwife of LDDS, helped raise cash to purchase an Arkansas reseller by selling stock in investment packages of $10,000 to $25,000, many to local businesspeople they knew through church connections. Several were financed through State Bank & Trust. LDDS agreed to pay the note back over 60 months at prime interest rate plus 1 or 2 percent. In exchange, the investor received 4,995 shares. Many local investors held onto their stock for several years, cashed in, and "made a mint," said Dunnaway. Many antebellum homes in the Brookhaven Historic District have been beautifully refurbished, a testament to those windfall profits. Stories have circulated about early investors tucking stock certificates inside lockboxes and not realizing until years later that they had made millions.

Not everyone was as enthusiastic to plunk down large sums of money, especially businesspeople in McComb, a city of 13,000 located 25 miles south of Brookhaven. Like many neighboring towns, they were friendly rivals. In those early days, Ebbers, Aycock, Dunnaway, Singleton, and Thornhill were jokingly referred to as the "Brookhaven mafia."

"We laughed at what those Brookhaven boys were doing," said a McComb businessperson. "They'd never done much of nothing." Alan Kitchens, co-owner of Kitchens Brothers Manufacturing Company in Hazlehurst, recalled that Ebbers showed up on his doorstep one day and pitched the idea of investing $3,000 in LDDS. "When he told me he was building a new phone company to compete with the Bell System, I thought I was going to laugh out loud, but thank goodness I didn't," said Kitchens. "I just thought he was a little crazy." Kitchens did not invest.

"We did have very humble beginnings," said Carl Aycock. "It was probably stupid to invest in something we knew nothing about. But we know the Lord has blessed our business. It's definitely not anything we did. He gets the credit."

Ebbers' uncompromising management style was evident early on. The company's first accountant, Marshall E. Jenkins, an independent public accountant from Tupelo, didn't last long. "We handled the books for a very short time while the offices were located here," said Jenkins. "When they moved south, they found someone else." The second accountant was Doug Grissom, a church friend of Dunnaway. A CPA and controller for the local hospital in West Point, Grissom held a master's degree in accounting. "After a while, his style and Bernie's conflicted, so he resigned," said Dunnaway.

Ebbers' methods were unorthodox, especially when situations involved the "Brookhaven Mafia." "When I was on the board . . . (Bernie) would have Debra, his secretary, call down here, and see if we were all available for the next day, or that afternoon, or something," said Singleton. "And Max and Danny, and Carl and myself would jump in the car and run up here (to Jackson, Mississippi). And he would run a deal past us. And he would want us to sign off on that deal, and get us all on speakerphone with the investment banker out of Atlanta, and we'd lay out all the numbers. And of course it was not a board meeting because the board wasn't there."

Because of limitations with the switching equipment, most of the accounts that LDDS signed up early on were small and midsize businesses. "In the beginning, if we had someone that ran $2,000 a month in long distance, we were tickled to death," said Waldron. The company's first T-1 customer was the University of Southern Mississippi (USM), which Eddy landed in June 1986. With its sprawling campus located in the heart of Hattiesburg, USM's striking main entrance on Hardy Street featured a world-famous rose garden. The school's football stadium, affectionately known as "The Rock," was home to such outstanding Golden Eagles football players as Louis Lipps and

Sammy Winder, who turned professional in the mid-1980s. Beginning in the 1987 fall season, it would be the stomping grounds for a relatively unknown star high school quarterback, Brett Favre, where a sea of black and gold pompons would cheer him on before he headed to the NFL's (National Football League's) Green Bay Packers.

Landing the account was a coup and an impressive addition to LDDS's calling card. "The company already had some of USM's business before I was there," said Eddy. "Unfortunately, it wasn't profitable. It took us three and a half months to figure out how to make it work . . . because our technical people didn't know how to make it work."

In 1985, approximately 13,000 students were enrolled at USM. The student body plus nearly 1,000 teachers and administrators represented monthly billings of $20,000 to $30,000. LDDS wrested the account from MCI by offering long-distance phone service for seven or eight cents a minute. USM then sold the service to students for an extra penny. Within four years, the university made enough money from those long-distance profits to pay off a million-dollar PBX system, which had replaced an antiquated, problem-ridden system installed in January 1982. The venture also allowed USM to finance the installation of fiber optics in 1987, the first entity in the state to do so. "We were making money, the students were saving money, and it worked out fine. Good service. No problems at all," said Thomas Bateman, director of telecommunications for USM from 1979 to 1988. Several USM professors and coaches—basketball coach M.K. Turk among them—made money by selling WorldCom stock at a profit during its meteoric rise.

Early LDDS customers had to punch in a seven-digit access number (950-1450) and a five-digit security code before dialing an area code and phone number to make a long-distance call. Sometimes, the company put an automatic dialer in place so customers did not have to dial so many digits. Originally, the customer was billed for the automatic dialer charge. Later, LDDS began picking up the tab.

The first fraud against LDDS came from the USM campus, when some Middle Eastern students gained access to a few of the five-digit security codes and made long-distance phone calls to relatives in Saudi Arabia and Afghanistan. "They ran up some terrible bills," said Bateman. "Of course, they'd always deny it, but we had a system that would point it right out to you." The fraud prompted LDDS to change the security code to seven digits.

Years later, after Ebbers had donated millions of dollars to Mississippi College, the University of Mississippi (Ole Miss), Tougaloo College, and Jackson State University—all Mississippi institutions—some USM administrators were miffed that Ebbers had overlooked the university for scholarships and endowments. Mimicking an old Southern saying, a professor said, "The feeling was that Bernie didn't dance with the one that brung him."

By the mid-1980s, AT&T still had roughly 85 percent of the long-distance market. More than 400 long-distance companies shared the rest, of which MCI was the greatest competition. One of the biggest challenges during that time was advertising—or a lack of it. AT&T and MCI were marketing heavily. LDDS was not. Because Ebbers had been successful marketing motels with billboards posted along the highway, he was not easily persuaded to invest in advertising. Until the MCI merger, LDDS spent less than half a percent of gross revenue on marketing. The company had steered away from costly marketing and publicity campaigns. To stimulate growth, it was focusing instead on mergers and acquisitions, cost-effective technology, and customer programs. Ebbers reluctantly agreed to work with an advertising manager from New Orleans, who displayed a striking array of professionally designed TV, radio, and print advertisements. Key LDDS personnel, who met with the ad man in a local hotel room, were impressed. The results of his work for LDDS's first advertising campaign, though, were unimpressive.

"We were supposed to be on the cutting edge of something new, and the pitchman for this ad campaign ended up being an old man with gray hair and a flat-top haircut, standing in the rain talking about long distance," said Waldron. "He used the name AT&T eleven times and LDDS three times. It was an ad for AT&T! It wasn't until the MCI merger that Bernie really started advertising."

Future WorldCom CFO Charles T. Cannada met Ebbers in the summer of 1986 on business unrelated to LDDS. Ebbers and several others had invested in a pineapple farm in Costa Rica and needed an accountant. By then, Ebbers was thinking about taking the company public and asked Cannada to consider coming on board at a later date. Meanwhile, Scott Sullivan, who would later report to Cannada, had been promoted to manager at KPMG in record time—four years—and was handling major clients such as General Electric. John Sidgmore had been promoted to vice president and general manager of General Electric Information Services (GEIS) North America, where he was responsible for tripling the $240 million business segment's net income after three straight years of decline. He left in 1989 to run Intelicom Solutions, a small, privately held communications software company based in Bethesda, Maryland. After building annual sales to $100 million, it was sold to Computer Sciences Corporation in 1992. Sidgmore remained president until early 1994, when he took over UUNET and became one of the elite dot-com millionaires in earnest.

Meanwhile, Ebbers learned that Steve W. Grantham, Sr., president of TelaMarketing Communications of Mississippi, Inc. (TMC), was willing to sell his long-distance company. The Mississippi PSC had approved TMC as an intrastate WATS reseller on July 5, 1983, just months before LDDS was formed. By the time Grantham was ready to sell it, the company had a healthy revenue stream. Months before, Diana Day had left the company to work for Ebbers and knew the intimate details of the operation. A franchise outfit, TMC had locations in Evansville, Indiana; Louisville, Kentucky; and Montgomery, Alabama. Even though TMC would have been a wise acquisition and would have provided the company with its first short-haul digital microwave, cash-strapped board members were reluctant to approve the purchase. "Nobody wanted to borrow more money or encourage more debt, so Bernie took a big risk and mortgaged everything he had to buy TMC outright," said Dunnaway.

Grantham, who was working with other long-distance resellers in the south, sold TMC to Ebbers for approximately $2 million in March 1987. Ebbers raised the funds through a Chicago firm that had financed his motels. Later, after TMC was folded into the LDDS portfolio, again by Ebbers' design, "that's when Bernie got way ahead of everybody else with the most stock," said Dunnaway. "And rightly so."

Day, the daughter of Ole Miss standout quarterback Eagle Day of Jackson, who had tossed the football around with Dunnaway when he was a high school quarterback in Columbia, was a tremendous asset in marketing LDDS and would later play a prominent role in the company's growth. In the formative years of LDDS, each state was considered an independent unit, and directors were responsible for all operative details except writing checks. Day was director for Tennessee, and Eddy was director for Mississippi. "Diana and I were door-pounders," said Eddy. "That was our strength. We would go out and close sales. That was the whole deal."

Ebbers became a master puppeteer. "In the early days, (Bernie) was very much in control," said Singleton. "I can remember specifically when he led us into a board decision that . . . we were not going to be a centrally operated company . . .

and I thought it was a great idea. At the time though . . . I questioned if he would be able to operate that way. I remember thinking and saying to some of my friends on the board that, 'I don't believe he can do that. I don't believe he'll ever be able to keep his hands off' (but) . . . he cultivated a very effective culture."

Rumors circulated widely that Ebbers, then married, and Day were an item, though it was never confirmed. One source, however, witnessed an affectionate public peck on the cheek. "Good question," quipped a former longtime associate when asked why the pair never married. "No one could understand why, when the company was having problems, trying to stretch money, all of a sudden Diana comes up driving a Jaguar while the rest of us were driving Oldsmobiles and Chevrolets," said a former coworker, who failed to mention that Day's father was a car dealer and served on the state motor vehicle commission. "Diana was such a beautiful and brilliant lady," said another, "and I often wondered why she didn't marry. I'm sure she had lots of offers." One associate said that Day didn't marry until she was 39, and didn't have a child until she was 42, adding, "She gave her life to the company and what does she have to show for it?" Another observed that "being retired in her mid-forties, living on a beautiful farm (Daystar Quarter Horses in Nashville), where she and record producer husband (Alan Cartee) host benefits, and having a beautiful child is not a bad life."

Eyebrows were raised toward Ebbers after board members arrived for a ribbon cutting in Jackson, Tennessee, and found empty liquor bottles lining the office where Ebbers had been working. "Some of them were unhappy about that," said a board member, who added that watching a company formed by dedicated Christians with a slipping CEO was disheartening. Other coffee shop gossip, though never confirmed, circulated that Ebbers was keeping two women in Jackson while his wife and three daughters were living in Brookhaven.

At an annual shareholders meeting on April 23, 1987, Ebbers extolled the benefits of potential savings of microwave and fiber connection, the potential elimination of the switch in Jackson, Tennessee, the status of several acquisition candidates that LDDS was courting, and the status of a public offering with J. C. Bradford. He passed out 1986 financial statements that reflected the combined operations of several smaller predecessor carriers and were prepared by the accounting firm Arthur Andersen. Annual revenues for LDDS in 1986 totaled $8.6 million, resulting in net income of $903,957, or nearly 11 percent. He explained that in the first quarter of 1987, revenues were $3.8 million, reflecting a net income of $612,119, or approximately 16 percent. He warned shareholders that income for the second and third quarters would be lower because of anticipated increased conversion-line costs. Board members Aycock, Dunnaway, Fields, Singleton, Thornhill, and David Giffen, a relative newcomer from the Jackson, Tennessee, operation, nodded in agreement.

Ebbers talked about how the new ABC switch would be delivered at the new LDDS office in Jackson later in the month and eliminate the need for the switch in Hattiesburg. He had already started moving offices to Jackson, a better geographic location, he said, for an emerging regional company. In a succession of LDDS board photos, Ebbers had literally begun standing further apart from other board members, and this move was no different.

At the meeting, shareholders unanimously approved increasing the number of shares from 10,000 to four million. "This was necessary in view of the corporation going public in the next four to six months," wrote Dunnaway, the corporate secretary. They also unanimously approved a thousand-to-one stock split to eliminate fractional shares that existed among the shareholders.

In June 1987, LDDS acquired Southland Systems of Mississippi, Inc., a long-distance reseller in Jackson, owned by attorneys and brothers Wade and Jimmy Creekmore, who also had an interest in Cellular South, which would become one of the nation's largest privately held wireless providers.

That same year, Dunnaway resigned from Master Corporation, then owned by Ebbers, Aycock, and Thornhill. At one point, the number of motels in Master Corporation's portfolio was in the teens, but after the 1986 Tax Reform Act took away long-term capital gains tax advantages, Ebbers started selling properties, retaining about a dozen. An old pal of Ebbers said he thought Ebbers owned a motel in the New Orleans area at one time, but it was never confirmed.

Around this time, Chicago-based Heller Financial provided LDDS with an infusion of approximately $10 million with no personal liability for the shareholders. After a second and possibly subsequent infusions, Heller Financial had loaned the company reportedly more than $50 million and held stock warrants equal to 20 percent of LDDS. Analysts speculated that Heller Financial, which was eventually absorbed by General Electric Capital Corporation in 2001, exercised its options too early. "They left a lot of money on the table, but at the same time, they made a tremendous return on their investment," said Dunnaway.

The extra cash allowed LDDS to pursue meatier long-distance resellers throughout the south and west. In August 1988, LDDS purchased another TMC franchise. John A. Porter sold it to LDDS for 60 percent cash and 40 percent stock. Because TMC was one of several franchises, Ebbers viewed it as an opportunity to get a foothold on other TMC resellers throughout Mississippi and Tennessee. When Porter was going to be named chairman of the board, replacing Ebbers, one shareholder remarked, "We can call John the chairman, but we know who'll be running the show." It became customary for Ebbers to rotate board members of acquired companies, each time retaining total control. During his tenure, Ebbers never served as WorldCom chairman.

In the early years, Ebbers nurtured a family atmosphere, where every employee knew the game plan and clocked as many hours as necessary to get the job done. Some outsiders never understood how he inspired such loyalty. Others saw Ebbers' style as management by intimidation, which became markedly evident when he was contradicted. But growing pains challenged everyone including Ebbers. "Everybody worked hard in the beginning and did the best they could," said Waldron. "It was a learning experience for all of us."

At times, Ebbers was a benevolent employer. "Somebody who worked for us . . . wound up in trouble with the law," said Singleton. "It was a white collar crime of some kind. I can't remember now what the deal was. (Bernie) led us as a board to continue to pay that salary and provide for that family because I think the guy was in for 18 months or something. It was not an extremely long sentence. But we fed that family. And that's very Bernie. Very Bernie. On the other hand, if somebody didn't perform, he would escort them out of the building."

A customer service manager for LDDS recalled her first day on the job—March 28, 1987—began at 8 A.M. and ended at one o'clock the next morning. Ebbers and Day hosted a leisurely breakfast at the upscale members-only University Club in downtown Jackson. Afterward, they headed to the corporate offices where Day gave the customer service staff the task of laminating long-distance travel cards for the company's 500 accounts. Ebbers had purchased a laminating machine so travel cards could be laminated in-house to save money. "We stayed until we finished," said the manager. "My husband would call and say, 'Are you ever coming home?' This became typical. No one outside the company could understand our devotion. We were going to kick butt." The devotion to their jobs did not come without a price—physically, emotionally, or sometimes even financially.

Because LDDS did not have a 24-hour customer service switchboard like AT&T and BellSouth, the 22 customer service representatives took turns being on call. "We were the answering service for the entire company," said a former customer service employee. "I might be changing diapers in the middle of the night and get a call from a college student who couldn't call home with his calling card. It was not at all unusual to give someone like a bank president a home phone number to call if he needed anything."

The company often maxed out every switch because it was growing so rapidly through acquisitions and new accounts. When a switch malfunctioned, customer service representatives received an alert—three beeps on their pagers. They knew to immediately call and schmooze their key customers.

Keeping a tight fist on expenditures was critical to Ebbers' idea of making a profit. As acquisitions grew, only select employees from those companies were invited to join LDDS, and they quickly learned to toe the line. Even mundane costs were scrutinized. If the office staff ran out of toner for the fax machine and it was not in that month's budget to replace it, they usually had to buy it themselves and get reimbursed later. Additionally, employees did not always get paid on time. Paychecks for some departments were distributed up to a week late, but paychecks for the sales staff were never delayed. "Bernie made us all feel that we would definitely be compensated one day," said a former manager. "No one even thought about abusing sick days."

Their inability to credit customer accounts on a timely basis often irked customer service personnel. Sonny Evans, a vice president in the San Antonio office, allocated the amount of credits allowed for customers in any given month. After those were used up, not another penny could be credited until the following month no matter what the circumstances might be. Some customers would wait as much as two more billing cycles for credits to show up on their bill.

No one questioned Ebbers about the policies and procedures. "If you go out in a schoolyard where there are a bunch of kids, the kid that gets his way all the time is the one everybody wants to flock around," said a vendor. "Bernie was like that. He was going to do things his way, and you played by his rules or you didn't play."

In 1987, revenue climbed to $18 million. In 1988, sales topped $95 million, counting LDDS purchases. Ebbers had his eye on the future. He had learned a very simple acquisition formula that guaranteed success. A reseller who was interested in selling to LDDS called the office and was faxed a short questionnaire, requesting a financial statement and a few other items. "We could look at it in no time and decide what we could pay," said a former LDDS accountant. "If his revenue was good and he was priced right, paying him six times annual revenues for his company was the standard. The best he could get on his own was three or four multiples. We got to take, say, 12 times revenues off our next quarter's bottom line. It was a beautiful deal. And we found people like that all day long."

When Mike Lewis put his St. Louis, Missouri-based company, Comlink 21, on the selling block, there were three potential buyers—TMC, Advantage, and LDDS. Lewis chose LDDS. "We were proud of our company," he said. "The other companies were just dollars and cents. They didn't seem to care about our corporate culture or our employees. That was a real turnoff to me. The bottom line ought to drive any sale, but I felt there were certain things that ought to be preserved. The other companies had their way of doing things and that was that. Bernie and I might have been more on the same wavelength."

Ebbers called his way of making deals with CEOs "saving face." "You run into a lot of CEOs, heads of companies, whose egos wouldn't fit in this room," he said. "One of the things I do that's effective is I don't play like I have an ego. A lot of deals go bad because of social things [like] who's going to report to whom, who's going to have what title. I'm willing to accommodate them, give them the position they need." Besides, if the reseller made too many demands, Ebbers would simply walk away from the deal.

So far, Ebbers had been able to mostly swap stock in private deals, but some cash was almost always required. To play in the big leagues, Ebbers knew he needed another tool: the ability to use LDDS stock to buy out other companies. For several years, he had worked on a plan for LDDS to become a public company and he had the key personnel in place. When he heard that Advantage Companies, Inc., a public company known more for its publishing arm and hotel business than its long-distance service, was on the brink of bankruptcy, Ebbers gathered the board members around a table and gleefully announced, "Now boys, it's time to go public."

You couldn't write this script and have somebody believe you.
Danny Dunnaway, LDDS Board Member, 1995

L DDS became a public company with a spot on the Nasdaq system when it acquired Advantage Companies, Inc. (ACI) in a stock-for-stock deal on August 14, 1989. The stock price was approximately 84 cents. ACI was an odd mix of businesses: a publishing firm, hotel holdings, and a long-distance reseller in 11 midwestern and southern states. "Advantage Companies probably started off in the publishing and hotel business, then this little telecom arm actually grew to be much more significant and valuable, to the tune of tens of millions of dollars a day," said a former LDDS accountant. At the time of the merger with Advantage, LDDS reported combined annual revenues of approximately $116 million.

Diana Day was dispatched to Advantage's 22,000 square feet of plush offices in Nashville, Tennessee, to bring Advantage

Companies out of bankruptcy and to sell off its publishing division. In October 1989, Charles Cannada joined LDDS as CFO. Ebbers also gained a friend and board member, Stiles A. Kellett, Jr., who was chairman of Advantage when LDDS bought it. Ebbers now had the currency with which to transact and craft even bigger deals, and the talent with which to do it. The deal making began in earnest.

"People began to get on the train," said Singleton. "And the train got bigger. And the bigger it got, the faster it ran. The faster it ran, the easier it was to get somebody on it and the higher the stock went. There was always a deal cooking. We were buying something every time we had a board meeting, it seemed."

"LDDS was very aggressive about going after business, especially after the company went public," said Mississippi Public Service Commissioner Nielsen Cochran. "They were in here every month filing petitions to acquire phone companies. That struck all of us as being unusual. When you start growing in this industry as quickly as they did, which was astronomical, and acquiring as many companies as they did in a relatively short period of time, well, it's almost unheard of. There was always conversation that at some point in time, they were going to have to start paying off debts."

As head of a public telecommunications company, Ebbers now was at odds with major network providers. When negotiating for network capacity, LDDS was being charged premium rates. Even with increasing volume, the cost was squeezing profit margins. Ebbers realized the company needed to own rather than lease lines, particularly fiber-optic lines, which had tremendous ability to move data. LDDS would save money and could service larger accounts more efficiently by using the Internet to move data, voice, and video via fiber-optic lines. Then it could overtake competitors that were burdened with large staffs and endless mounds of old copper telephone wiring and whose client base reflected LOLITAs (shoptalk for Little Old Ladies In Tennis Apparel), or mostly fixed-income customers who spent little money on long-distance calls.

Ebbers knew that packet-switched data was drastically different from voice transmission, which was delivered in unpredictable spurts requiring large bandwidth for short bursts. Via the Internet, voice transmission was almost indiscernible. Technology guru George Gilder later called the telcos' failure to convert networks to packet-switched data perhaps "the greatest blunder in the history of business." He referred to a statement by former FCC Chairman Reed Hundt: "What we need is a data network that can carry voice, instead of what we have today, a voice network struggling to carry data." Ebbers understood.

Despite high-powered ideas, Ebbers ran a laid-back shop. In fact, a new employee once mistook him for a fax machine repairperson. At the unimpressive one-floor, 6,000-square-foot corporate offices in Jackson, he surrounded himself with young, energetic workers who would wink, laugh, or nod at his antics on cue. When *Mississippi Business Journal* reporter Kevin D. Jones sat down to interview Ebbers, CEO of Mississippi's newest public company in the fall of 1989, Ebbers was dressed "in jeans and alligator boots, no tie," he wrote. "Are jeans normal dress for the CEO of a company with projections of $150 million in revenues this year?" Ebbers responded to Jones's observation. "What's normal? Let's go see what's normal around here." Ebbers hopped up from his executive chair for an impromptu inspection. "By hand count, a little more than half the males had ties. None sported a power tie; they had preppy suspenders," wrote Jones.

Ebbers told Jones that LDDS—on track to earn an estimated $4.8 million for the year, with an average revenue per employee of $360,000, more than double the industry standard—could absorb as many as seven more companies by the end of 1989. Mike

Lewis, whose St. Louis, Missouri-based company, Comlink 21, was acquired by LDDS in January 1988, told Jones: "People want to perform for Bernie. But he's able to do it without a stressful or structured environment." That is, unless staffers failed to do their homework. "Unless it's on paper, (Ebbers) doesn't want ideas," said Fields. "They learn not to come to Bernie until they know what they are talking about."

A simple detail revealed a telltale sign of some of the management problems to come. When Jones poked around LDDS offices, he noticed a large, empty glass-walled conference room past a crowded receptionist's desk. Wasted space in a prime location. Even though LDDS had acquired impressive furniture through acquisitions, much of it was in storage. This central room had been barren for a year. "The room was an afterthought," he wrote. "It's oddly shaped and has too many corners for a traditional table. On a recent Tuesday, a secretary was finally getting around to ordering some $50 folding metal tables so the room could be used for training." Ebbers' response? "We don't need to impress people."

Like many early LDDS employees, Mary Jo Beck, the owner of a local collection agency hired by Ebbers in 1989 to collect for LDDS, gushed about the homey atmosphere. "There were times when we all had meals together as one big happy family," she said. "We'd cook and Bernie would come eat with us. He was always helping others in need. When someone's house burned, he helped out with a donation. It was good." Another longtime employee that Ebbers liked said he "felt fortunate to work in the same building and ride the same elevator with the CEO of a Fortune 500 company. Any interaction was positive, whether it was a grunt or whatever. At least you were being noticed. I mean, (former General Electric CEO) Jack Welch probably didn't walk into a lunchroom where staffers dined."

With major accounts like USM under his belt, Eddy quickly moved up the ranks, working directly for Ebbers. During the height of Ebbers' early acquisition streak, he was named director of operations for the company. In 1990, LDDS acquired its two largest companies to date, and Louisiana became the largest revenue-producing state for the company. "When we did a deal, my whole mission was to go in and make the efficiencies where we could make the interest payments and merge the companies into the LDDS philosophy," said Eddy. "In Louisiana, for example, we did a phenomenal job. We kicked butt and took names. We signed up the crème de la crème customers, just like in Mississippi, where we had USM, Ole Miss, Trustmark Bank, and all the big-name accounts. In the old days, we probably did a better job integrating the companies because the bigger the acquisition, the more technical it became to integrate the billing systems, switches, networks, and accounting systems."

In August 1990, Ebbers noticed that Williams Telecommunications Group, Inc. (WilTel), and Microwave Communications Inc. (MCI) signed a long-term agreement to provide each with access to the other's fiber-optic network, giving WilTel access to more than 30,000 system miles. The deal would later benefit LDDS with an early, strong frame relay market presence.

On January 1, 1991, LDDS stock price was $1.32. That year, the company expanded services from California to the Great Lakes by acquiring National Telecommunications and MidAmerican Communications, and billed customers 3.6 billion minutes. Annual revenues totaled $719.2 million and operating income was $96.2 million. In 1992, LDDS scooped up Prime Telecommunications and TeleMarketing Investments, both long-distance carriers with clients in the Midwest, Southwest, and the West. The company entered into an alliance with Bell Canada that would later play a key role in the company's growth. Canada's leading communications provider, Bell Canada served seven million residential and business customers, including major corporations, in Ontario and Quebec.

By this time, John Sidgmore was president and CEO of CSC Intelicom, the largest independent software company in the telecommunications industry. Formerly known as Intelicom Solutions, CSC Intelicom generated approximately $100 million in sales annually and employed nearly 600 people around the world.

Scott Sullivan had moved from the accounting industry to the more lucrative telecommunications field. At KPMG, he had kept the books for New York real estate magnate Francesco Galesi, the owner of Telus Communications, Florida's largest privately held long-distance company. Impressed with Sullivan, Galesi signed him as CFO. Not long after Sullivan moved to south Florida, Advanced Telecommunications Corporation (ATC), a long-distance reseller based in Atlanta, acquired Telus Communications. With a fiber network from Miami to Atlanta to manage, Sullivan assumed the No. 2 finance position and continued to handle accounting operations from company offices in Boca Raton.

Ebbers met Sullivan in 1992, when LDDS made its first big fiber buy with the acquisition of ATC and its 11 subsidiaries. Before the ink was dry, Sullivan was vice president and assistant treasurer of LDDS, reporting directly to Cannada. Galesi, who had a 25 percent interest stake in ATC, landed a seat on the LDDS board, and would become one of "Bernie's Boys." The stock-for-stock acquisition was valued at approximately $850 million and propelled LDDS from a long-distance reseller in 27 states, with annual revenues exceeding $263 million, to the nation's fourth-largest long-distance provider.

So far, LDDS had expanded through approximately 35 acquisitions of companies operating near or within its existing service area, meeting its goals of growth by acquisitions of contiguous systems. "We only bought companies in contiguous states," said Eddy. "The reason was network efficiencies. We could hook a switch in Jackson with a switch in New Orleans, buy DS-3s, and run circuits between them a lot more cost effectively. It was all a synergistic opportunity deal and it worked." DS-3 lines, sometimes referred to as T-3 lines, are used mainly by Internet Service Providers (ISPs) to connect to the Internet backbone and for the backbone itself.

After each purchase, the plan was always the same: Eliminate the fat, preserve earnings, and support the stock price. Ebbers still did not believe in expensive advertising campaigns or pricey executive perks. He continued to lease lines at wholesale and resell them at attractive retail prices. Instead of telemarketing, he employed local salespeople, theorizing that the personal approach reduced customer turnover, decreased bad debts, and produced a steady stream of customer referrals. By the end of 1992, LDDS had billed 4.9 billion minutes, generated revenues of $948.1 million, and reported operating income of $139.1 million.

In 1993, the company jumped into markets in the Northeast, California, and Europe through acquisitions and began looking to expand service into virtually untapped Latin America markets. In March, LDDS acquired Dial-Net Inc., whose operations covered half of the United States. In July, Ebbers entered negotiations with Jeffrey Sudikoff, CEO of IDB Communications Group, Inc., to buy the innovative global satellite company. Based in Culver City, California, IDB had initiated activity in Russia when Sudikoff secured a contract to transmit a Billy Joel concert from Moscow. He broadcast Gulf War images to televisions around the world. Ebbers' patience in the deal would later be rewarded.

In a three-way merger deal on September 13, 1993, LDDS acquired full-service long-distance providers Metromedia Communications Corporation, based in East Rutherford, New Jersey, and Resurgens Communications Group, Inc., based in Atlanta, in a $1.25 billion cash and stock transaction. With Metromedia, LDDS inherited a beefy, talented sales force and a digital microwave network from New York to Texas. After the merger, the repertoire of the company—now renamed LDDS Communications—included switched and dedicated long-distance products, 800-services, calling cards, operator services, private lines, frame relays, debit cards, conference calling services, advanced billing systems, and broadcast fax services to residential and business customers throughout the nation and to foreign countries. By year-end, LDDS billed 6.9 billion minutes and generated $1.4 billion in revenues and $238.8 million in operating income.

"I was writing business stories for the *Clarion-Ledger* at the time LDDS really started taking off and sometimes I was the only reporter—or me and WLBT-TV—that showed up for press conferences so I got to know Bernie and for some reason he liked me," said Lee "Scoop" Ragland, senior public relations account executive for GodwinGroup, an advertising agency based in Jackson, Mississippi. "I remember Bernie's secretary calling me the night the Metromedia merger went through and telling me that Bernie was on the line. It was late and I was tired. I had been writing an obit, so when Bernie came on the line, I said, 'Bernie, is this for real?' and he said, 'Yeah, now start typing,' and he read the press release to me over the phone."

Ebbers kept his eye on IDB, a promising outfit that would extend his international reach. In 1994, Sudikoff had been named Merrill Lynch Entrepreneur of the Year. However, after IDB's first-quarter earnings of $8.8 million matched analysts' predictions, the company's accountants, Deloitte & Touche, abruptly quit because of "an inability to rely on management's representation" of its numbers. As a result of subsequent investigations, IDB stock nosedived, and Sudikoff and IDB president Edward Cheramy were indicted on charges of insider trading and securities fraud. After pleading guilty to two counts of insider trading and one count of failing to disclose stock trades to the SEC, Sudikoff was ordered to pay $3.8 million in fines and sentenced to a year in a minimal restriction correctional facility and three years' probation. Cheramy's guilty plea of one count of insider trading earned him $350,000 in fines, three years' probation, and 500 hours of community service.

On December 30, 1994, Ebbers snapped up the company for a bargain in a stock-for-stock transaction valued at approximately $936 million. The deal included its international division, IDB WorldCom, which provided service to customers in Lithuania, Moscow, Siberia, Azerbaijan, Kazakhstan, Uzbekistan, the Baltic nations, Ukraine, Moldova, and Belarus. The purchase would later inspire another, more permanent, name change. By year-end, LDDS's revenues had spiked 50.6 percent to $2.2 billion. Its operating income totaled $269.4 million, and 11 billion minutes had been billed.

By 1995, Ebbers appeared supremely confident, especially after LDDS swallowed its first big fish—its key supplier—WilTel. The $2.5 billion cash deal with the Tulsa, Oklahoma-based company was justified with immediate, substantial savings in operating costs and boosted LDDS's annual growth rate from the high teens to the low twenties. Inheriting WilTel's stable of engineering talent was a bonus. "We only have 5 percent of the market, so we're kind of like a gnat on an elephant's back," Ebbers said. "A gnat on steroids."

WilTel was originally established as Williams Oil & Gas, and had become the nation's fourth-largest fiber network by running single-mode fiber lines down pipelines abandoned as a result of natural gas deregulation in the early 1980s. With its 11,000-mile fiber-optic cable network, LDDS could serve even the largest corporations with both voice and advanced data capabilities. "The MCI acquisition probably had more pizzazz and flash, but the WilTel transaction was probably the best deal we ever did," said a former board member. "We bought a subsidiary of a large public company that didn't want to sell to us. We said to ourselves, 'They just don't understand. WilTel belongs in *our* shop.' We'd talked for months. They wanted to break off negotiations, so we sent them a letter with a $2 billion cash offer. We had a confidentiality agreement, but under SEC rules, a formal offer was disclosable. We were following the rules of the game. They just didn't like the rules. They had a lot of pressure on their stock at the time because they had an oil and gas pipeline company on one side and telecom on the other. It was a two-headed monster for them and neither side understood the other. The stock wasn't as effective, so the shareholders basically told them to sell so they could realize that value."

After the grueling, complex, and time-consuming WilTel merger, Cannada stepped down as CFO, citing exhaustion and burnout. "In 1994, Scott and I did the WilTel and IDB transactions as a tag team," said Cannada. "I was the A team. He was the B team. Even though we had a lot of fun and worked well together, the long hours were starting to affect my personal life. I told Bernie I didn't need this. He was gracious enough to give me another role with a fair amount of responsibility and I was always appreciative of that."

Sullivan stepped up to the CFO position and continued to commute from his home in Florida to an upscale waterfront condominium at The Breakers overlooking the Ross Barnett Reservoir. Located in nearby Ridgeland, it was the closest substitute to harbor living that Sullivan could find in central Mississippi. A workaholic by nature, Sullivan frequently logged 20-hour days. Associates said it was not unusual to receive phone messages from his office time-stamped between two and three o'clock in the morning. "I wanted to tell him to get a life," said a former senior executive, "but his wife was back home in Florida and they didn't have any kids, so I guess he had nothing better to do."

On a rare weekend that he stayed in Mississippi, Sullivan and a Chicago investment banker, who was a Civil War buff, headed to property near Champion Hill Battlefield in Edwards, not far from the Vicksburg Military Park. With a metal detector, the unlikely duo spent hours scouring the grounds at "Uncle Bob's place," family land owned by the Cannada family. "A metal detector? That seemed so out of character for Scott," said a former executive. "It made us realize we didn't really know him."

Even though Sullivan was extremely popular with Ebbers, he irritated division managers, whose books he repeatedly verified. At first, division managers viewed the double-checking as unnecessary and demeaning work. Later, they began to suspect Sullivan was pushing the envelope with his aggressive accounting tactics. "We'd send in one set of numbers and then see different numbers in the final financial reports," said a former executive. "No one would listen to us when we complained."

"I hated the work," admitted a former property tax accountant, who was hired in 1992 and left the company three years later. "LDDS had decided to save money and do a lot of tax work in-house. They'd just hired an Arthur Andersen tax consultant to run the department and I was brought in during a hiring binge for about $3,000 or $4,000 less than competitors were paying. We were expected to work at least 60 to 70 hours a week—two hours overtime was mandatory—and not just during busy seasons. We often worked till midnight while other departments left at five o'clock, and because we were salaried, there was nothing we could do about it. The paperwork was endless, just massive amounts, because LDDS was buying so many companies. We had offices in places we never knew about. We'd get calls from people we didn't even know existed."

As a result of the long hours and low pay, the turnover in the tax department was exceptionally high. "I never once regretted leaving," said the accountant. "I didn't like the manager, who was all about work and nothing about morale. She was so dedicated to her job that she had no life and assumed nobody else wanted one. I'd gotten engaged and married while I was there and wanted a life outside work. It was a very cliquish group and you were either in or out, and I guess I was out. About six or seven months after I left, they started giving out stock options and I thought, 'Crap, that figures.'"

The WorldCom accounting department was inundated with work when David F. Myers dialed Cannada. The two men knew each other from Ole Miss, where both had studied accounting. Before that, Myers had gone to the now-defunct Woodland Hills Academy, a private church school in Jackson. After college, Myers went to work for Ernst & Young and Cannada took a job with Arthur Andersen. Both offices were located in downtown Jackson, and their paths crossed occasionally with mutual clients. When Myers jumped to Lamar Life Insurance Company and Cannada moved to LDDS, they kept in touch. In the call to Cannada, Myers explained that Lamar Life, where he was CFO, was merging with another company, and one of his staff accountants was looking for another job. "I asked David, 'What's your situation?' and he said, 'Well, I don't know yet,'" said Cannada. "I told him, 'You need to talk to Scott Sullivan. He needs some help.' I always had a lot of respect for David. I introduced the two of them, and a few months later (August 1995), he was hired."

In May 1995, with a global vision in mind and many of America's largest corporations as its customers, Ebbers renamed the company WorldCom and loosened the promotional purse strings enough to sign NBA superstar Michael Jordan, then a three-time Most Valuable Player, as its spokesperson. "Michael Jordan came and asked to be a part of our company," said Ebbers. "[We told him] we can't afford you, but if you want to be paid on the basis of how the company performs, we'll be glad to have you." The season before, Jordan had pushed himself to regain the status as basketball's preeminent player and was at the top of his game with the Chicago Bulls. He later won two more coveted MVP titles. "You build a team carefully," said Jordan. "You make sure all the parts fit. But when the right opportunity to make a deal comes along, you jump on it. Come to think of it, that works for basketball, too." The teamwork strategy paid off handsomely, and WorldCom gained an even bigger slice of the market.

Some WorldCom employees scoffed at the teamwork theory. "How could we work as a team when there was no order in the company? Each department had its own rules and management style. Nobody was on the same page. In fact, when I started in 1995, there were no written policies," said a former WorldCom travel department manager, who added that 12-hour days were the norm. "Who was a staff person in the travel department to tell a vice president he couldn't travel first class or stay at the Ritz?"

Life-size cutouts of Jordan lined the walls of the marketing department, yet Jordan, who was publicly chastised by Jackson city councilman Kenneth Stokes for "not wanting to visit Mississippi," never made an appearance at corporate headquarters. "I never saw Michael Jordan, but what did he need to come here for?" said the manager.

Ebbers was becoming increasingly active politically, doling out hefty sums to Democrats and Republicans, but WorldCom paid dearly for one mistake. The company coordinated contributions from more than 100 LDDS employees for a Mississippi Public Service Commission candidate. Even though board members believed no laws were broken because the donations came from individuals, WorldCom pleaded guilty in U.S. district court in 1995 for failing to report a felony. Federal law prohibits telecommunications and other regulated companies from donating money to PSC candidates.

Even after a roller-coaster year, WorldCom ended 1995 on a very positive note. "Two years ago, the big three wouldn't have given us a second look," said Ebbers. "Now they're looking over their shoulders." That year, LDDS billed 19.4 billion minutes, and reported revenues of $3.63 billion and operating income of $676 million. Including service to the United States Congress, the company processed more than a billion minutes monthly. More than 7,000 people were employed in 160 offices worldwide. The company ranked as the nation's largest overseas private network services provider, with more than 40 percent of the international private line market. WorldCom had also provided global communications links between ground controllers in Moscow and Houston and astronauts and cosmonauts aboard the space shuttle Atlantis and Russia's Mir space station that summer. Who would have thought that this tiny start-up company from a rural community in the poorest state of the union would be responsible for linking Washington to Moscow via the Cold War "hot line"?

The Ultimate Drug

If people told you all day long, year after year, how great you were, pretty soon, you'd believe it. You might even be duped into believing you did it all yourself.

An early WorldCom investor who bowed
out in the mid-1990s

Power was the drug of choice for Ebbers, who relished refining his deal-making prowess. He would be richly rewarded in 1996, when the *Wall Street Journal* would rank WorldCom No. 1 among 1,000 corporations in return to shareholders over the previous decade, the company would be added to the Standard & Poor's 500 index, and *Fortune* magazine would name Ebbers a rising star.

In the winter of 1996, WorldCom received permission to provide local telephone service in California, Connecticut, Illinois, and Texas; signed contracts to provide long-distance telecommunications services to GTE Long Distance, Ameritech

Communications, Inc., and Southwestern Bell Mobile Systems, Inc. It also entered an agreement to become a major provider of data telecommunications services for Plano, Texas-based Electronic Data Systems Corporation (EDS), a global information services company. All of this was possible as a result of the passage of the Telecommunications Act of 1996.

The bill, which President Bill Clinton signed into law in February 1996, deregulated the telephone industry, allowing companies to compete in the local telephone market against the Bells, therefore eliminating the final barriers to competition and making it possible for WorldCom to form business alliances. After passing the bill, congressmen were wary of the outcome; one congressman was overheard telling another: "Now that we've given everything to both sides, wonder how long it will be before we have to revisit this decision."

Homecoming 1996 on the campus of Mississippi College was an exhilarating time for Ebbers. After the Choctaws marching band played the alma mater, blue and gold balloons were released, banners were unfurled, and a hot-air balloon emblazoned with the school logo drifted across the night sky. As 5,000 students and alumni listened intently, Ebbers, chairman of the New Dawn capital campaign committee, took the microphone at Robinson-Hale Stadium and announced the official kickoff of a fund-raising campaign with an $80 million goal. "The time has come for us to decide whether we are going to reach our potential, or just settle for being mediocre," said Ebbers. "Personally, I have never just settled for anything, and I do not believe that the alumni and friends of Mississippi College want that, either." Mississippi College President Howell Todd followed Ebbers' announcement with one of his own: An anonymous donor had pledged a challenge gift of $25 million. Without a name being mentioned, everyone knew that it was Ebbers.

To coincide with the kickoff of the capital fund-raising campaign, a freelance photographer was dispatched to Ebbers' office to take his picture for the alumni magazine, *The Beacon*. It was one of the rare days that Ebbers had worn a suit to work. The photographer was wearing faded, rumpled jeans. "Bernie was so pissed off," said the photographer. "He was fully cooperative, but he didn't say a word to me. Not one word. His secretary said I was lucky he didn't go off on me. Apparently, she'd heard him do that more than once."

The same photographer was driving a golf cart one day for Ebbers and Todd and attempted to make small talk. "I just happened to say, 'I read that article that Allan Sloan did on you last week for *Newsweek* and thought it was rather good.' Before I even finished the sentence, Ebbers cut me off. He said, 'Never met the son-of-a-bitch in my life.' Later, I went back and read everything I could find that Sloan had written about WorldCom to see why Bernie had that reaction and he had done nothing but call Bernie a genius." Similar comments were beginning to surface from people who worked with Ebbers. The public accepted his image as an easygoing, God-fearing cowboy. Only those who dealt closely with him on a daily basis were fully aware of his rages over petty details.

"Bernie was a John Wayne type character," said a WorldCom higher-up. "He always seemed to be the nice guy, but people were scared and intimidated by him. Unfortunately, people glorified him and that wasn't realistic."

"Bernie was a paradox," said Singleton. "He wore the clothes of a good old boy. And he kind of wanted to be one of the good old boys. But . . . he was always somewhat confrontational, and in-your-face, compared to most of us in the Deep South . . . and that created some problems for him sometimes. Conversely, he could be extremely compassionate. I've seen him in church, not infrequently, just weep. And he is very caring of anyone he would perceive to be an underdog, while on the other hand, if he . . . smelled competition, he became another person. He could be rude. In competition, he is fierce and, in a business sense, he'll cut your heart out. I know of times in merger situations where it would come down to the eleventh hour and he'd close the book, get up and walk out of the room. And leave the other party just sitting there. He usually won in those cases."

Soon after the Telecommunications Act of 1996 was passed, Salomon Smith Barney telecom analyst Jack B. Grubman emerged as a rising star on Wall Street and a great friend of WorldCom. Grubman and Ebbers shared similar rags-to-riches stories. Neither boasted upper-crust backgrounds, Ivy League degrees, summers in the Hamptons, or winters in Vail. The son of a city construction manager and a fashion retail clerk, Grubman grew up in the blue-collar neighborhood of Oxford Circle in northeast Philadelphia. A one-time amateur boxer, Grubman graduated from Boston University before joining AT&T in 1977, jumping to Wall Street in 1985, and landing at Salomon Smith Barney in 1994. He met Ebbers in 1990, when he began covering LDDS, WorldCom's predecessor. A star telecom analyst, he sometimes pocketed as much as $20 million a year.

But Grubman's penchant for exaggerating—even when it was unnecessary—became evident early on. Grubman claimed to have grown up in a more historic south Philly neighborhood and to have attended the Massachusetts Institute of Technology. But those discrepancies did not send up red flags. Instead, Grubman would help raise $190 billion for WorldCom, Qwest, Global Crossing, and 78 other telecom companies. High-powered CEOs of pet companies would later become routine recipients of hot initial public stock offerings, with Grubman justifying his actions by saying, "What used to be a conflict is now a synergy. Someone like me, who is banking-intensive, would have been looked at disdainfully by the buy side 15 years ago. Now, they know that I'm in the flow of what's going on."

From 1996 to 2000, Ebbers would receive 869,000 shares in 21 companies and make $11 million—the largest allocation was 205,000 shares of Qwest Communications, a telecommunications firm that went public in June 1997. Sullivan would receive 32,300 shares in nine companies. Grubman was tied so closely with WorldCom that he even advised Ebbers on takeover strategies, attended at least 10 corporate board meetings, and maintained a "buy" rating on WorldCom stock while it plunged 90 percent from its peak in June 1999. "Jack was always saying that WorldCom was going to eat AT&T's lunch and that AT&T couldn't get out of its own way," an executive told the *New York Times.* "He was very snide and, naturally, that got to Mike [Armstrong, CEO of AT&T]."

One of LDDS's earliest acquisition coups involved MFS Communications Company. The largest of the local carriers, MFS owned local fiber-optic networks in the United States and Europe and enabled large businesses to connect voice and data to long-distance networks without using the local phone company or paying access charges. Established in the early 1990s by construction executives at Peter Kiewit & Sons in Omaha, Nebraska—James Q. Crowe and Royce J. Holland among them—who built local phone networks around the nation, the "alternate-access" local-calling networks accommodated business customers in 50 major cities in the United States and Europe. "Because MFS competed with the local Bell companies, their business opportunity was to stay below the radar," said a marketing director who joined WorldCom in 1994. "If they advertised, it brought focus on them from the regulators so their objective was to provide a needed service in the market while staying behind the scenes." Ebbers liked that game plan.

An unexpected bonus for MFS had come the year before, in May 1995, when Internet giant UUNET Technologies, Inc., completed the third most successful initial public offering on Nasdaq for the year. Under John Sidgmore's leadership, UUNET had become the world's largest Internet company, offering a comprehensive range of Internet access options, applications, and value-added services to businesses, other telecommunications companies, and online service providers. In the summer of 1995, two highly publicized events would fuel LDDS's growth: the emergence of Windows 95 and the Netscape browser. The Internet began growing 1,000 percent annually. "No one has ever seen this kind of growth," declared Sidgmore. "In fact, my network engineers tell me, 'John, if you're not scared, you don't understand.' This is mind-boggling, explosive growth." In 1997, Melanie A. Posey, a senior Internet analyst at International Data Corp., told a reporter, "We're getting to the point that if you want to do anything on the Internet, you can't avoid dealing with UUNET." Since Sidgmore joined the company in June 1994, company revenues had skyrocketed from $6 million to $300 million. More than 15,000 people were employed worldwide.

MFS acquired UUNET for nearly $2 billion on August 12, 1996. WorldCom snapped up MFS in a stock swap valued at approximately $12 billion—seven times the company's assets—without immediately realizing the incredible value of the UUNET data network. When the deal was consummated, Sidgmore, who stayed on during both transactions, quipped, "How many times can you sell the same company?" But Grubman, who endorsed the deal, had the last laugh. When the acquisition closed on August 26, 1996, WorldCom stock was $14.58 and Ebbers was the emperor of fiber.

By acquiring both companies, WorldCom inherited end-to-end bandwidth, global networks, and an accelerated revenue growth. It acquired local network access facilities via digital fiber-optic cable networks in major metropolitan areas in the United States and in several major European cities, a network platform that consisted of company-owned transmission and switching facilities, and network capacity leased from other carriers primarily in the United States and Western Europe. Over the next two years, Ebbers would build the first pan-European fiber network, representing more than 80 local fiber-optic rings in U.S. and European business centers.

"With the Telecommunications Act, it was clear that competitors were going to be offering a full array of services," said Ebbers. "We made this move because of fear of getting squeezed out of the marketplace altogether. [Landing UUNET] was good fortune. MFS had already acquired UUNET, and because of lack of technical understanding, I probably didn't realize how important UUNET was at the time because our interest was on the local side. UUNET certainly has been a big plus."

Six months after the MFS acquisition, Ebbers allayed concerns about seamlessly integrating different networks and offering integrated services when he told Internetweek.com that the effort was going "phenomenally well." He added, "We are able to provision customers' requests for circuits or frame relay or ATM services through one organization."

Considered one of the most powerful people in networking, Sidgmore stayed during both acquisitions, but refused to move to WorldCom's corporate headquarters in Mississippi. Instead, he retained his office in Washington, DC. Sidgmore, who headed WorldCom's Internet division, and James Crowe, who earned a spot as WorldCom's chairman, board member, and employee with the MFS merger, shared a similar vision for World-Com—"a very aggressive bias toward the Internet," Sidgmore said. "We both believed that the Internet was going to dominate communications, and that the real objective was to build an infrastructure quickly to be able to support that rapid growth."

But signs of friction emerged when Crowe sent Ebbers an "ongoing relationship" memorandum on February 11, 1997. "I will continue to be an employee of the company, reporting to you, however I will not have line responsibility," he wrote. In exchange, he would devote one day a month "to such business as you direct" to earn his $120,000 annual salary. Crowe would be paid $10,000 per day for work for "even a fraction of an extra day spent on such tasks." He would have a $75,000 budget for community and charitable donations and sponsorships to allocate at his discretion, use of his office in Omaha, Nebraska, and his secretary Dinah Sink, and would remain board chairman until November 23, 1997. Until then, he would not exercise his stock options. And by the way, Doug Bradbury and Terry Ferguson would be fired by the end of the month.

Instead of waiting until the fall, Crowe abruptly resigned on June 26, 1997, and launched Level 3 Communications, Inc., a data upstart company that received funding—and endorsements—from Grubman, and would later came under fire for, among other things, a lack of customer service. Andy Zmolek, manager of network architecture for a Denver-based software company, described working with Level 3 as "provisioning nightmares compounded by customer care reps that changed every month or two and support desk staffers who don't understand Telecom 101 and won't escalate technical issues without serious arm-twisting." About Crowe's resignation from WorldCom, Sidgmore commented: "It was clear, even before the merger happened, that Jim and Bernie were not going to get along together. They had completely and utterly dissimilar views on the world. Bernie was strongly focused on growth with profitability. Jim had run MFS for 10 years and never made a profit. So they had a very different view of the world and . . . just didn't get along."

To make room for WorldCom's new larger family of employees, Ebbers announced a major expansion of the downtown

Jackson corporate headquarters in April 1996. Since Ebbers had moved offices from Hattiesburg to Jackson, the company had grown rapidly through mergers and acquisitions and employees were scattered in leased offices around the metropolitan area, with corporate staff separated by a half hour's drive time. But Ebbers was not chummy with Jackson city council members, who many people say bungled the WorldCom deal. Citing a lack of support and hassles with zoning, he called off the downtown project, a $30 million expansion that called for building a 12-story, 250,000-square-foot tower adjacent to the existing building, and a 1,400-car parking garage connected by an elevated walkway over Amite Street. Instead, in September, he announced that WorldCom would build a 420,000-square-foot international headquarters complex in Clinton, near his beloved alma mater. The 84-acre suburban campus would leave room to expand the facility and, many people speculated, to build a new home arena for Ebbers' hockey team, the Jackson Bandits. The vast chrome-and-glass edifice, with its four buildings connected on every floor, a full-service cafeteria, and an on-site gymnasium, would dominate the landscape on the south side of Interstate 20.

"The WorldCom campus is quite an interesting juxtaposition because Clinton is a very old, traditional, conservative town, Mississippi College has all these historic buildings, and the downtown streets are still brick," said Clinton Mayor Rosemary Aultman, who was elected in 1993 as the first female mayor in the city's then 142-year history, and has served ever since. "Yet across the interstate, we have this sleek, high-tech, modern building that springs out of the ground. It's a unique blending of old and new, traditional and high-tech."

Mississippi College, which had created a telecommunications-engineering curriculum to train future technical employees, and Hinds Community College, located in nearby Raymond, were used as training grounds for new corporate and field employees. The Jackson International Airport was located a half-hour away, and Hawkins Field, a smaller airport, was even closer to park the occasional corporate jet.

Before Ebbers bought the Clinton property from Mississippi College, school officials had to take care of a potentially sticky situation. A dozen or so bodies were buried in the undergrowth at one of the city's earliest, though long forgotten, cemeteries—some referred to it as Hilltop Cemetery—located on the property where a parking lot was supposedly planned. "The proper legal notices were posted in the local newspaper, but nobody noticed," said a former Mississippi College employee. "So in the middle of the night, the bodies were disinterred, put in brand-new caskets and reburied in the Clinton Historic Cemetery." Established around 1800, the Clinton Historic Cemetery was one of the oldest cemeteries in central Mississippi, with families of pioneer settlers, college presidents, and Confederate soldiers buried there.

"Before WorldCom developed it, nobody really knew where the cemetery was because it was kinda lost on a hilltop," said Mike Allard, a renowned historian from Clinton. "You practically had to have a four-wheeler to get to it. When [school officials] discovered it, they said they really wouldn't disturb anything. Next thing I knew, they were trying to notify families of descendants that might still be living in the area and talking about relocating the bodies. Why not let people lie where they are?"

An area with an infamous past and present, the same plot of land was close to the site of Clinton's dueling grounds—and two legendary duels. The first duel took place between Judge Isaac Caldwell of Clinton and Major John B. Peyton of Raymond after Peyton cast the overriding vote against naming Clinton as the state capital in 1829. Clintonians had helped put Peyton in office, and Caldwell was understandably bitter about the results. However, the famous duel resulted in no serious injuries to either party. The second, most historic duel, took place between Caldwell and Col. Samuel Gwin, registrar of the Land Office at Mount Salus after Gwin supporters defeated Caldwell's senatorial candidate in 1835. During the duel, both men fell, with Caldwell dying within a couple of hours and Gwin living for about a year. One of the men was reportedly buried at the Hilltop Cemetery. A woman, perhaps his spouse, was allegedly murdered and buried there, too. "Seems like them grounds is haunted," quipped one local resident. "Nothing good ever happened out there." In the end, the parking lot was located elsewhere and the original cemetery site was not developed.

The entire WorldCom project was kept under wraps even to people generally in the know. Mayor Aultman said the city did not become involved until the company anonymously requested rezoning for the property, then agricultural. "We knew it was intended for a corporate facility, but we didn't realize it was for WorldCom until after we had a meeting with Brooks Warren, who did property acquisitions for WorldCom and other corporations, and things began to click," she said. "Soon after, I remember [Mississippi College president] Dr. Howell Todd and I met with property owners on Quail Wood Drive, which backed up to the WorldCom site. Nobody really knew at the time who was buying it, even though there was some questioning, especially by the media. Property owners were concerned that it might be an auto dealership, with bright lights and loudspeakers. Dr. Todd specifically said it was a very clean corporation with little activity at night and on weekends. Before it was over with, the project was probably the worst kept secret because everyone knew WorldCom had scrapped plans to do additional development and renovation in downtown Jackson. It all began to fit. Their plan all along was to have a campus concept where employees felt they were at work but removed from the hustle and bustle. Bernie wanted a less stressful environment for them."

WorldCom was a stellar corporate neighbor from the very beginning, said Mayor Aultman. "Every step of the way, World-Com was very cognizant of keeping the city informed and making sure all the guidelines were met," she said. "They didn't ask for any special exemptions or exceptions. After they were up and running, they asked for a 10-year tax exemption, to which they were entitled. We made some intersection improvements around the site, but they didn't ask us to do any bonding for infrastructure. They did it themselves. Fortunately for us now (in 2002), the city holds no bonds, no investments, nothing that relates to that facility." In 2001, Clinton Public Schools, which WorldCom internal auditor Cynthia Cooper attended, received $449,000 in tax money from the company.

Around the time Mississippi College and WorldCom were celebrating the deed exchange, Kid's Town Playground, an elaborate community-designed facility in Clinton that had cost approximately $250,000 to build, burned to the ground as a result of teenage vandalism. It had been open for only two months. Community leaders immediately made plans to rebuild the park for roughly $125,000. Days later at the deed-signing ceremony, Ebbers whipped out a personal check for $50,000 to help the community rebuild the playground.

"People who have read about Bernie Ebbers know he had a less than auspicious beginning," said Mayor Aultman. "He had what some people would consider fairly menial jobs and some scrapes along the way, but you only had to spend a very short time with him to realize that he was very grateful for people who helped him along the way and people who had made a real difference in his life. That's why he's as devoted to Mississippi College as he is because he will tell you his life turned around at Mississippi College. He got some focus and some people gave him direction. He had a real heart for the underdog and people who needed help."

When negative comments appeared in the local newspaper about the three young men who had been playing in the park when the fire was set, Ebbers called Mayor Aultman and told her to "get control of those people." "Bernie rarely put any strings on anything," she said. "That was not his style. This time, though, he said, 'I've been where those kids are, not in this same type situation, but I can tell you this is not helping them. I gave the money to get the community focused on the positive side. We don't need to focus on the negative side.' He wanted people to move on."

Also in 1996, WorldCom acquired a 30 percent stake in Dublin-based TCL Telecom, entered the cellular resale market by acquiring Choice Cellular of Phoenix, Arizona, one of the top cellular resale companies in the nation, and acquired BLT Technologies, Inc., a top supplier of retail prepaid phone cards. It was the year that Sullivan, then a four-year company veteran, became a board member. A founder of LDDS, who lost his seat on the board as a result of Sullivan's ascent, said, "Know how I found out I was no longer a board member? My picture wasn't in the annual report. No phone call from Bernie. Nothing. A phone call would've taken less than two minutes—and would've shown some respect. But that's just Bernie." By the end of 1996, WorldCom was a $5.6 billion company with half a million customers, approximately 15,000 employees worldwide and a ranking of No. 309 in the Fortune 500. Over a 10-year period, WorldCom averaged an annual return to shareholders of 53 percent. Only Oracle Corporation boasted a higher average return.

On a hot, hazy July day in 1997, after nearly three decades of marriage, Ebbers filed for divorce from his wife, Linda, in the Lincoln County Chancery Court. He moved to a double-wide trailer on his expansive soybean farm, where he kicked back as a bachelor for a brief while. Ebbers moved his membership across town to Easthaven Baptist Church after he was asked to step down as a deacon at First Baptist Church in Brookhaven because of the divorce. Linda continued her involvement in the local community and at First Baptist Church, which remained her church home after the divorce, and at Mississippi College, also her alma mater, where she was a magnanimous supporter. "Linda is so generous with her time and her talents," said Dr. Lloyd "Bo" Roberts, CFO of Mississippi College. "She is just a wonderful person who supports the college faithfully."

Speculation swirled that, for quite a while, Ebbers had been courting a much younger woman—a pretty, slim blond WorldCom salesperson, Kristie Webb, the wife of a well-respected local assistant district attorney and the mother of a young daughter. Ebbers and Kristie were frequently spotted around town together. "Everybody knew Kristie always had a crush on Bernie," said one of Webb's coworkers. "I don't know if she was dating him before he got divorced. I mean, he had a wife and three daughters, and the next thing you know, he's getting a divorce and marrying her. Diana (Day) married some music executive."

Earlier that summer, Ebbers made known his plans to distinguish WorldCom from its competition. "We will not be forming international alliances and consortiums with the likes of Deutsch Telecom and France Telecom like Sprint did, or merge like BT and MCI did, or what AT&T hopes to do," said Ebbers. "We intend to go it alone, build our own facilities, sell our own products and collect the revenues that we produce ourselves."

At that time, WorldCom was completing 9,000 miles of additional domestic fiber to complement its existing 12,000 miles. The company was in the second year of a 42-month process of building local facilities in 85 U.S. cities. A double-loop undersea cabling system that was being laid between the United States and Great Britain would handle 30 gigabits per second to propel WorldCom in the European market. Three-year plans called for building local networks in 35 European cities as part of a pan-European network. And UUNET was adding Asynchronous Transfer Mode (ATM) backbones, a network technology based on transferring data in cells or packets of a fixed size, for Internet traffic. The multiyear project cost was $2.5 billion a year. "We do not see a need for more acquisitions because we are participating in all markets with the infrastructure that we're building," said Ebbers. "But I won't rule out acquisitions that would increase our shareholder value."

After all, Ebbers commandeered two of three pivotal telecom technologies—fiber, Internet, and wireless—and was a worthy world competitor. Technology guru George Gilder explained WorldCom's 'Q factor': "The U.S. establishment telcos command an apparent capital edge of over fifty fold, with a global-installed base of plant and equipment worth roughly $263 billion, compared with Ebbers' roughly $5 billion. Altogether, the international telcos command more than $1 trillion worth of capital assets or 200 times WorldCom's stake. But look at the famous 'Q factor,' the ratio of market value to replacement cost as conceived by Yale economist and Nobel laureate James Tobin. It can serve as an index of the entrepreneurial dynamite in a capital stock. With a market cap of some $264 billion and a similar capital installed base, the 'Q' of AT&T and the Baby Bells is approximately one. With a replacement cost of some $5.5 billion and a market cap of some 33 billion, Mr. Ebbers' pre-MCI 'Q' was 6.5. The telco establishment constitutes a Maginot monopoly."

That fall, a cocksure Ebbers, who still relied primarily on handwritten faxes for communication, strolled into the ballroom of the Pierre Hotel in Manhattan to inform the world that WorldCom planned to buy America's second-largest long distance provider. Even though Ebbers grudgingly agreed to pay cash in lieu of stock to buy out British Telecom's 20 percent stake in MCI, which it had owned since 1993 when MCI and BT formed global joint venture Concert Communications, he had wrestled the MCI deal from BT by coughing up 30 percent more—all in stock, of course. Led by Sir Iain Vallance, BT's bid for MCI, which included $4 billion in cash, would have been the largest-ever foreign investment in a U.S. company. "Who was this Ebbers man suddenly gazumping them?" asked the *Independent-London*.

That same day, Ebbers announced a deal to purchase Brooks Fiber for $2.9 billion, a move that would boost World-Com's presence in the local calling market. Soon after, Brooks Fiber shares soared. A month earlier, Ebbers had unveiled plans to buy CompuServe from H&R Block in an elaborate $1.2 billion stock deal and swap its online service for America Online's ANS network service subsidiary, a move that would jolt capacity for WorldCom's UUNET Internet services division. All was well with the world. Ebbers had "Kingmaker" Grubman in his corner.

Masterstroke

On a whim I said, "We might be able to help out."
Scott Sullivan, Chief Financial Officer, WorldCom, 1997

Sullivan grew excited when he heard that the MCI/ British Telecom merger was floundering, after BT cut its offer. While waiting to board a flight from Washington, DC, to Mississippi, Sullivan bumped into Eduardo Mestre, an investment banking executive at Salomon Smith Barney who was representing Brooks Fiber Properties. WorldCom and Brooks Fiber were having trouble agreeing on a purchase price, and when MCI came up in the conversation, Mestre grumbled to Sullivan about arbitrage losses in the MCI/BT deal. Earlier that day, BT had lowered its bid because MCI was having trouble maneuvering through the local business climate, a problem similar to one WorldCom had conquered when it acquired MFS. "On a whim, [Sullivan] said, 'We might be able to help out . . . but we wouldn't get involved unless we were absolutely sure we could pull it off.' "

During the flight, Sullivan began running numbers when the notion struck him that WorldCom could outbid BT, even though both companies—BT and MCI—were at least three times larger than WorldCom. BT's initial deal with MCI for $21 billion would have been the largest foreign investment ever in a U.S. company. But BT expressed concerns about MCI's dissipating Internet presence, particularly after its costly and disastrous $2 billion dalliance with media giant News Corporation, owned by Rupert Murdoch, an Australian. BT thought MCI was overpriced. Sullivan knew that MCI was worth more to WorldCom than to BT because WorldCom could meld the long-distance company's assets with its own local network. "I was convinced that we could unseat BT," Sullivan told his alumni magazine. "We could offer a higher price than BT, and make it more beneficial to WorldCom's shareholders. (But) we wouldn't get involved unless we were absolutely sure we could pull it off." Ebbers was exuberant.

Ebbers knew that MCI would be a coup in many ways. It was also a homegrown company with meager beginnings. Microwave Communications Inc. was the brainchild of telecommunications pioneer John D. "Jack" Goeken, a high school graduate and Illinois native who once quipped, "I didn't go to college because I'm not very smart." He later received honorary doctorates from the University of New Hampshire and Drexel University—"schools I couldn't get into as a student," he said. In high school, Goeken fixed radios. As a newlywed, he also repaired TVs to make extra money. "My dad was a Lutheran minister, so the only people that had TVs back then were taverns, and I couldn't go there," he said, with a laugh. "The first TV I ever got to see was one at the Central Presbyterian Church that went bad. They called and asked if I could fix it. I said 'oh, sure,' even though I had no idea what those vertical and horizontal hold knobs meant. When I figured that out, I went into the two-way radio business, fixing those."

Goeken was a General Electric manufacturer's representative selling two-way radios from Springfield, Illinois, in the early 1960s when the idea occurred to him to build microwave towers along Route 66 between St. Louis and Chicago. The move was originally intended to boost radio sales to truck drivers and dispatchers. "It was hard to sell radio systems in Chicago because of the frequency congestion and St. Louis had lots of customers, but in between, there were very few users," said Goeken. "So I came up with the idea to put a microwave between the two and the only reason we filed an application was to increase our two-way radio business."

Illinois Bell, Southwestern Bell, AT&T, General Electric, and Western Union pounced. They immediately filed petitions to shut down the company, with AT&T's complaint predicting, "There is no need for this type of service and the company is going to go bankrupt," and "it was impossible for this type of system to work." Goeken knew he was onto something big when AT&T disparaged the plan. "If that was true, why would AT&T, with its influence in the financial markets from paper clips to vehicles, fight this?" he said. "And the FCC was more anxious to get rid of us than AT&T was. I mean, who wanted to get blacklisted from AT&T?" Bankers were not overly impressed with the revolutionary idea, and AT&T's political stronghold on the industry stymied Goeken's progress. Undaunted, Goeken and four partners invested $600 each for a total of $3,000, and MCI opened for business in 1963. "All we asked for was the right to fail," said Goeken. "We didn't ask the government to guarantee anything."

To raise money, Goeken decided to sell stock in MCI. "We figured that anybody who bought stock would have to be dumber than us," said Goeken. "But we knew it would take a lot of money to stop these guys." To get around FCC blockades to obtain a license, early investors placed money in an escrow account that was invested in T-bills. "The FCC finally agreed to grant us a license as an experiment," said Goeken. Those who held onto the original MCI stock at $1,500 a share—sold when the company went public despite no earnings—saw the value rise to more than $60 million a share in 2000 as part of MCI WorldCom. "I had a secretary I couldn't pay so I gave her MCI stock in place of a paycheck. About 10 or 15 years later, I heard that she sold that stock for $2.7 million. And I didn't even get a Christmas card."

By the mid-1960s, the company was sputtering and Goeken's original partners left. "There was no money and they gave up," he said. When he couldn't afford to pay his attorney, Goeken wrote many legal arguments himself, longhand on a legal pad. "My lawyer, who had already stuck his neck out but had partners to answer to, felt sorry for me and let me use his library for research," said Goeken. "He didn't know that many nights, I slept on the couch because I couldn't afford a hotel room."

In 1968, Goeken tapped financial guru William G. "Bill" McGowan to help raise money and to expand the network coast-to-coast by acquiring land leases on which to build the towers. Together, they "built (MCI) from a firm grown out of dissatisfaction with AT&T's long distance service between Chicago and St. Louis into today's multibillion international long distance telephone corporation," wrote the Associated Press.

AT&T tried to disconnect MCI when it began offering Execunet private lines with customer-owned switches in 1974. After a court intervened, AT&T tripled its interconnection fees. MCI challenged AT&T's monopoly in a March 1974 lawsuit citing violation of the Sherman Antitrust Act. MCI was awarded damages in 1980, and the breakup of AT&T followed in 1984. "If I can take on one of the world's largest corporations and win, with no money, no political influence and not much else, and start a company that becomes the nation's second-largest long distance . . . it just shows that anybody can do anything in this country," said Goeken.

Claiming differences in strategy with McGowan (Goeken wanted to build a solid technology base; McGowan only looked at the bottom line and wanted to focus solely on capturing a sliver of AT&T's $50 billion annual revenue), Goeken stepped down as president in 1974 and left the company in 1977. "Financial people have no vision, so instead of becoming a whole new industry, we became a discount telephone company," said Goeken. He went on to develop the FTD Mercury Network, a flower distribution system for streamlining the order process, and launched AIRFONE and In-Flight Phone, phone systems for airplanes (he also has a pilot's license). In addition, he organized the Goeken Group, a $60 million-a-year incubator company that funds start-ups for helpful and innovative health, safety, and security products. "I wanted to do things no one else was doing," he explained.

When McGowan underwent a heart transplant in April 1987, Bert C. Roberts Jr. took over as CEO. A native of Kansas City, Missouri, Roberts attended Johns Hopkins University in Baltimore, where he earned a bachelor's degree in electrical engineering. McGowan remained COO until his retirement in December 1991; he died in June 1992. Over the years, excess had bloated the company's overhead. By the time MCI was for sale, it was the nation's second-largest long-distance provider, but it was bogged down with one of the industry's cushiest overheads—30 percent of revenues. Ebbers would later drastically slash that percentage.

Before most businesspeople had their first cup of morning coffee on October 1, 1997, an energized Ebbers dialed Roberts from his New York hotel room. He wanted to tell Roberts, who wasn't in, that WorldCom's unsolicited takeover bid for MCI would proceed. Even though Roberts returned the call around 8:30 A.M., Ebbers took a jab at Roberts at a press conference later in the day by telling reporters that Roberts needed to get to the office "a little bit earlier" if he ended up working for him. Roberts' phone response was apparently more palatable than that of AT&T director Walter Elisha, who snubbed Ebbers by allegedly asking his secretary, "Ebbers who?"

By mid-October, GTE, the nation's second-largest local phone company, had aggressively offered $40 per share—in cash—to outbid WorldCom for MCI; and BT, which already owned a 20 percent interest in MCI, proffered an 80 percent stock deal. If the MCI WorldCom deal went through, Ebbers knew he could skim the best customers while other phone companies were scrambling for reposition. The nation's top long-distance carrier, AT&T, had not yet replaced former CEO Bob Allen. Without MCI, BT would lose access to the U.S. telecom market, which was a cornerstone of its expansion strategy. The leading U.K. operator would need a new partner to fill the void. GTE would need a partner to expand domestically and internationally. The five Baby Bells needed a long-distance or international partner. Sprint, with its local, long-distance, and wireless presence as well as its international partners France Telecom and Deutsch Telekom, was a prime takeover candidate.

So Ebbers was triumphant when he announced on November 10, 1997, that the MCI WorldCom merger, valued at approximately $42 billion, was the richest in history and boasted that "not one red dime is needed" to pull off the then biggest takeover in U.S. corporate history. It was the ultimate power play over rival BT. WorldCom paid BT roughly $7 billion cash for its 20 percent stake by raising $6.1 billion in August 1998 from a public debt offering, selling MCI's Internet assets to Cable & Wireless, and selling MCI's 24.9 percent equity stake in Concert Communications Services to BT. At the end of the day, World-Com stock closed at $19.86. "We were exuberant," said Sullivan. "This was putting a stamp on communications history." Bragging rights for the richest deal were short-lived because 1998 ended up as a year of megamergers, and the MCI WorldCom deal actually finished eighth.

Overnight, Ebbers infatuated Wall Street, prompting *Time* magazine to report: "WorldCom is here to stay. It's a smart addition to any portfolio." Daniel F. Akerson, who left MCI as president in 1996 to head Nextel Communications, Inc., a wireless venture that would later play a key role in changing the direction of WorldCom, said, "Ten years ago, WorldCom was a mouse among elephants. Now it is literally bringing the elephants down." Ebbers became known intermittently as the Bill Gates/Ted Turner of telecommunications, or simply the "Man from Mississippi." Technology guru George Gilder predicted in October 1997 that Ebbers would "release many trillions of dollars in wealth in Internet commerce and communications . . . (and) is a hero of the dimensions of Rockefeller and Milken." Dave Neil, vice president and research director at Gartner Group, called the MCI acquisition "a stunning event," adding that "over the years, Ebbers had demonstrated how an entrepreneur with an idea could change the structure of an industry."

Industry watchers said WorldCom was positioning itself to challenge the long-dominant AT&T. Tom Aust, a telecom analyst with Citicorp Securities, Inc., told *BusinessWeek* that the merger was "a big PR grab—a move to say we are a player." Many Europeans considered the merger a bad omen; an editorial in *Information Society Trends* blamed the U.S. stock markets for "enabling a second-rank company such as WorldCom to become a global giant in a matter of a few years."

Ebbers insisted the merger was vital not for its size, but because "it led to increased shareholder value . . . captured in the anticipated synergies" and "it joined two companies with highly complementary strengths and assets . . . transforming the industry from a monopoly utility business into an intensely competitive market." By swallowing a conglomerate three times its size, WorldCom would become the only

U.S. carrier offering a full range of services with local service in 102 U.S. markets. Its place as the nation's second-largest long-distance carrier would be secure. Its estimated revenue of $30 billion would include control of more than half of all U.S. Internet traffic.

Globally, the combined group would have offices in 65 countries and would be the leading Internet provider. MCI also plugged a big hole in WorldCom's capability to offer businesses systems integration through its subsidiary, SHL Systemhouse, a leader in bundled voice and data network packages for heavyweight corporate customers. Overall, the plan was very simple: Consolidate and then improve the network between Europe and the United States while saving $20 billion over five years. In the end, WorldCom won over even MCI shareholders, who would own a 45 percent stake in the new combined company.

Longtime WorldCom shareholders were ecstatic. "It was truly the case of the minnow swallowing the whale," wrote Nancy Lottridge Anderson, CFA, a financial columnist for the *Mississippi Business Journal.* "Before the announcement, people around the country said, 'World Who?' After network news coverage and national news headlines, WorldCom has become a household name, inspiring awe and respect."

However, not everyone was thrilled. WorldCom shareholder Rev. Jesse Jackson, head of the Rainbow/Push Coalition, opposed the plan; and his presence at a special shareholders' meeting in March 1998 to vote on the proposed merger created quite a stir. "We checked our watches and waited for Bernie's appearance," wrote Anderson. "He strode in, confident and chipper as usual. Unusually, though, he skipped his Western attire in favor of a Wall Street business suit. He meeted and greeted, shaking hands and slapping backs. This was the Bernie of Mississippi folklore. Bernie milled about the front of the room with an unlit stogie in his mouth while his employees handed him paperwork and rigged him for sound. Just before 11 o'clock struck, he walked in. I punched my client. 'There he is. Time for the fireworks.'"

Despite the standing-room-only crowd, Jackson and his entourage moved to reserved seats as the meeting began. "Bernie started the meeting, reading from his assigned script," Anderson wrote. "His usual banter during this time was missing. When he asked for a count of the shareholder votes present in person or proxy, I was surprised to hear this figure represented 78.4 percent of the total outstanding. This vote had certainly created some interest. After an announcement of the proposal, the floor was opened for discussion. On cue, Rev. Jackson stood and went to the podium."

While Jackson espoused concerns about "the lack of blacks on the board for WorldCom and the lack of black representation on Wall Street," Anderson noticed the posters of World-Com spokesman Michael Jordan on the wall. "Hmmm . . . Rev. Jackson had some good points. I'm just not sure why he was making them there," she wrote. In the end, Jackson was a nonfactor. When shareholders overwhelmingly approved the merger, the crowd applauded.

Ebbers planned to sell off MCI's residential telephone service, an increasingly unprofitable sector, but regulators strenuously objected. They were concerned that WorldCom would limit fiber-optic competition by acquiring MCI's Internet division, which would have given the company 60 percent of America's fiber-optic backbone. When Ebbers bought MCI's residential and long-distance services and inherited a wealth of debt, but sold the Internet network to pacify regulators, "he threw away 14 years of strategy out the window," said Discovery Institute's John C. Wohlstetter. The United Kingdom's Cable and Wireless picked up the choicest parcel, the Internet network.

"Ebbers was told by regulators that he could acquire the low value part of MCI, but not the high value," said Wohlstetter. "Up until then, his strategy had been predicated on focusing on the high value segment, and it was Sidgmore's statement that they intended to sell off Granny and jettison MCI's 20 million residential lines that set off the mini-earthquake in Washington. Had he not said that, they might've wound up being able to do it later. Essentially, Bernie took the low value end because, above everything else, he wanted to make the deal."

"(Ebbers) had no interest in content," wrote Gilder. "His interests lay strictly in conduits. His aim was to compete with the telco oligopolies, many of them owned by foreign governments, by using Internet facilities to reduce drastically the costs, first of fax and data, and later of phone traffic. But the Justice Department looked only at the bogus 60 percent U.S. Internet 'control' figure and saw danger. Once again, in the name of halting an alleged monopoly, the U.S. government repressed a competitive threat to real monopolies, from the European telcos to the U.S. Baby Bells."

Six weeks before the MCI/WorldCom merger was complete, MCI acquired a nearly 52 percent voting interest and an almost 20 percent economic interest in Embratel Participacoes S.A., Brazil's facilities-based national and international communications provider, for approximately $2.3 billion in a two-year cash payout. The acquisition gave the companies access to Latin American markets. Soon after, WorldCom would expand its position in Mexico and link the two regions when it acquired a 45 percent interest in Avantel, a company that built Mexico's first all-digital fiber long-distance network.

When MCI and WorldCom officially united on September 14, 1998, the combined businesses represented the first major phone company to offer long distance and local service across the United States since the breakup of the former AT&T. By landing a whale, WorldCom dotted the world map. The company jumped from fourth to second place in the long-distance business. Now the very model of a twenty-first-century phone company, the deal allowed WorldCom to offer businesses one-stop shopping for virtually all communications needs. The combination of offerings catapulted WorldCom into position to be the first carrier to provide a seamless digital network, with the ability to eventually move all sorts of traffic across a singular digital path. "I think the world changed today," said fund manager Bruce E. Behrens. "This changes the dynamics of the industry." The all-in-one company was poised to be the biggest threat to the Baby Bells in the $100 billion local telephone market.

The new 17-member board of directors comprised 11 outside members and six officers of the company. In addition to Ebbers, Sidgmore, and Sullivan, the board included Clifford Alexander Jr., James C. Allen, Judith Areen, Carl J. Aycock, Max E. Bobbitt, Stephen M. Case, Francesco Galesi, Stiles A. Kellett Jr., Gordon S. Macklin, John A. Porter, Timothy F. Price, Bert C. Roberts Jr., Gerald H. Taylor, and Lawrence C. Tucker.

WorldCom was able to capitalize on MCI's innovative—and often magical—marketing concepts, such as the Friends & Family plan. "Advertising wasn't WorldCom's thing," said a former WorldCom marketing executive. "Advertising really started with the MCI merger because that company recognized its importance." Even then, Ebbers was unhappy about doling out marketing money, said a WorldCom marketing manager, an eight-year company veteran. "He didn't buy into it," he said. "Especially after we spent hundreds of millions of dollars on advertising after the MCI merger and saw no increase in sales as a result of it, it only made his belief stronger that he was right." According to *Advertising Age,* MCI spent nearly $219 million in 1998 on network TV advertising alone. "When I first started in 1994, we had 11 people in my department," said the marketing executive. "By the time I left in 1999, there were 600 to 900 people in the department. In that short five-year span, there was a lot of change."

By the end of 1998, WorldCom had successfully completed multibillion-dollar acquisitions of three rival companies—

MCI, Brooks Fiber, and CompuServe. These purchases were increasingly sophisticated. They added significant scale to the company and consolidated its leadership position in the industry. The company organized its businesses into three geographically based units—United States, European, and Asia-Pacific operations—with each reporting to top-tier managers in the United States. The base for network operations and public affairs was in Dallas, Texas. The human resources division was located in Boca Raton, Florida. The legal department was in Washington, DC, and the headquarters for financial operations was in Clinton, Mississippi.

While Ebbers and Sullivan were getting kudos, others were skeptical. "Even though the MCI deal was a huge coup, perhaps it wasn't the wisest move," said a former WorldCom board member. "If the objective was to be big, a survivor and a world class telecom company, it was a good move. If the objective was to maximize shareholder value in the long term, I'm not sure it was a good move. It looked good the first year after we did it because the stock price responded extremely well. When the MCI deal was done, it was going to be very difficult to sell out to anybody because the company was going to be too big, with too much market capital. With over $100 billion of market cap, nobody could touch you. It became evident that WorldCom was never going to sell out, despite what Bernie said about selling the company two years from now. He'd been saying that for a decade. This wasn't supposed to be a 100-year commitment for everybody. But Bernie didn't care about selling. He was having too much fun, at the top of the game. Nobody wants to get off when they're riding that high."

After mulling it over, Ebbers decided to retain title sponsorship of the annual PGA tour event, Heritage Classic. Since 1969, it had been held annually at the Harbour Town Golf Links in the Sea Pines Resort of Hilton Head Island, South Carolina; MCI had been the title sponsor since 1987. Even though it was uncharacteristic for Ebbers to loosen the purse strings for what he thought were unnecessary promotional events, the prestige and hobnobbing opportunities proved irresistible to him.

"Bernie was here all the time, on [No.] 18," said tournament director Steve Wilmot, referring to the hospitality booth on the famous lighthouse hole. "I think he really enjoyed himself here. It was always nice to see him on Easter Sunday, when we have a church service on the 18th green. He was always a part of that." Documented proof showing that MCI made more than $300 million the week of the tournament might have influenced Ebbers' decision to remain involved in the PGA tour event. "When you're talking about spending a couple of million dollars on TV, a couple of million with us and a couple of million on entertaining, that's a pretty good return on investment," said Wilmot. "It's good business."

The $2.9 billion Brooks Fiber purchase, effective January 29, 1998, extended WorldCom's local calling network in nearly 40 new markets and accelerated its local city expansion by at least a year or two. It was a custom fit with WorldCom's core strategy of offering end-to-end communications, such as being able to complete a phone call from New York to Paris without needing to use another company's services. "It became apparent that we would not make money by reselling local services," said Sullivan. "We realized early on that we'd need to build local capacity, or acquire those assets."

The CompuServe merger, effective two days later, and the acquisition of ANS Communications from America Online, Inc. (AOL), enhanced WorldCom's Internet and systems integration capacity and sealed its position in the fastest-growing segment of the telecommunications industry. H&R Block, the tax-preparation people, owned CompuServe, an ailing online service provider, which Ebbers snagged in an elaborate stock swap deal worth approximately $1.3 billion. WorldCom picked up the Internet backbones of CompuServe and AOL by inking a five-year deal to become AOL's largest network service provider in exchange for a small wad of cash—$175 million— and AOL receipt of CompuServe's Interactive Services Division, which provided Internet access to AOL subscribers in the United States, Canada, Europe, and Japan. Structuring the deal this way reduced Block's taxable gain by roughly $400 million, and AOL and WorldCom were able to save about $300 million by writing off CompuServe's assets. "[CompuServe and AOL] had a mixture of business and consumer customers that didn't quite fit, so we worked with AOL to come up with something that benefited everyone," said Sullivan, who admitted the deal was even more complex than the MCI merger.

The elaborate three-way asset swap was master planned by Sidgmore, who predicted that voice traffic would account for less than 10 percent of all telecommunications traffic by 2002. At the time, long distance still accounted for 95 percent of WorldCom's revenues. The acquisitions helped ready the company for a profound industry shift, which Sidgmore compared to the transition from telegraph to telephone.

Under Sidgmore's guiding hand, MCI WorldCom's Internet division prospered, with revenues totaling approximately $1.3 billion a year—six times that of AT&T's WorldNet. WorldCom also operated two MAEs (metropolitan access exchanges) in the East and West, where first-tier Internet Service Providers (ISPs) exchanged traffic with their peers. With its rapidly growing Internet division, the company was primed to shift revenues from the telcos onto the Internet through its Internet Protocol (IP), fax, data, and voice offerings. In July 1998, MCI World-Com became the first alternative operator to provide voice and data communications services in the Brussels area over its own fiber-optic network.

But it was Sullivan who was richly rewarded. For his acquisition coup of MCI, Sullivan, only 36 when he engineered the deal, received the *CFO* Excellence Award for mergers and acquisitions in 1998 from *CFO* magazine, which also honored him with an elaborate feast in posh Palm Beach, where Ebbers was a surprise guest.

Sullivan relished the newfound glory and respect. He and his wife, Carla, often socialized at the Boca Raton Resort Club, where he played golf and occasionally joined pals on deep-sea fishing trips. They dined at glitzy restaurants, appeared at fancy soirees, and were involved in community service organizations, such as the Children's Museum of Boca Raton. They were VIP guests at the Super Bowl, Orange Bowl, Olympics, Final Four, Stanley Cup, Masters Tournament in Augusta, Miami Dolphins home games, and other high-profile sporting events.

Sullivan had been offered a seat on the Oswego College Foundation Board of Directors in 1996. Under his leadership as national chair of The Fund for Oswego in 1997–1998, contributions increased 9 percent and reached $1.3 million. It was much less than the tens of millions that Ebbers donated to Mississippi College, but impressive enough for Oswego faculty and alumni. He received the 1998 Anniversary Class Award "for outstanding career achievement and contributions to his alma mater and to society."

By the end of the year, Sullivan's reported $19.25 million package—a base salary of $4 million plus $15.25 million in stock option profit—topped *CFO* magazine's list of the 25 highest-paid CFOs. He told *CFO* magazine, which named him a "compensation champ" in 1998, that instead of a pay increase, he wanted the opportunity to score larger cash bonuses. "I'd prefer that any day," he said. "I'm willing to lay it all on the line in terms of performance." In 1998, WorldCom revenues totaled approximately $17.6 billion. Between 1999 and 2002, Sullivan would collect $45 million in bonuses and stock sales. He paid $2 million for 4.3 acres in the tony Boca Raton community of Le Lac and began construction on a mansion so lavish that it was only three-quarters finished when Sullivan was led away in handcuffs in July 2002.

WorldCom's rising fame and fortune caught the eye of many critics, the loudest of whom was perhaps the Rev. Jesse Jackson. In addition to objecting to the MCI/WorldCom merger at the special shareholders' meeting in March 1998, he visited Tougaloo College, a historically all-black college located near company headquarters, where he complained loudly that Ebbers had virtually ignored African Americans. LeRoy Walker Jr., a prominent African American businessperson, Tougaloo board member, and owner of 16 McDonald's restaurants in the metropolitan area, quickly corrected him. Ebbers had donated more than a million dollars to Tougaloo College, Walker pointed out. He had also helped acquire a country club and donated computers to be used by disadvantaged black youth. Black churches had also reaped the benefits of Ebbers' generosity. He would later bail out Jackson State University, another traditionally all-black school, when missing computer inventory came into question. To cover the losses, Ebbers simply handed the university a check. Because African Americans represented the majority in Jackson, "Bernie knew who to cater to, at least in the local community," said a former WorldCom executive. A humbled Jesse Jackson left Mississippi in search of another corporate target.

As street-smart as Ebbers was with some decisions, he blurred the lines on others, particularly in pacifying shareholders closer to home. "When everything was going well, which it did for a very long time, Bernie was happy," said a former executive. "When it didn't, Bernie didn't want to hear about it." Ebbers knew that Mississippians were among the most charitable Americans, giving away a larger portion of their income than others. Their generous spirit led them to invest in WorldCom, and early investors were richly rewarded. Investors since 1990 enjoyed an unheard of 225-to-1 return by the third quarter of 1997. That year alone, WorldCom stock increased nearly 66 percent, and Ebbers relished reading letter after letter from shareholders thanking him for building the value of the company, which allowed them to send their children to college, build their dream homes, or retire early.

Not everyone was on the bandwagon. "I may be the only guy of means in Mississippi that never bought WorldCom stock," said a Jackson telecommunications executive. "All these people would say, 'Man, you don't own it?' and I'd say, 'Guys, that's the worst run company in America.' They'd look at me like I was crazy. 'Oh, Bernie knows what he's doing,' they'd say, and I'd go, 'Yeah, right.' And look what happened."

Pride also played a role in the majority's decision to back WorldCom, Mississippi's only Fortune 500 company. But the primary reason for their unyielding faith in WorldCom, either as a customer or a shareholder, was the Christian connection. "In this part of the country, people would rather do business with a Christian than anyone else," said Ronny Smith, a Brookhaven car dealer and a student in Ebbers' Bible class.

At board and stockholder meetings, Ebbers always led meetings with a prayer, a tradition that especially endeared older Mississippians, many of whom had invested their life savings in WorldCom stock and doled out starter shares for weddings, anniversaries, graduations, and birthdays. They didn't realize that Ebbers was known to stay up drinking half the night with colleagues, even before board meetings.

Some Mississippians had a cultlike devotion to Ebbers and stubbornly held onto their stock until it was virtually worthless. But the Christian basis for the company was slowly eroding and so was Ebbers' demeanor. As his power increased and the trappings of success grew abundant, he dismissed obstacles, or what some former executives referred to as his "Christian conscience." An early investor who bowed out in the mid-1990s said: "If people told you all day long, year after year, how great you were, pretty soon, you'd believe it. You might even be duped into believing you did it all by yourself." With tears in her eyes, a trembling 90-year-old widow and staunch Ebbers defender asked: "How could anything go wrong with God at the forefront of this company?" The answer would soon be unveiled: Ebbers' Jekyll-and-Hyde personality.

At least a dozen people who dealt closely with Ebbers mentioned that he seemed to have a dual personality. Others said his treatment of people depended on the pecking order. "He wasn't prejudiced against race, religion, or anything like that," said a former employee. "It simply depended on how important you were to his agenda." A few people suggested that Ebbers might be manic-depressive or have a bipolar disorder, though it was purely speculation based on his extreme mood swings. "It would be very interesting to have him tested," said a former associate, who has known Ebbers for nearly two decades. "I'd love to see the results."

7

The Honeymoon Is Over

Sidgmore was so pissed off about Nextel that he took his ball and went home.

Former executive, WorldCom, 1999

MCI WorldCom kicked off 1999 by announcing plans to focus on the industry's fastest growing segments—international, U.S. local and long-distance phone services, and the Internet—and to triple the size and scope of its pan-European long-distance network connecting city networks. Significant initiatives were underway in Brazil and Mexico, and the company was eyeing opportunities in the Asian market, specifically the Pacific Rim. MCI WorldCom was already a fully licensed telecommunications operator in Japan and Australia and was constructing local facilities in Tokyo and Sydney with planned growth in Singapore and Hong Kong.

Even though North America continued to be the company's bread and butter, Europe was a fast-paced, high-profile area. In early 1998, MCI WorldCom had embarked on a project to provide Belgium, the most densely populated country in Europe and home to the European Commission, with a national backbone that traversed the country from France to the Netherlands. By January 1999, the network was operational and MCI WorldCom launched its first facilities-based national network of voice, data, and Internet services in Belgium. That deployment became the blueprint for similar operations in the United Kingdom, France, and Germany.

In January 1999, the United States Supreme Court gave MCI WorldCom and the rest of the telecom industry the green light to pursue local competition after it affirmed the Federal Communications Commission's (FCC's) nationwide authority to implement the local competition provisions of the Telecommunications Act of 1996. A group of incumbent local exchange carriers (ILECs) led by GTE, and a group of state regulatory commissions, had separately challenged local competition rules adopted by the FCC in August 1996. The United States Court of Appeals for the 8th Circuit had overturned key portions of the rules, and in November 1997, the FCC, through the Justice Department, had asked the Supreme Court to review those rulings. A key impact of the Supreme Court decision, which issued the application of local competition pricing rules nationwide, was a dramatic reduction in the money local competitors had to pay for unbundled loops in many major urban markets. The Supreme Court ruled that ILECs must offer combinations of unbundled network elements for competitors and allow requesting carriers to "pick and choose" individual pieces of interconnection agreements for use in their own pacts.

Through its government markets division, MCI WorldCom snared numerous sizable contracts to provide voice, data, and

Internet and conferencing services in 1999, including an eight-year, multibillion-dollar deal with the Department of Defense and long-term contracts with the Social Security Administration, the Department of Commerce, and the Department of Labor. The Departments of Interior, Agriculture, and Transportation were already on board. WorldCom's clout continued to grow.

On-Net, the new global service announced two weeks after the MCI/WorldCom merger, allowed business customers to combine voice and data traffic from local U.S. and international locations onto one seamless network. The effort was going well, thanks to strategic partnerships with providers like Bell Canada, who agreed to promote the plan. "Everybody else in the marketplace is drooling to copy us," said a senior vice president. "They can't because they don't have the asset base that we do."

In April, MCI WorldCom purchased the remaining two-thirds stake in Proceda Technology, one of Brazil's leading computer services providers, from Partech, the holding company owned by Equifax, Andrade Gutierrez, and SOCMA Americana. SHL Systemhouse, a MCI WorldCom subsidiary, had acquired the other one-third interest in 1996. The acquisition accelerated the future information technology (IT) strategy and growth of Proceda, which held a $8.5 million contract with Petros, the pension fund management company of Brazilian oil and gas conglomerate Petrobras, and a new $100 million five-year contract with UNNISA, a leading credit card processing company. One of the leading IT companies in Brazil, Proceda was considered to have the best systems outsourcing strategic positioning in the industry, with annual revenues of more than $70 million. Proceda's blue-chip client list included Ericsson, Ford, Visanet, and BMG. WorldCom's tentacles continued to spread.

Two days after WorldCom's stock price was at its height of $64.50 on June 21, 1999, WorldCom outbid Cerberus Capital

Management to acquire Wireless One for $36 million. Based in Jackson, Mississippi, Wireless One was the largest provider of wireless cable TV services in the southeastern United States. It owned, developed, and operated wireless video, data, and voice over Internet protocol systems. Three months earlier, Wireless One had filed for bankruptcy protection and MCI WorldCom already owned a portion of it. When the acquisition was completed a month later, WorldCom was able to provide digital broadband wireless access services in Wireless One's 67 markets, which represented about 700,000 businesses and 7.7 million households in 11 states. In September, MCI WorldCom completed the acquisition of another company in which it was a majority stockholder: CAI Wireless Systems, Inc., a developer and operator of wireless telecommunications transport systems. At the same time, WorldCom was melding systems with MCI, it inherited a different billing system with each merger.

Even before the MCI WorldCom merger, Roberts learned that Ebbers' joshing about getting to work earlier was a mere hint of future circumstances. Roberts and other top executives were quickly demoted from first-class executive status with a seat on the corporate jet, limousine service, lavish feasts, cocktails on arrival, and luxurious four-star hotel accommodations. Instead, they were relegated to traveling coach class, scrounging for discount airfares, hailing taxis and renting economy cars, adhering to ridiculously low per diem food allowances, and bunking at budget motels. When visiting the home office from Washington, DC, Roberts and other executives often received instructions to book rooms at low-rent Mississippi hotels owned by Ebbers, such as the $59-per-night Hampton Inn, instead of upscale hotels. They also were told to drive 30 miles to Baltimore to save money on a round-trip fare to Jackson on Delta Airlines. Ebbers had already sold three of MCI's cushy corporate jets. Roberts was lucky in one respect. Other than Ebbers, he was the only executive left with a company car.

Roberts had his first sampling of Ebbers' heavy-handed management style when he and other MCI top brass were invited to a conference to learn more about WorldCom. Ebbers hosted the low-key event in Destin, Florida, an upscale resort town located on the Florida panhandle, and a favorite retreat for Mississippi executives and their families. There was a running joke in northeast Jackson, where many upper-crust executives lived, such as former Netscape CEO James Barksdale, that when Jackson Prep and St. Andrew's private schools let out for summer vacation and holidays, they emptied into Destin.

At this conference, there was no buffet line or beachfront view of the emerald green Gulf of Mexico. Also, MCI executives were told to scotch plans for unscheduled breaks during Ebbers' presentation, where he shared plans for immediate cost reduction measures and informed the group that he would personally supervise their spending through monthly revenue statements, or "MonRevs," as WorldCom folks fondly called them. Among other restrictions, the new system reduced business lunches without receipts from $25 to $5. Also, there would be no more gathering around the watercoolers. Those luxury items would soon disappear.

On the campus of Mississippi College in the spring of 1999, Ebbers gained a trophy wife when he married Kristie Webb in the Provine Chapel, an antebellum building completed in 1860 and spared from the torches of General Sherman. Renovated nearly a century later, world-famous architect Frank Lloyd Wright called the chapel with striking white pillars "one of the finest pieces of antebellum architecture extant in America." Ebbers was low-key even at the wedding, where he wore pressed Levi's and a formal black tuxedo jacket with tails. When he found out about a talented but financially strapped local musical group, Ebbers reportedly paid the musicians $100,000 to perform at the wedding. Another rumor circulating was that rock pianist Elton John, who was touring solo in 1999, played a song or two at Ebbers' engagement party in exchange for a sizable donation to John's pet charity. Jack Grubman was among the few guests who witnessed the intensely private Webb-Ebbers betrothal celebration.

In September 1999, *Forbes* named Ebbers the 174th richest American with a $1.4 billion net worth. He was on a first-name basis with world leaders, including President Bill Clinton, who gave a speech, "Doing the Morally Right Thing Happens to Be Good Economics," at WorldCom offices in Ashburn, Virginia, on March 1, 2000, and told employees: "I came here today because you are a symbol of twenty-first century America. You are an embodiment of what I want for the future." When its market capitalization peaked at $115 billion in 1999, WorldCom was the fifth most widely held stock in the nation, the 14th largest company in the United States, and the 24th largest in the world. Ebbers seemed untouchable.

But MCI and WorldCom executives failed to unite, creating internal conflict and turf battles that hindered the company's progress. In its wake, many well-paid but disillusioned key executives, including nearly a dozen marketing heavyweights and former MCI president Tim Price, then president and CEO of MCI WorldCom's Communications Group, exited the company. Price had been credited with MCI's successful but costly sales promotions, including the Heritage Classic, an annual PGA tour event.

"MCI was much more open and willing to take chances, to let people propose an idea and move forward with it, or as we used to call it, the Catholic way of doing business—do something and then ask for forgiveness later—but at WorldCom, it was not that way," said Kate Lee, an internal communications executive who joined MCI in 1988. "If the idea didn't come down from the top or one of the favored people, it didn't happen. Thinking was not encouraged. Over the years, a lot of creative MCI people left because they felt stifled and I can understand why."

It was evident early on that Price and Ebbers differed greatly in spending philosophies. To gain and retain customers, Price believed it was vital to spend money marketing the company. Ebbers did not. "We have a head start (over competition)," said Sullivan. "But we are not going to be defensive. We have to keep doing what got us there in the first place."

Even the ultimate deal-making troika—Ebbers, Sullivan, and Sidgmore—who worked together to mastermind several celebrated complex deals in 1997 and 1998, splintered after a failed deal with Nextel Communications, a wireless phone company that Sidgmore believed was a necessary piece of the WorldCom puzzle. Even though Ebbers had declared the Internet "a gorilla which is going to take over the entire industry," his actions spoke louder than words.

"I liked Bernie," said Sidgmore, who talked Ebbers out of selling UUNET in 1996. "I had a lot of respect for his accomplishments, his vision of the world. And WorldCom, of course, then became this huge, huge company. The piece that Bernie didn't get right away was the Internet piece. He understood the value of the MFS local infrastructure, but he wasn't focused really on the Internet. I convinced him that the Internet really was going to be the dominant piece of the company. And he basically told me that I would run the Internet, all the technology and the international stuff . . . in other words, all the new businesses. And he would run the telephone company in the U.S. And he was fantastic. We got along famously and we were very successful together. We bought dozens of companies together . . . MCI, CompuServe and many others . . . and he was easy to work for because he gave me freedom and flexibility, never got in my way."

Those warm and fuzzy feelings vanished after the nixed Nextel deal. "Sidgmore wanted the Nextel deal, but Sullivan didn't," said a former top lieutenant. "Bernie said it didn't matter, to flip a coin. This was a senior management flare-up that we weren't used to having. We'd always gotten on board the same ship and moved forward. But here we were, with John and Scott at opposite ends of the spectrum and no room for reconciliation. The Nextel deal was agreed to. Bernie had said yes. When I walked into Scott's office and told him they took the deal, Scott blew up. He said he didn't want to buy that piece of shit property and said he was going to leave. I went back to Bernie's office and told him his CFO was pissed off and he'd better do something about it. Bernie was real good about getting other people to smooth things over, but this time, he had to do it himself. So Bernie backed out of the deal to appease Scott, which really pissed off the Nextel guys and Sidgmore, because it was Sidgmore's baby."

Another factor that made it easy to side with Sullivan was the media's growing enchantment with Sidgmore. Ebbers enjoyed his perch on the pinnacle and made sure that none of the other executives had much face time in the press. "Bernie has never liked Sidgmore," a former senior WorldCom executive told *BusinessWeek*. "He's a monarch and wants courtiers and vassals. Sidgmore is neither." When Sidgmore began nabbing the spotlight, and his quotes popped up in prominent financial journals and magazines, Ebbers' resentment began to grow. "So when Sidgmore said, 'I think I'll take my toys and go home,' Bernie said, 'Here, take them and go. I'll give you this title and a paycheck, but don't show back up for a while,'" recounted the former executive. "Bernie couldn't afford to get rid of Scott. Scott was critical."

Some analysts believed Sidgmore was a more vital player. "He's the brains behind the whole Internet effort," said Sajai Krishnan, a partner in the San Francisco consulting office

Booz, Allen & Hamilton. When Ebbers publicly announced on May 6, 1999, that the Nextel deal was dead—he had backed away from bidding on AirTouch Communications earlier in the year—critics claimed that WorldCom was making a huge mistake by failing to pursue the wireless phone business. "We don't need wireless to continue the growth we're experiencing today," insisted Gary Brandt, vice president of investor relations for MCI WorldCom. When Ebbers acquired Digex without consulting Sidgmore, the relationship soured further. The escalating tensions were poorly timed. Even though Sidgmore retained the ceremonious title of vice chairman and dispensed "big picture" advice, Brian Brewer, WorldCom's senior vice president for business marketing and the most senior Internet executive after Sidgmore, ran the show. Sidgmore's focus was no longer solely fixated on WorldCom. He later remarked, "I think that was the beginning of the end of the company."

But Ebbers didn't mind. "The story goes that when the Nextel deal died, [Sprint CEO] Bill Esrey calls Bernie from his ranch out West and says, 'You didn't want to do that deal anyway. You want to do my deal.' Bernie got all excited and had Scott run some numbers," said the former executive.

Sprint would have been a prize, rich in history and staying power. In 1899, Cleyson L. Brown founded Sprint's predecessor, Brown Telephone Company, in Abilene, Texas. After the Depression, the company was renamed United Utilities and moved to Kansas City, Missouri. By the 1950s, it was the second-largest non-Bell telephone company in the United States. In 1972, the company, then based in Westwood, Kansas, was reorganized as United Telecommunications. In 1986, the company officially launched domestic long-distance service under the Sprint brand name with the nation's first 100 percent digital, fiber-optic network. By the time Esrey phoned Ebbers, Sprint served approximately 26 million customers in 70 countries and employed about 75,000 employees worldwide.

"Even though the SEC had told us they weren't going to let two more companies like ours get together, Bernie was emphatic," the former executive continued. "He told us, 'We're going to do *this* deal.' And Bernie always got his way. If you gave him the right answer, he'd pat you on the back and tell you how good you were. If you gave him the wrong answer, he'd give you a pile of shit. The Sprint lawyers had told him it could be done, so we went down that disaster road for several months. I didn't like the Sprint deal and I decided it was time to leave."

"The Scott and Bernie Road Show," complete with slick slide presentations showing WorldCom's ever-rising stock, remained a huge hit on Wall Street. Ebbers, in scruffy cowboy attire, would kick back in an executive chaise while Sullivan, in polished coat-and-tie, would point to propped-up share charts, showing arrows shooting through the roof. "They were a great tag team," said Ram Kasargod, a senior analyst with Morgan Keegan in Memphis. Annual meetings "felt like a big pep rally," said stockholder Marcia Weaver, a former Jackson councilwoman. Ebbers invariably deferred to Sullivan to "see if the numbers work."

In the corporate headquarters, where Sullivan and Ebbers had adjoining offices, jokes floated around that Sullivan often finished Ebbers' sentences. They ate lunch together almost daily in the company cafeteria and became so connected that they alienated other executives. "They often seemed to be two men with one brain," said Patrick McGurn, vice president of Institutional Shareholder Services in Rockville, Maryland. Sullivan—an analytical, levelheaded executive with bean-counting abilities—was the brains behind WorldCom's flashy merger and acquisition strategy. "Scott was one of the sharpest business minds of the last decade," said a staff accountant. An ace negotiator, he was considered to be Ebbers' chief confidant, adviser, and strategist about issues ranging from customer trends to market share. Ebbers, towering nearly a foot above Sullivan and almost two decades older, was a brazen, free spirit who furnished the brawn. "I don't think WorldCom would be where it is today without (Scott)," Ebbers once said. "Scott was . . . very sure of himself," said David Singleton, a former board member. "The last time I was at one of (WorldCom's corporate meetings), Bernie invited me in there, and I sat by Bernie, and Scott was right across, and people were popping questions, and it was really Scott doing all the answering. And he did it with such confidence, and such capability that for me, I was totally satisfied he knew what he was talking about, and he was on top of it."

Ebbers and Sullivan even shared investments. Soon after the initial offering of Rhythms NetConnections, a telecommunications company whose shares were underwritten by Salomon in April 1999, Sullivan tried to cash a six-figure check made payable to Ebbers, but endorsed to Sullivan. On the memo line, Rhythms NetConnections had been referenced. When questioned by Philip L. Spartis in Atlanta, the Salomon broker who handled WorldCom employee stock option plans and the accounts of Sullivan and other company executives, Sullivan told him, "We're splitting profits on a stock sale."

Around the same time, "Bernie's List" was making the rounds. Even though he wasn't keen on using computers, Ebbers scrolled daily reports that showed who was exercising stock options and selling shares. Bernie's List comprised shareholders who were blocked from doing transactions until Ebbers granted approval. "If you were at headquarters and you were below top-tier management and sold shares, you would get a call from Bernie," explained Spartis. In September 2002, the broker turned over to New York Attorney General Eliot Spitzer seven spiral notebooks and three calendars detailing daily conversations with clients and other Salomon employees from 1997 to 2001. With his list, Ebbers could keep the share price high by barring sales of stock. Without his intervention, stock prices could fall, depleting Ebbers of the deal-making currency he desperately needed to keep revenue growth high. When former CFO Charles Cannada bought his wife a white-and-blue, $32,000 Chevrolet Suburban by selling company stock in 1992, Ebbers chastised him. But Ebbers cashed in $59.5 million worth of his own company stock from 1991 to 1995 and Sullivan cashed in tens of millions of dollars in stock, including stock worth $18 million in August 2000. Sullivan didn't even get a slap on the wrist. "Bernie needed Scott," said a former executive. "Scott could get away with anything."

Two years earlier, Spartis had tried to talk Sullivan into setting up a deferred compensation plan that Salomon would manage, but Sullivan rejected it because the plan required the use of a "rabbi trust," which makes company officers liable if the company goes broke. "Scott said if we can do it without a rabbi trust we might think about it," said Spartis. "It was kind of disturbing to me, talking about bankruptcy and WorldCom in the same sentence in 1997."

In preparation for an analyst meeting in New York, Ebbers and Sullivan were contemplating what to do with $1 billion in proceeds from an assets sale. It had been two years since the company had laid out its full executive team corporate strategies to Wall Street and the highly anticipated meeting was scheduled for June 2, 1999. At the most recent shareholders meeting, Ebbers had announced that MCI WorldCom investments had brought greater returns than AT&T, GTE, or Sprint. Stock prices had nearly doubled within the past year, from $44.38 on May 20, 1998, to $86.75 on May 20, 1999. During the same time period, MCI WorldCom had quadrupled its market capitalization, acquired an Australian Internet service, a Brazilian phone company, sold its computer operations, issued more than $6 billion in bonds and moved into its new headquarters in Clinton. "We spend so much dang time planning things and not getting much done," Ebbers once complained.

On August 6, 1999, MCI WorldCom's network went haywire and Ebbers' resulting public relations blunder would make a lasting impression. For 10 frustrating days, more than 3,000 ISPs, banks, and businesses, including the Chicago Board of Trade, lost their Internet connection when one of WorldCom's major data networks failed. Even though the problem was eventually fixed, and MCI WorldCom offered customers two days of service for every one lost, the company's seemingly sudden dominance in the marketplace caught many people by surprise. "I had no idea Bernie had so much control," said one Mississippian. "That's scary."

The brownout left small ISPs with angry customers, canceled accounts, and bruised reputations. "This damaged my standing," said Brian Janus, owner of RuralNet in Oskaloosa, Kansas. WorldCom's publicity team recommended that Ebbers immediately hold a news conference and publicly apologize. He reluctantly stepped forward a week later, but instead of acknowledging wrongdoing, Ebbers blamed the error on Lucent Technologies, its software design partner that routes data over its wires. Even though Lucent accepted the blame, industry watchers perceived MCI WorldCom's delayed response as calculated and insincere and its customer service as inadequate. It was one of the first signs that the mighty conglomerate had merger excess bloat.

Alex Rubenstein called WorldCom's response standard operating procedure. "After the AT&T frame-relay outage, WorldCom sales reps were calling to let everyone know about it," he wrote in a threaded discussion on the Internet on May 26, 2000. "But when WorldCom had a frame-relay outage, you couldn't reach a WorldCom salesperson for days and then they didn't know anything. After the abovenet IP network outage, WorldCom salespeople were calling letting everyone know about (that too). But when WorldCom/UUNET had IP network problems, the sales druids knew nothing about their own network."

For the first time, analysts sharply criticized Ebbers' acquisition tactics, saying he paid too much for Florida-based Intermedia Communications and its majority stake in the coveted Web-hosting firm, Digex. WorldCom's plan to increase its focus on data and Internet operations and move away from long-distance business hinged on acquiring Digex, whose clients included Ford and Sony. Ebbers considered the move pivotal, even though he paid $4.1 billion for Intermedia and had to cough up a $165 million settlement to Digex shareholders who filed a lawsuit against WorldCom.

When the Internet's rapid expansion began to plateau in 1999, WorldCom was stuck with billions of dollars worth of bandwidth it could not sell. To make matters worse, the world economy was slowing down and companies like Qwest and Level 3 Communications were buying capacity and building bandwidth on spec for untapped routes, for example, in South America. "(Other companies) weren't concerned about not having buyers," said a former WorldCom accountant. "They assumed they'd find them. When they didn't, the industry ended up with a glut of excess bandwidth." Because the company no longer leased bandwidth, it couldn't be written off as a business expense. Even though the bandwidth/extra capacity was going unused, WorldCom accountants deemed it a capital expense. The aggressive accounting tactics would later land the company in a world of trouble.

It seemed like a good idea when WorldCom bought SkyTel Communications, an international leader in wireless messaging that was headquartered in Jackson. An industry pioneer, SkyTel had been the first wireless messaging company in the nation to offer alphanumeric paging, international paging, two-way, and text-to-voice messaging. Via its subsidiary, Mtel Latin America,

SkyTel had also tapped into the Latin American market, where less than one percent of the population had pagers.

Established in 1989, SkyTel had amassed 1.6 million customers through an aggressive marketing campaign and had partnered with eBay, eLink, DataLink, Big Planet, Inc., Bloomberg, and Office Depot. Before joining the company, SkyTel President John Stupka helped build Southwestern Bell's cellular phone service. SkyTel Chairman John Palmer and Vice Chairman Jai Bhagat worked with Mobile Communications, a cellular and paging company, before the cellular division was sold to BellSouth. SkyTel was a spin-off of that venture.

Ironically, WorldCom tipped the media about the merger with SkyTel after journalists discovered the company had registered the domain name, www.skytelworldcom.com. Within 15 minutes of the news, SkyTel's stock jumped 16 percent to $21.88. WorldCom spokeswoman Barbara Gibson said the domain name filing was a blunder. Many analysts never believed a merger between the two companies would occur. "I remember that WorldCom's general counsel chief spokesperson denied that anything was going on," said *Clarion-Ledger* business reporter Robert Schoenberger. "When it actually turned out to be true—the merger was announced four days later—he had to resign."

The $1.8 billion acquisition, which closed in October 1999, was a window to a wireless market for MCI WorldCom, already the largest reseller of SkyTel paging services. MCI WorldCom inherited talented SkyTel CEO John Stupka as director of its wireless division, who would later unwittingly play a role in uncovering the corporation's book-cooking tactics. But analysts' predictions held true: Even though its two-way paging systems were profitable, SkyTel wasn't a good fit for a global telecommunications firm. Because wireless phones and services plans plummeted in price over the following three years, two-way messaging didn't take off as an inexpensive alternative to wireless phones.

Surprisingly, the merger of two companies based in the same city was a poor fit for employees. SkyTel personnel were less than thrilled about the merger, and many refused to acknowledge WorldCom as its parent company. "The SkyTel people were downright bitter about the merger," a former WorldCom travel department employee said in 2002. "Anytime somebody takes over your company, some people are bound to be bitter. But with this merger, they would never say they worked for WorldCom. Even now, if you ask them where they work, they'll say SkyTel."

It was a matter of pride, said a five-year SkyTel veteran. "Initially, there were high hopes about being bought by a multimillion-dollar company," he said. "We thought World-Com was going to invest in us and that never really materialized. Neither did better benefits, which you think you'll get as a result of working for a larger company. The benefits actually got a little bit worse and we had to pay more for them. There were other benefits we lost, so there weren't a lot of positives associated with the merger."

SkyTel employees had also heard about Ebbers' nearly absurd cost-cutting measures. "For example, travel reimbursement was very different," said a former travel and expense employee. "On the SkyTel side, before the merger, we had more flexibility in traveling. We could choose a direct flight or one after seven o'clock in the morning and we could eat pretty much what we wanted within reason and get reimbursed. At WorldCom, you had to take the cheapest flight, no matter what time of the day or night the flight was or how many connections there were, and depending on the city, per diem meals were $20 to $30. You couldn't eat but one meal in New York on that." Other SkyTel employees claimed the policy wasn't always enforced. "It depended on Tier approval," said one. "Tier 2s could run their own game plan. Ours did."

A former SkyTel product manager said WorldCom "essentially left our division alone" for the first year and a half after the merger. "After that, all advertising, trade show efforts, and product placement was pretty much eliminated," he said, and he insisted that a SkyTel pager displaying vital information in *Serving Sara* (a Paramount movie released in August 2002 starring Elizabeth Hurley and Matthew Perry) was not WorldCom-endorsed. "Motorola has efforts along those lines and uses our pagers," he said. "It was probably their product placement."

In August 1999, building on the success created by its MCI 5 Cent Sundays plan, the company rolled out its newest residential calling plan, MCI 5 Cents Everyday, hawked by Michael Jordan and Looney Tunes characters from Warner Brothers. Even though the campaign was successful, MCI WorldCom as well as other long-distance providers came under fire for its sales tactics. The personal touch of local salespeople had been replaced with telemarketers who were less than scrupulous.

Even though MCI WorldCom praised the U.S. appeals court decision to delay implementation of its rules for handling "slamming" complaints (the FCC had adopted its antislamming rules in late 1997), the company found itself slapped with lawsuits based on piles of complaints for the unauthorized switching of consumers' long-distance carriers. Later, it would agree to pay the largest ever penalty of its kind—$3.5 million to settle slamming charges in California. "There was never enough information about WorldCom that would indicate to us they were switching deliberately to deceive people in Mississippi," said state public utility commissioner Nielsen Cochran. "We did find a lot of computer errors involved in switching customers. We also found some overzealous telemarketers who would not take no for an answer. But we can't regulate arrogancy."

When a customer filed a slamming complaint and the Mississippi Public Service Commission requested a third-party verification tape to confirm the switch was legally done, MCI WorldCom was almost always able to supply it, said Cochran.

Speculation swirled that Ebbers was mounting a run for governor, perhaps as a Republican candidate. He was immensely popular—considered an icon, and sometimes a savior, in the Mississippi public eye—and his private life was shrouded in mystery and intrigue. Mississippi has a long history of unusual leaders, and four of the last five divorced in office. "Power is quite the aphrodisiac," quipped one political pundit.

Around that time, media scrutiny intensified on Ebbers. A controversy emerged over whether he was indeed a U.S. citizen. Some Mississippi journalists became so enamored with proving that Ebbers was still a Canadian citizen that it became a game to prove he wasn't. Ebbers seemed to enjoy toying with the media while working both sides of the political fence. He contributed more than $15,500 to Democrats, including the Clinton/Gore 1996 primary campaign, the Mississippi Democratic Party, and United States Representative Bennie Thompson, the only black congressional delegate from Mississippi. At the time, Republican Governor Kirk Fordice and fellow Mississippi Republicans were lobbying support for the Dole/Kemp ticket. Ebbers' split support did not sit well with the GOP state chapter.

Reporters searching for verification of Ebbers' citizenship status were often given the runaround. When WorldCom's public relations minions bothered to return phone calls to reporters about the issue, they would confirm that he was an American citizen, but declined to provide proof. Even journalists calling in favors in high places were told, "Sorry, can't help on that one." In a news analysis, former *Mississippi Business Journal* editor Buddy Bynum summed up: "Ebbers may in fact be a U.S. citizen. But his reluctance to share any of his personal background is disturbing and simply raises more questions. Sorry, Mr. Ebbers, not even a man of your elevated station in life can have it both ways."

For unknown reasons, Ebbers decided not to run. If he had, political observers thought he would have been a shoo-in over Fordice's successor, Democrat Ronnie Musgrove, who did not win by popular vote but was voted into office in January 2000 by the Mississippi House of Representatives, which the Democrats controlled.

Musgrove also divorced in office and cleverly dodged allegations of an intimate relationship with a press secretary, even after reporters obtained questionable documents, including copies of his cell phone bills. These showed countless calls to her at all hours of the day and night, long after the press secretary had quit her job and moved to another state.

In the end, the only governorship Ebbers held was as Mississippi's Best Western representative.

8

The Courting of Sprint

In October 1999, Ebbers really sent jaws to the carpet.

The Independent—London

In September 1999, BellSouth, the dominant local phone company in the southeastern United States, bid $100 billion to buy Sprint, the nation's third largest long-distance provider, and sent a signal that it could not afford to be left behind in the emerging global telecommunications market. With the clock ticking, Ebbers bid $115 billion for the Westwood, Kansas-based conglomerate. The deal, as later announced on October 5, 1999, was worth $129 billion, including $115 billion in equity and $14 billion in debt, and was heralded as the richest merger in world history. WorldCom's stock price was $43.53. Because Ebbers had never failed to close a deal, few people questioned him. Ebbers had already dropped MCI from the corporate name and was running the 14th largest company in the United States. At the end of 1999, the company reported $37.1 billion in revenues and net income of $4 billion.

Jimmy Heidel, then executive director of the Mississippi Department of Economic and Community Development, later renamed Mississippi Development Authority, called the proposed merger "a dream come true for the state of Mississippi." Heidel continued, "When I go to national conferences and meetings and the words 'Mississippi' and 'WorldCom' are mentioned in the same sentence, I don't have to show a map any more. Corporate America is recognizing that the road to the future in high technology runs through Mississippi."

The merger announcement of WorldCom and Sprint spurred building activity around WorldCom headquarters as real estate developers readied for economic prosperity. The real estate inventory swelled with new planned unit developments (PUDs) featuring homes starting at $150,000. Half-million-dollar executive spreads were not uncommon. The construction schedule was expedited for a Clinton north-south parkway, a direction in which traffic flow had been stymied since the advent of the automobile. National retailers and restaurant chains took a sudden interest in the area. "At this point, WorldCom's growth will be limited only by its ability to fuel this great machine," said Nancy Lottridge Anderson, CFA, a financial planner and president of New Perspectives, Inc. in Clinton.

WorldCom was an ace for the entire state of Mississippi, which began attracting tech-savvy companies and professionals over competitive nearby technology hot spots like Atlanta, Memphis, and Birmingham, and high-tech hubs, such as Boston, the Silicon Valley, and North Carolina's Research Triangle. "(Bernie) is the Ted Turner of the telecommunications industry," said telecommunications analyst Peter Bernstein, "and Jackson, Mississippi, is the hot bed of the communications industry." Ironically, Ebbers' local involvement diminished as the telecom cluster in central Mississippi and the

Mississippi Technology Alliance grew stronger, facilitated by Harvard Professor Michael Porter's game plan. After the Mississippi Legislature approved $17.5 million for a state telecommunications conference and training center in 1995, Ebbers flippantly said he had no need for it. The upswing was that by the time WorldCom filed for bankruptcy protection, the telecom cluster was a thriving, self-sufficient entity and had emerged, for the most part, unscathed.

"Once LDDS folded its merged companies into WorldCom, they removed us from their vendor list," said Gerard Gibert, president and CEO of Venture Technologies, Incorporated, of Ridgeland, Mississippi, one of the top technology solutions companies in America. "Decisions for purchases of information technology products and services were no longer being made in Jackson. That was just as well because [WorldCom] was very difficult to work with. They were notorious for terrible billing practices. They were constantly late paying their bills and were awful about billings to their customers. To me, that's a gauge for the quality of management of a company. In WorldCom's case, they've been poor on both counts since inception. There's probably not a WorldCom customer in America that doesn't have complaints about the inaccuracies of the company's billing process. It was only a gut feeling, but I really felt like it was simply a matter of time before the whole thing crashed, just because of that."

The Sprint deal was important to Ebbers partly because of its wireless unit, Sprint PCS. Even though WorldCom was the second-largest long-distance provider in America and carried more Internet traffic than any other company, it lacked a nationwide wireless network. Sprint's huge wireless phone business would allow WorldCom to offer the full array of telecommunications services. WorldCom was also betting on a separate piece of Sprint technology—Multichannel Multipoint Distribution Service—that could allow the company to reach millions of customers without having to lay wires. WorldCom had picked up the technology when it acquired wireless telecommunications transport systems operator CAI Wireless Systems, Inc. "Packet switching" technology allowed a single circuit to accommodate more than 100 phone conversations at once, compared with "circuit switching," which could accommodate only one.

In a speech titled, "Strong Enough to Fight Back," given at a National Press Club luncheon in Washington, DC, on January 12, 2000, Ebbers announced plans to sell the benefits of a new service provider—the result of the proposed WorldCom-Sprint merger as an "all-distance carrier." "If you're not all-distance in this business, you won't go the distance," he said. "That means providing local, long distance, international, data, Internet, wireline, and wireless. All services, all distances." Ebbers' philosophy seemed to work. By February 10, WorldCom announced it had nearly tripled its earnings in the fourth quarter of 1999. During the first quarter of 2000, the company increased revenue by 14 percent and earnings by 80 percent. Industry watchers were happy. "Bernie does a wonderful job of not disappointing people," said Philip Wohl, an analyst with the New York-based S&P Equity Group. But WorldCom began using a different accounting method to keep what would amount to more than $7 billion in spending out of its financial reports, beginning sometime between 1999 and the first quarter of 2000. By starting the year on such a positive note, a weakened WorldCom seemed unimaginable.

But trouble was brewing. At the same time that Ebbers was courting Sprint, Internet growth had shifted considerably from 1,000 percent a year to 100 percent. Profits leveled off and WorldCom's stock price began to tank as demand for its data network services began to sink. The telecom industry meltdown continued. Selling basic local-phone service was becoming wildly unprofitable. Within a four-year period, long-distance phone calls in North America plummeted from 15 cents to a bargain two cents a minute. The long-distance price war took its toll on WorldCom. The year before, WorldCom had won a bid to provide long-distance service to discount retail giant Kmart. "We won the bid, fair and square," Ebbers said. To retain Kmart as a customer, AT&T offered to provide the same service for $5 million less. When Ebbers found out, he offered to undercut AT&T even deeper, but in the end was forced to raise the white flag. At that point, he couldn't make a profit from Kmart anyway.

Kinks in the regulatory system had emerged, prompting Allan Sloan to write in October 1999, "The FCC is making a valiant attempt to hold the current system together, as it's legally charged to do. But it's like trying to stuff a 42-inch waist into 36-inch shorts. It kind of works, if you don't look too close, but there are still all sorts of unsightly bulges." The situation was mirrored at WorldCom. The nearly $30 billion in debt piled high during the spectacular spending spree was beginning to weigh heavily on company coffers.

Analysts began criticizing Ebbers' management style. Business writer Dana Blankenhorn called Ebbers "basically an old-style telephone guy, heavy on finance and cost-cutting but weak on operations and marketing. He can buy, he can squeeze, but he can't build. That's fine when customers have limited choices—and the merger with Sprint was designed to limit those choices further—but the world has changed."

Shareholders still loved Ebbers. At a packed-house special meeting held April 28, 2000, to bless the WorldCom-Sprint merger, Ebbers was a folksy host. "(He) apologized for the lack of chairs. No one seemed to mind," wrote Nancy Lottridge Anderson. "First, Ebbers introduced board members and paid homage to the man who started the original company, LDDS, . . . then proudly introduced us to the 'most important person in the room,' his infant grandson. The actual meeting took about 10 minutes. Business was dispensed with quickly, with Ebbers quipping his way through the script. Two ladies in front heard the adjournment motion and turned to me wide-eyed. 'Don't worry,' I said, 'Now comes the good part.' With that, the floor was opened for questions, and Ebbers displayed his flair for handling even the most annoying questions with poise and humor. In the middle of all the one-liners flowed information and visions of the future world. That this revolution could be emanating from Clinton, Mississippi, lent a surreal atmosphere to the meeting."

The Sprint deal began to sour after regulators in Washington, DC, and Brussels raised objections. They claimed the deal was anticompetitive even though AT&T still had a 57 percent share of the residential long-distance market, and the combination of Sprint's 8 percent and WorldCom's 19 percent would make them better able to break AT&T's dominance. Regulators were also concerned with Internet traffic. WorldCom's 37 percent and Sprint's 16 percent market shares would have dominated Web traffic, even though SBC was allowed to acquire PacBell and Ameritech, giving the company a monopoly on virtually every local phone call west of the Mississippi River, and Bell Atlantic was allowed to acquire Nynex and dominate the fiber across the eastern seaboard. SBC and Bell Atlantic were working to satisfy regulatory requirements that, once done, would have allowed them access to the long-distance market.

Combining Sprint's wireless network with its Internet services would have allowed WorldCom to converge services to businesses at a faster pace. Messy details related to the proposed WorldCom/Sprint merger prompted some congressional leaders to rethink the Telecommunications Act of 1996, which unwittingly contributed to industrywide consolidation when it removed restrictions between local and long-distance services.

To make the merger work to satisfy competition watchdogs, Ebbers would be forced to sell off huge chunks of Sprint and WorldCom. Both companies agreed to sell off Sprint's

Internet division, the nation's second-largest backbone network. Ebbers, however, vowed he would never sell UUNET, which provided Internet access, Web hosting, remote access, and other services to more than 70,000 businesses in 114 countries. It also owned and operated a global network in thousands of cities throughout North America, Europe, and the Asia-Pacific Rim region. But WorldCom and Sprint were unable to demonstrate to the FCC that it was price, not brand, that prompted consumers to switch long-distance carriers.

By late spring, WorldCom shares started to tumble. Then word began to spread that the predator from Mississippi was becoming bait itself. Deutsche Telekom was mentioned as a possible suitor, but it was struggling to complete its purchase of VoiceStream, a wireless provider in Seattle, Washington. Also mentioned was Spain's Telefonica, the leading telecommunications service provider in the Spanish-speaking world, which WorldCom had partnered with in March 1998 as a European business network distributor, and whose chairman and CEO, Juan Villalonga Navarro, had joined the board of directors in November 1998. So was BellSouth.

When the U.S. Department of Justice filed suit to block the deal on June 27, 2000, Esrey told Ebbers that fighting the government in court was "not a realistic alternative." At a press conference in Washington, DC, Attorney General Janet Reno said the proposed merger "threatens to undermine the competitive gains achieved since the department challenged AT&T's monopoly of the telecommunications industry 25 years ago." European Union Competition Commissioner Mario Mont said his proposal to the commission would be to prohibit the merger by a July 12 deadline. But Ebbers was not ready to give up.

By the time Ebbers officially called off the blockbuster wedding on July 13, 2000, WorldCom's stock price had slipped to $46.07. "After the Sprint merger fell through, our stock dropped so bad," said a former travel department employee.

"Everybody was so upset about it because they had stock options. We knew the value of working there would eventually go down. Then when the layoffs started, morale went down. What we didn't get was, why did Sprint's stock go up?"

Mississippi Business Journal editor Jim Laird said: "Love it or hate it, you can't leave it. The WorldCom-Sprint deal was our little big merger. It was Mississippi's big gulp of the 'New New Thing.'" Howard J. Schilit of the Center for Financial Research and Analysis, said: "The kiboshing of the Sprint merger was, for all intents and purposes, the end of WorldCom. When you have companies that have to make acquisitions to survive, once the music stops, the dance is over."

In a prepared statement, Ebbers blasted FCC Chairman William Kennard and Joel Klein, assistant attorney general of the Justice Department's Antitrust Division: "Opposition to this merger just adds to the list of Kennard-Klein policies that ultimately will reduce innovation and choice, and raise the cost of telephone services for residential customers, particularly those in rural America." Analysts eschewed Ebbers for making remarks that could hinder future mergers. "That was not a smart thing to do," said Lisa Pierce, an analyst with the Giga Information Group. "I presume that Bernie might want to buy something in the future, and that's not going to help him in any future go-rounds." Indeed, the statement would come back to haunt Ebbers for an entirely different reason.

On Wall Street, however, Ebbers' tone was different when he made this humbling statement: "We recognize that we, as a company, have let you down. I have let myself down. We certainly don't look at this as the best day of our life . . . [The attempt to acquire Sprint] ended up a mistake—and I am certainly accountable for that mistake . . . I'm sure with the recent performance of this stock, people have a legitimate right to ask if I have a right to lead this company."

The merger with Sprint would have allowed WorldCom not only to replenish its reserves but to increase them substantially. Without sufficient excess reserves to draw down as a device to increase earnings going forward, the company began converting significant portions of its line-cost items into capital expenses, conversions that would lead to the June 26, 2002, disclosure of $3.8 billion in improperly booked income.

With no dial tone between WorldCom and Sprint, Ebbers was left with two other vexing problems—no wireless strategy and voice service revenues that accounted for 54 percent of its $38 billion in revenues. "WorldCom's focus and primary goal was to acquire Sprint PCS," said Stacey Wall, president of Pinnacle Trust in Ridgeland, Mississippi. "This was not a cheap proposition. However, it would have provided WorldCom with a lock on the premier global integrated-broadband communications provider. If WorldCom could have held on to the current agreement with the option to acquire PCS at a 10 percent premium to the share price in several years, it would have been a home run."

Initially, WorldCom employees were somewhat relieved that the deal did not go through, said Ronald E. Drabman, director of training and psychology programs at the University of Mississippi Medical Center in Jackson. "When your company is in play, you always wonder if it is you that will be downsized. However, with the rumors that WorldCom [might] be sold, anxiety was much increased."

While Ebbers' attention was focused on the Sprint deal, customer service had steadily declined. Ebbers had accumulated a grab bag of companies but had not spent the money to integrate billing, sales, or service. Andy Zmolek, manager of network architecture with a Denver-based software company, said the result was "like dealing with 100 islands, even though sales and marketing tries to present a unified front."

On ConsumerAffairs.com, one of many outlets for frustrated consumers, WorldCom customers complained about billing errors and deteriorating customer service despite claims in the company's 1998 annual report, where Diana Day-Cartee, president of customer satisfaction and service operations for WorldCom proclaimed: "No situation is too difficult. No question unsolvable. When you ask, you can consider it done."

Clifford of Wesley Chapel, Florida, apparently did not think so. He wrote: "MCI does not appreciate the consumer's business nor do they respect the consumer's precious time. It takes a lot of effort to call, be put on hold, discuss your case (and) then end your conversation dispirited. I vow never again to deal with MCI and warn other consumers of their tactics." Deborah of Charlotte, North Carolina, received a bill from WorldCom for long-distance charges at a rate of .289 cents per minute, substantially higher than the nine cents a minute she had agreed to pay. "I called MCI immediately and, after waiting on hold for a long, long time and listening to their advertisements, I got connected to a customer service representative . . . (who) said that when I moved 11/1/99 . . . I neglected to call them to tell them that I wanted the same calling plan . . . and they switched me over to the standard rate." The preprinted change of address form she mailed to the company a week before the move was apparently insufficient, she wrote.

After Susanne of Choctaw, Oklahoma, received a long-distance phone bill with charges of 59 cents a minute for using a MCI calling card, she began the first in a series of lengthy and fruitless calls to WorldCom customer service to dispute what she deemed "highway robbery." "My time is worth about $17 per hour to me, but evidently nothing to MCI," she wrote. "On two separate occasions, I stayed on hold about 40 minutes, only to be told that their computers were down and I would have to call back another time." After several exhausting conversations with WorldCom about overbilling, Ilona of Brooklyn,

New York, wrote: "I would not recommend MCI to anyone and will never use them again."

In many ways, WorldCom had become a follower, not a leader, and industry watchers were taking note. The company was already established as a late arrival to the wireless market and missed important trends such as high-end corporate Web site management. Ebbers admitted: "We dropped the ball. In the MCI transaction, we spent a year before regulators, another year integrating the companies. Then we jumped off the diving board with Sprint. It was our mistake. We did not keep up on the cutting edge of the development of new products."

Shareholder value—and faith—plummeted. WorldCom stock fell 20 percent in a matter of hours after the company slashed its growth expectations for the rest of the year, prompting Wohl to say, "(Ebbers) disappointed me for the first time." A former WorldCom employee wrote on an ebulletin board: "WorldCom was just one big ponzy scheme that fell apart after the Sprint deal fell through."

WorldCom regional vice president Chris Eddy, who at one point supervised all the billing systems, mergers, security development, and marketing of integrated companies for the company, called some of the news articles written about the poor integration of merged systems "slanderous bullshit."

"People don't realize how technically challenging it is to merge a network and billing and accounting systems," said Eddy, who has also done extensive consulting work for CLECs (competitive local exchange carriers). "Shoot, it could take five years. People were given the impression that we weren't trying to get it done. It's just a massive undertaking. MCI had more different billing plans than you could imagine. The same thing with a lot of other customer bases, like WilTel's. When we bought ATC in 1992, I was in charge of that one and it was seamless, but it's typically just not something that happens overnight. It's amazing to me how quickly the banking industry can do it . . . but in the telecommunications industry, when you're integrating switches, billing systems, and accounting systems, the idiosyncrasies of the different plans that these customers are on . . . it's a very complicated deal."

Administrative details were often overlooked during the melee, said former WorldCom executive Kate Lee. "With mergers and acquisitions, you'd knock off the big synergies, as Bernie would say, very quickly, and then you would start working your way down to the lower dollar items," she said. "A lot of that would get pushed off to the side because another new big merger or acquisition would come along and we'd end up with a big pile-up. Tracking the ownership of the company's PCs, for example. You never knew who had what. As a manager who worked inside the company for a long time, you just looked around and said, 'Okay, on to the next thing,' and the inconsistencies never resolved themselves."

When the calendar flipped to 2001, shareholders hoped that 2000 was simply a bad year. But some say Sullivan was in a bind. It is alleged that he continued manipulating the books to artificially boost revenues by reducing expenses. A former WorldCom board member said the Sprint deal "took the eye off the ball for a little while, but it's not the real reason the company went south." Internal pressures continued to mount in the feckless family of employees as a mass exodus of key executives continued. By stitching together dozens of companies, WorldCom never operated as a single, seamless enterprise. "Don't think of WorldCom the way you would of other corporations," said a former high-level employee. "It's not a company, it's just a bunch of disparate pieces. It's simply dysfunctional." Poor management decisions were the norm. For example, when executives couldn't agree on opening three centers MCI had in place to handle network ordering and provisioning—making sure the system had necessary equipment for it to function properly—the company opened a dozen centers and hired more people to run them.

Even Eddy, who had faithfully served Ebbers for 11 years, was eventually ready to make a change. "When I found myself spending 55 percent of my time dealing with HR [human resource] issues and 40 percent of my time doing reports that nobody read and 5 percent of my time doing what I liked, which was dealing with customers, and had a six-month old and a three-year old and didn't want to travel anymore, I got out," he said. "The company grew to the size where I couldn't make a difference and I decided it was time for me to go."

WorldCom seemed incapable of functioning properly and rivalries ensued between the divisions, particularly among executives from different corporate backgrounds, known internally as Legacy MCI executives or Legacy WorldCom executives. Units became fiefdoms, and communication between divisions of the communications conglomerate was strained. To some insiders, Ebbers seemed to bask in the chaos. "When the Sprint deal fell apart, everything fell apart," said a Legacy WorldCom executive. "We had a nice groove we had fallen into over the years. We'd buy a company, then for some months, it was always an 'us versus them' mentality with the new company until another merger came along. That's typical. We did so many deals that every year we had another set. When the next year's deal came along, the old deal was over. With WilTel, we had a lot of difference in that process because we went two years without a major transaction, so the 'us versus them' camps stayed longer. Even though it was a much smaller deal, MFS was different because of the type of business they were in. UUNET was a piece of that. There wasn't much long distance even though they rode the backbone of the company.

"Then MCI comes along. A totally different animal. The Sprint deal would probably have quelled the 'us versus them.'

But MCI had three to four times more people than WorldCom did. They had an attitude and arrogance. They looked at us like, 'Who are these upstarts? They don't know what they're doing,' and to some extent, they were right. Their attitude was that 'we're the best of the best and we're going to do it this way whether they like it or not.' However, we thought we could do some things more efficiently. Maybe less formally. They were a very structured company, with various levels of management throughout. We got rid of some of that, which they considered sacrilege. And the next deal that should have brought everybody together never happened." Ebbers was running out of things to buy.

The entire company culture changed with the influx of MCI employees, many of whom made it abundantly clear they were not pleased with the changes. Just like troubling racial issues that simmered beneath the surface but were rarely discussed in public anymore, the "North versus South" issue reflected the same mentality. In the South, conversations are peppered with niceties, usually initiated with a mostly sincere "How are you doing?" A generally laid-back attitude prevails. Northerners were viewed warily, and were seemingly brash and hypocritical. "They weren't real compassionate," said a native Mississippian who worked at corporate headquarters in Clinton during the influx of MCI employees from above the Mason-Dixon Line. "If you got sick, they were like, 'What do you mean you're sick?' and when I was pregnant, their attitude was, 'If you're going to have a baby, you'd better have it right here because we're in a hurry. We've got to get to a meeting.' Before the MCI merger, it was a real homey, cozy atmosphere. That all changed. In Clinton, when you passed people in the hall, you didn't know them. They didn't wave, talk, nothing. People started leaving in a constant stream." Some insiders compared coalescing the polar-opposite corporate cultures with mixing oil and water.

"The reason they could be acquired is that MCI was over-spending," said a former WorldCom travel auditor. "You wouldn't believe the stuff people would do and then try to say it was for business. They wouldn't have receipts for almost anything. Bernie was like, 'I want to make sure this is for business and not some frivolous thing, like you took your family out.' Nobody likes travel auditors. When we dug into it, we found that, most of the time, it really wasn't for business."

MCI reimbursed employees more than 30 cents per mile and paid for mileage from home. WorldCom paid much less and enforced stringent restrictions. "The policy was pretty strict," said the former travel and expense auditor. "We paid 24 cents a mile. That covered wear and tear on the car, and oil and gas. We'd pay parking fees at airports, but we didn't pay for mileage from their home to the airport."

Travel and expense auditors often referred employees to higher-ups to substantiate an expense. "Bernie started putting the law down," said the auditor. "He required receipts for everything. Major policy changes were updated on the internal online bulletin board. If someone tried to slip in a receipt for a Palm Pilot or anything else that wasn't approved in the policy handbook, we'd pick up the phone, call, and say, 'Either you get a Tier 1 report to Mr. Ebbers, and you'll have to answer to him why it was okay to pay it, or you have to get a Tier 1 approval (one rung below Ebbers). Tier 1 executives knew that Bernie would have a fit because he got these huge printouts and they would have to answer to him. Believe me, when you had to spit out that Tier 1 approval was needed, they'd usually just eat it."

While Wall Street was charmed when Ebbers preached frugality to his staffers, industry watchers thought it might be a bit much. "Bernie is running a $40 billion company as if it were still his own mom-and-pop business," a WorldCom exec told *BusinessWeek*.

Even though Ebbers was strict in many areas, others seemingly were given free rein. Billing and research analyst Jeffrey Vendeventer, who joined WorldCom in 1998, was told to book revenue as it came in but to drag his feet on refunds. Some customers, who were owed as much as $300,000, complained for up to two years before action was approved. When Vendeventer resigned, he commented, "How could this place stay in business? It was a shell game."

"The billing of telecom services already is as convoluted as it can possibly be, especially when you're in the corporate world with a lot of data lines and circuits in addition to long distance, and when you start looking at all these multiple locations, accounts, and phone numbers, you have no idea if the bill is right or not," said a former WorldCom corporate customer. "Consultants make good livings auditing bills just to make sure you're billed right. I remember the (WorldCom) CFO made a statement a few years ago, 'Well, we feel pretty good now. We're down [from more than 40] to only six billing systems.' Yeah, well, talk to any WorldCom customer and they'll tell you their bills were still messed up."

Departments were buying new equipment without first checking the inventory. Oddly enough, an existing inventory review wasn't required prior to making a purchase. In 2001, this inefficient practice led to unnecessary spending of some $3 million on fiber patch cords. Tony Minert, a former telecommunications reporting manager known for cost containment measures, alerted Myers and Yates in an e-mail: "There seems to be no regard for cost." Interestingly, the same e-mail communication suggested the notion of shifting the operating costs of leasing network capacity to capital expenditures.

During the downward spiral of WorldCom stock, executives grumbled that losses on stock holdings in the company would outpace base salaries. Middle managers weren't happy either. Most employees had signed on with WorldCom for lower than industry average salaries because of the lure of matched stock options. The prestige of working for a world-class telecommunications company was losing its luster. Plus, Ebbers continued phasing out employee perks. The watercoolers were long gone. Free coffee was next. He stopped subsidizing home long-distance phone bills. Free travel cards were no longer distributed. Year-end bonuses dwindled, and then were gone for most of the lower-level employees. Even the office plants withered. Some employees had to wait up to four months to be reimbursed for expenses instead of the usual week or two. "It wasn't that bad," said a longtime WorldCom marketing director. "We had coffee. But it was never a happy place to work. Anybody that tells you it was ever fun, I'd like to know what they did. Even in our heyday, we were forced to work really hard—10, 12, or 15-hour days—but we had money and it was a swap-out. After the bust, there was a lot of hard work, but not as much money in the bank. That's okay. At least I didn't have to cut grass in the rain today. Coming from a lower-middle-class family, I know my dad worked much harder than I do on a daily basis."

Because of WorldCom's burgeoning growth, working for the company became even more demanding. "We were all demanding," said a former Tier 1 executive. "We were all running at 100 miles per hour, but that's what it took to get the job done. The people that couldn't stand it needed to get out of the way because there simply wasn't another option. That's why I got out of the way. Let someone else with energy do the job. Working 18 to 20 hour days? I didn't want to sacrifice that much."

In an attempt to expand the demographics of WorldCom's customer base, Ebbers chose unwisely, and industry watchers—and Hollywood—noted his reluctance to right the situation. WorldCom drew harsh criticism for its sponsorship of *WWF Smackdown!* a weekly cable program known for its violence, sexual content, and foul language. In the first of a round of phone calls to WorldCom, former wrestling announcer and Parents Television Council (PTC) chairman Steve Allen asked the company to boycott the show. In reply, company spokesperson Ginger Fitzgerald stated that the company was "fully aware of the content of the program" and that it was "perfectly acceptable."

No action was taken until the media made it a glaring issue. Sportscaster Bob Costas said: "There was a time when I was a wrestling fan in small doses . . . I thought it was funny . . . they were bold slapstick characters. There was a tongue in cheek and a twinkle in the eye. It has become . . . cultural sewage. It's belligerent, it's mean-spirited, it's anti-woman, it revels in the worst possible racial stereotypes, and it is vulgar in the extreme. And there is nothing puritanical about saying that." On June 15, 2000, bowing to pressure after a slew of big-name companies like Wendy's, Ford, Coca-Cola, Procter & Gamble, and AT&T yanked advertising dollars from the show, WorldCom dropped its sponsorship of *WWF Smackdown!*

By September 2000, Ebbers' spot on the *Forbes* 400 wealthiest Americans list had fallen to No. 368. The next month, WorldCom's sagging stock prices forced Ebbers to sell three million shares of stock to raise an estimated $84 million to pay off investment debts when personal loans were called. "I am much more a stockholder than an employee," Ebbers told *Fortune* magazine. "The value of my stock is worth a lot more to me than my job and my salary. I've often told the board I may have to fire myself for the sake of my stock." But in November 1999, Ebbers received 20,000 shares of KPNQwest, Qwest's European outfit, a transaction that drew harsh criticism because the shares represented 2 percent of the shares Salomon set aside for the firm's entire network of individual investor clients.

Ebbers didn't mention that during the stock-driven 1990s, he either personally guaranteed or pledged WorldCom stock as security for more than $1 billion in personal and business loans on behalf of Mississippi College, Douglas Lake Land & Timber Company, Douglas Lake Cattle, BC Yacht Sales, Joshua Timberlands, and Master Hospitality Services. As the price of WorldCom stock decreased, and Ebbers' margin calls increased, so did WorldCom's loans to Ebbers. The compensation board authorized the first loan of $50 million to Ebbers in September 2000. He would wait two months before signing the promissory note. As WorldCom stock continued to fall, it triggered additional margin. In December 2000, the company extended Ebbers' loan to $75 million. By April 2002, the loan amount had escalated to $408.2 million. Each time, the compensation committee's surprisingly brief minutes reflected the same statement that the loan was in the best interest of WorldCom and its shareholders.

Following Ebbers' advice to stay home, Sidgmore spent the better part of 2000 focusing on two start-ups—eCommerce Industries and Strategy.com—based in Vienna, Virginia. Sidgmore's former executive assistant, Paula Jagemann, had created eCommerce Industries (ECI), a privately held start-up that sold office supplies business-to-business on the Internet, after WorldCom bought MFS and she refused to move to Jackson, Mississippi. "We came up with the idea of trying to be the technology vehicle for all of these little companies who had to wind up with an Internet presence and needed software to run their businesses so they could compete with the big guys, but they couldn't afford the capital required to do that on their own," said Sidgmore, chairman of ECI. "So we came up with the idea of actually building the technology for all the office products dealers." As chairman of Strategy.com, Sidgmore helped guide the wireless data company to a separate entity from MicroStrategy, a data-mining firm that sold only to businesses managed by Sidgmore's frenetic pal, Michael Saylor.

Sidgmore was still vice chairman of WorldCom, but was largely inactive. "My role at WorldCom has changed over the last two years from a totally operational focus to a more strategic role," Sidgmore said in 2000. "And as I sort of managed that evolution, I created a little bit of space for me to go out and work with some small technology-driven companies that are of high interest to me. Two years ago, I just simply decided that I did not want to be the CEO of a huge telecom company. So little by little, I have extracted myself. And I don't think my role going forward is going to change at all. I'll still be vice chairman. I'll still be involved in the strategic planning and development of the company."

When Sullivan was preparing a quarterly earnings statement for the company's toughest quarter in years in mid-October 2000, he e-mailed Sidgmore a note that said WorldCom was in a "really scary" situation with escalating costs and declining revenue in key growth areas. The glut of network capacity was forcing down prices, competition was cutthroat, and dot-coms, once key clients, were folding. America Online, one of WorldCom's largest customers, was growing at an unbelievably slow pace because Internet traffic growth had significantly slowed, with much of the data carried on leased lines, not lines owned by WorldCom. "Wow! I had no idea that the revenue growth had deteriorated that much," Sidgmore wrote back. "It's going to take some pretty fancy explaining."

When Sullivan produced the quarterly financial report on October 26, 2000, he reported a strong 12 percent increase in overall revenue. He glossed over a few "challenges," and told analysts the company's operating margin, a key Wall Street benchmark, had improved. To help make that calculation, Sullivan had reclassified two revenue sources totaling approximately $225 million, including fees and equipment sales, as cost reductions. Technically, the maneuver didn't violate accounting standards, but it manipulated them. Sullivan would later be charged with ordering finance officials to use company reserves to offset operating costs by $828 million, another earnings boost. Operating costs generally cover the basic expenses of running a business and must be recorded at the time they are incurred. Capital costs typically include one-time purchases such as real estate or equipment, and the expense can be spread over longer periods.

In a live online interview with the *Washington Post* on July 11, 2002, Sidgmore had another take on the situation: "My positions at WorldCom were reflective of my involvement in operations. Obviously, the board reviewed highlights of the financial condition and key ratios at each board meeting. There was nothing to suggest that this problem was looming, and I was totally taken by surprise and outrage."

9

Hockey, Pals, and the Farm

*Quite frankly, it's made it easy to pick up the phone and call
people and say, "I'm with the hockey team that J.L. and Bernie
own" and everybody takes my calls.*

Brad Ewing, General Manager, Jackson Bandits, 1999

Ebbers sometimes seemed to be all work and no play, but
he took advantage of his newfound fortune and bought
toys he could only dream about while growing up poor
in Canada. He enjoyed sharing his fortune with choice family
and friends. On several occasions, Ebbers' parents visited
him in Brookhaven, but no one recalled seeing his siblings
around town.

One of Ebbers' first sizable purchases was a hockey team.
An avid hockey fan from his younger days in Canada, Ebbers
and pal J. L. Holloway formed Mississippi Indoor Sports LLC
(MIS) and bought the Chesapeake (Maryland) Ice Breakers,
moving the hockey team from Washington, DC, to Jackson.

135

Ebbers and Holloway each owned 45 percent of the team. Lenny Sawyer and Sherman Muths, minority owners of the Mississippi Sea Wolves, a hockey team on the Mississippi Gulf Coast, owned the remaining 10 percent.

Ironically, Ebbers chose "Bandits" as the team franchise name, in a nod to the nineteenth-century outlaws famous for robbing wealthy travelers on the historic nearby Natchez Trace. The Jackson Bandits represented one of nine hockey teams in the Deep South that had been formed in the East Coast Hockey League over a five-year period. As soon as the team's inaugural schedule was released, season tickets—$11 per home game—sold briskly, with floor boxes selling out practically overnight. The enthusiasm for hockey was unusual in a sports culture dominated by football.

Despite messy weather fueled by Hurricane Irene festering in the Gulf and a 4–1 loss to the Florida Everblades in Estero, Florida, for their debut game, fans loved the Jackson Bandits. Their first victory came the next night, when the Bandits beat the Jacksonville Lizard Kings 4–2. "Football is practically a religion in Mississippi, and for people to be so interested in the hockey team, I have to think it was simply because of Bernie," said a local sports fan. "At that time, he was quite a celebrity. Hell, he was almost bigger than Elvis. People knew if they wanted to see him, he'd be at the games."

When the Bandits held their first home game October 23, the 6,620-seat Mississippi Coliseum was sold out. Ebbers and Holloway relished the action and the attention despite a 5–1 loss to the Baton Rouge Kingfish, with Mike Bayrack scoring Jackson's only goal. "Quite frankly, it's made it easy to pick up the phone and call people and say, 'I'm with the hockey team that J. L. and Bernie own,' and everybody takes my call," Brad Ewing, general manager of the Jackson Bandits and a 15-year pro sports veteran, said in 1999. "People recognize that we've got good, solid ownership and support the team in some facet, whether it's season tickets or sponsorship. That's quite a luxury for me."

Nineteen months after plans were announced to build a new arena, the Bandits secured a necessary land lease to construct a 7,500-seat multiuse arena on a site adjacent to Mississippi Veterans Memorial Stadium, an underused football arena that serves as home to Jackson State University, a historically all-black college. Among other sites on a short list, Ebbers and Holloway had considered building a sportsplex on property adjacent to WorldCom headquarters in Clinton, but there was a sticking point—the city's beer ordinance—that the Clinton city council would need to address. Instead, the pair secured a 25-year lease with an additional 25-year option near the stadium, and the Bandits sought the $25 million necessary to build the arena. Even though the team sold 23 of 30 luxury suites and planned to sell 1,200 club seats, and the state and the city cosigned loans for $16 million, the team had not made a profit in three seasons. By the time WorldCom filed bankruptcy, the plan still had not materialized. The Bandits continued to play at the cramped and spartan Mississippi Coliseum, where the average attendance of home games steadily declined from 4,108 in 1999 to 3,365 in 2001.

Shortly after Ebbers resigned from WorldCom in April 2002, the Bandits' front office began falling apart. Mike Sheehan, the team's radio announcer and public relations director, was dismissed in May in a cost-cutting move. Ewing abruptly quit in mid-July. That left Bandits Coach Derek Clancey, who subsequently inked a new three-year deal for an undisclosed sum in time to prepare for the 2002 season, which opened October 11 with the tagline, "Your town, your team, gotta be there." The Jackson Bandits lost six of their first seven games of the season, but bounced back in November. By January 10, 2003 the Bandits were 21-17, with 32 games left in the regular season.

A search for new ownership to buy out Ebbers ended in September 2002, when Isaac Byrd, an African American trial lawyer and businessperson from Jackson, Mississippi, stepped in as a co-owner. Three years earlier, Byrd had been suspended from practicing law for five months, sentenced to four months' of home confinement, fined $10,000, and placed on a two-year probation for failure to file income taxes in 1992. Holloway welcomed Byrd as the "newest Jackson Bandit," which Byrd claimed he was "proud to be." Jacksonians Brian Fenelon, who worked with Ebbers, and William M. "Billy" Mounger II, a successful telecom executive, also had an interest in the team.

Ebbers and Holloway were great friends; both were wildly successful self-made men. The son of an oil-field roughneck, Holloway grew up poor, living on a dirt road in rural Mississippi in the 1940s. After his parents died, Holloway dropped out of Ole Miss in 1971 to sell construction equipment and soon established a reputation for upgrading and repairing worn-out drilling rigs. He bought Friede & Goldman, a New Orleans design outfit, and launched an IPO in July 1997. The company, which built and refurbished marine oil-drilling platforms primarily from its Mississippi Gulf Coast base in Gulfport, grew so dramatically through acquisitions in 1998 that it landed the top spot in *BusinessWeek*'s Hot Growth rankings for 1999. Holloway became a star when he completed the merger between Friede Goldman International and Halter Marine Group in November 1999. The new company, Friede Goldman Halter, rivaled the 11,500-employee workforce of Ingalls Shipbuilding in Pascagoula. Located 30 miles away, Ingalls was the largest private employer in the state. Considered a "gregarious negotiator," Holloway was a charismatic host to oil executives, whom he often indulged with hunting and fishing excursions; this social savvy served him well in business.

By the fourth quarter of 1999, WorldCom had tripled its earnings, and Friede Goldman Halter had boosted its earnings 60 percent for the year. Holloway was inducted into the Mississippi Business Hall of Fame that year: "Ebbers and Holloway were the Barry Bonds and Sammy Sosa of Mississippi business," said *Clarion-Ledger* reporter Rick Cleveland. "They had clout."

Even so, there were rumblings in the undercurrent about the duo's questionable business practices. "There was nothing I could put my finger on, but something didn't add up," said a Mississippi businessperson. "J. L. was a snake in the grass," a female financial analyst from Jackson, Mississippi, quickly retorted. "That's all there was to it." Both men would resign as heads of their respective companies within two weeks of each other, and both companies would file bankruptcy little more than a year apart. Friede Goldman Halter filed for bankruptcy protection April 19, 2001; Holloway stepped down as chairman on May 10, 2002. Ebbers resigned April 29, 2002; WorldCom filed bankruptcy on July 21, 2002.

On July 7, 2000, Ebbers, a former truck driver, pitched in $27.4 million to help pal William J. "Jack" Liles III take over KLLM Transport Services after KLLM's board of directors agreed to accept the bid of $8.05 a share. Liles had been involved in a tug-of-war for the Richland, Mississippi-based refrigerated carrier with rival shareholder Robert E. Low, president of Prime, Inc., in Springfield, Missouri. Liles had to withdraw his $8.25 per share offer in mid-May to buy all the KLLM common stock he did not already own because "one of his financial backers withdrew financial support for the bid for reasons not related to [KLLM] or [Liles]," according to Security and Exchange Commission (SEC) reports. The backer was widely assumed to be Ebbers. What transpired next is unclear, but at the midnight hour, Ebbers rushed in to help Liles win the bid against Low, and Liles was able to retain control of the company he had joined in 1974.

On July 31, 1998, Ebbers paid an estimated $66 million to buy the famed Douglas Lake Ranch in British Columbia from the family of the department store magnate, the late Charles "Chunky" Woodward, who bought it in 1959 and died in 1990. The Woodward family had turned the ranch, built circa 1884, into a private paradise, offering cabins, chalets, and yurts for rent, along with boat rentals, fly fishing schools, and horseback riding lessons. In the mid to late 1990s, the family contracted with a brokerage firm to sell the property, and one of its 37-page, glossy brochures sent to a short list of prospective buyers landed on Ebbers' desk.

Located in the Nicola Valley between Kelowna and Kamloops, 200 miles northeast of Vancouver in the foothills of the Canadian Rockies, Douglas Lake Ranch is Canada's largest and one of the world's largest working cattle ranches, with 164,000 deeded acres and 336,000 acres of crown land. It is home to some 20,000 cattle head, but is known best for its beauty and seclusion, with rolling pastureland, valuable timberland, well-stocked lakes, rustic fishing lodges, and recreational facilities. It has been host to occasional royalty (the Queen and Prince Philip visited in 1959), who no doubt appreciate the privacy of the property's private airstrip. The ranch even features a small town with its own general store, school, and church. The picturesque landscape is a magnet for location scouts. In June 2002, a new Honda commercial was filmed there. Ebbers would keep the ranch a family tradition by asking one of his brothers to help run it.

After conquering the mountains, Ebbers headed to the sea. His first yacht, a 60-footer, was aptly named Aquasition, and he routinely invited friends of the family to cruise the Mediterranean. In May 1999, Ebbers and his buddies bought Intermarine, a yacht-building shipyard with 150 employees in

Savannah, Georgia, for $14.4 million from Italy's Compart. An acquisition bonus: two extravagant luxury yachts worth a combined $25 million or so. WorldCom would wind up owning Intermarine after Ebbers stepped down as CEO.

Ebbers knew he could not go wrong buying land. Or so he thought. In September 1999, soon after Kimberly-Clark Corporation closed its pulp mill in Mobile, Alabama, Joshua Timberlands LLC, Ebber's private holding company, of which he owns 65 percent, purchased 460,000 acres of timberland in Alabama, Mississippi, and Tennessee, at $869 per acre for approximately $400 million. In a move that would be considered one of many potential conflicts of interest with WorldCom, Citigroup's Travelers Life and Annuities unit loaned Ebbers' company about $82 million toward the purchase. Its Travelers Property Casualty unit loaned Joshua Timberland about $52 million as part of a $489 million loan package with three other insurance companies that Citigroup did not identify. The loans were secured by timberland, not WorldCom stock, and the New York State Common Retirement Fund would later sue Citigroup to recover more than $300 million it lost in WorldCom investments. The Kimberly-Clark deal also included the Elberta Forest Tree Nursery, originally established in 1991 by Scott Paper Company and later managed by Kimberly-Clark after the 1995 merger of the two companies.

Ebbers tapped former Mississippi Secretary of State Dick Molpus, owner of Molpus Timberlands Management LLC, in Philadelphia, to manage the daily operations of the nursery. For good measure, Ebbers bought Columbus Lumber, a high-tech sawmill in Brookhaven. "Trees grow," Ebbers said. Because of declining timber value, which peaked in the south in 1998, the timberland was valued at roughly $700 per acre, or $322 million, when WorldCom filed bankruptcy in July 2002.

In November 2002, Ebbers came under scrutiny for taking at least $4 million in farm subsidies from 1998 to 2001 on three properties—Angelina Plantation, Pine Ridge Farm, and Joshua Timber—according to the United States Department of Agriculture (USDA) Farm Service Agency documents. Angelina Plantation, a 21,000-acre rice plantation in Monterey, Louisiana, owned by Ebbers and his brother, Jim, listed 20 producers and received $1.4 million in 2001. The set-up suggested "a Mississippi Christmas Tree at work here," said farm subsidy expert Ken Cook, president of Environmental Working Group, which retains a database on farm subsidies. A Mississippi Christmas Tree refers to a farm that on paper includes many subsidy recipients to gain maximum taxpayer funding, Cook said. "It's likely they are legitimate," he added.

When the Brookhaven Country Club in Ebbers' hometown wanted to add nine holes to its existing 9-hole golf course and spruce up the tennis courts at the private club built in 1934, local banks turned down the board's request for a loan. Ebbers stepped in with an approximate $2.4 million loan, reportedly at a point or two below the prime interest rate, and secured it with stock in the country club. In the fall of 1999, Mississippi-based Maxwell Golf Group was contracted to build 10 new holes on newly acquired property north of the existing course and to convert the existing nine holes to eight new holes and space for 18 to 20 new golf course home sites. A half dozen new tennis courts were added, and the clubhouse was renovated.

The end result was "a rural surprise," wrote a golfer from Grand Prairie, Texas, who played the course. "New layout, carefully landscaped and in really good playing condition. Conditions of the greens, tees . . . is exceptional for a newly redeveloped course. Placement is required off many of the tees to have a clean second shot, which is really interesting because there are not lots of trees or water in the casual sightline. From the backs, a good player needs to let it rip to have really good position to go for the greens. Putting surfaces are true, with just a little mystery to the line on several holes.

Water, moguls, bunkers, pampas grass, and native Mississippi softwoods are all eye appealing and come into play on errant shots. I really like what they have done with this course."

When word spread about the improvements and the board's benefactor, 130 new members joined within a 12-week period. But it did not stimulate enough cash flow. When the improved course reopened and the board was unable to repay the debt, Ebbers foreclosed on the loan and became the sole owner of the Brookhaven Country Club. "He had to protect his interests," explained a Brookhaven businessperson, shrugging his shoulders. Through one of his hotels, Best Western Brookhaven, he began offering golf packages that included a round of golf at the country club for a $25 green fee per person, $5 to $10 more than advertised on a Mississippi sports information Web site. "That's typical Bernie," said a local golfer. "His game is making money."

Even though Ebbers had several hometown business holdings, he was typically hands-off. "He doesn't jump into local politics," said a local banker. Brookites suggested that Ebbers derived the greatest joy from riding a tractor, tending his soybeans and cattle, occasionally castrating bulls, and listening to Willie Nelson—turned up loud. Between marriages, Ebbers set up camp in a modest double-wide trailer home on his farmland while planning a $1.8 million mansion and a 15,000-square-foot stone and cedar lodge on his nearby 960-acre property— Oak Hill Farm. It was located at 2116 Highway 84 East in Brookhaven and featured a pristine 100-acre lake. The lodge was designed by a Colorado architect to reproduce a villa that Ebbers favored in Vail.

People inevitably compared the lifestyle choices of Ebbers and Sullivan, with many people saying Ebbers was a down-home guy while Sullivan was more pretentious. True, Ebbers lived a bit more modestly and could often be seen hosing down his flashy Corvette or mowing his lawn or even his neighbor's. His home was accessed by a gravel drive from a flat stretch of two-lane rural highway leading into town. Brookhaven Hardware, a John Deere dealership he frequented, was located less than a mile away, and the Brookhaven Country Club was close by. Joshua Management, Ebber's private holding company, was situated in downtown Brookhaven, on the same block that housed a Christian bookstore, the original bank lender for LDDS start-up money and, ironically, a NexTel retail store. All that was missing was a white picket fence. For Ebbers, it was black wrought iron.

Sullivan preferred more prestigious digs. For many people, the $15 million lakeside mansion he was building on 4.3 acres at 6006 Le Lac Road, close to the Polo Club of Boca Raton, was an emblem of excess. The 16,410-square-foot Mediterranean Revival style home—white with a red tiled roof—had eight bedrooms. It featured 117 windows and 87 doors, nine refrigerators, four microwave ovens, a wine room and separate cellar, a half dozen Jacuzzis, a six-car garage, a library with adjoining galleries, a soundproof 18-seat movie theater, a game room, and a domed exercise facility.

The massive master suite featured a "mini pool"—an oversized garden tub measuring six feet wide and eight feet long—matching showers and toilets, and trailer-size closets. A storage room was created just for furs. Other amenities included a lavish pool with a Jacuzzi spa, a footbridge, a reflecting pond, wet bar pavilion, and an outdoor grilling area with its own wet bar, a two-story boathouse with a covered dock and office space, and separate living quarters for two maids. Some 7,100 square feet of terraces, walkways, and balconies featuring Corinthian columns, ornamental ironwork, concrete planters, and sculpted lions connected the property's many attractions. Unless the Justice Department or SEC won a case against Sullivan, it would remain his property, as long as he could pay for it.

At the pinnacle of his earning power, Ebbers was generous with contributions to his alma mater and various organizations, many times anonymously. It was widely known that he funneled millions of dollars to Mississippi College through gifts of WorldCom stock, and he was routinely present for ribbon cuttings of new and renovated buildings. When WorldCom filed for bankruptcy protection in July 2002, nearly two months after Ebbers resigned as CEO, many people wondered what the backlash would be for Mississippi College. "Even though there have been a few exceptions, none relevant in this case, we sell stock the day we receive it," said Dr. Lloyd "Bo" Roberts, senior vice president for administration and CFO for Mississippi College. "We have a policy to give a gift receipt, with an average of the high and low in the market that day, to the person who gives us stock. In Bernie's case, it was never a problem. We just sold it." Roberts declined to estimate the value of the stock Ebbers gave to Mississippi College, but bankruptcy court reports indicate the amount of stock cashed was at least $36.5 million.

Ebbers also made significant contributions to the Mississippi Baptist Children's Village and to the Mississippi Children's Home Society and CARES Center, perhaps because one of his three children with his first wife Linda was adopted. "Bernie had a big heart for helping people," said Chris Cherney, executive director of the CARES Center. "I can't say enough nice things about how much the Ebbers have helped us."

Ebbers routinely passed out meals to the homeless at Frank's World Famous Biscuits in downtown Jackson. "He was very down-to-earth, no airs or nothing," said restaurant owner Frank Latham. "In fact, when he came over for lunch, there would be three or four guys with him and he would be the worst dressed of them all."

Ebbers often held court over beef and drinks in an unimpressive secluded room accessible only through the crowded and noisy kitchen at Tico's Restaurant in Ridgeland, Mississippi, a nondescript building with inadequate parking. A map of the world—WorldCom's sales territory—appropriately covered an entire wall in the private cubby. Another wall was dotted with an eclectic mix of sports memorabilia—a dusty replica of the Ole Miss Centennial Team, a Jackie Sherrill-signed Mississippi State University football helmet, and shelves that were lined with golf trophies. They had been won by Thomas "Tico" Hoffman, a former professional golfer, who was the amiable proprietor of the popular eatery and Mississippi's unofficial government seat. An old style wall phone, with longtime Mississippi House of Representatives Speaker Tim Ford among the powerbrokers on the speed dial, hung prominently on the back wall. Wooden louvers that covered a row of windows allowed low lights to be seen glowing faintly in the wee morning hours. During legislative sessions, reporters could often size up the status of pending legislation by the hours that court was in session in The Room or the number of heavy-duty Ford trucks left behind in the parking lot.

Most times though, Ebbers wined and dined under an enormous stag's head in Tico's huge main room, where he was more visible. The elk, mounted on a dark paneled wall above a stone fireplace and illuminated by flickering neon beer signs, was a gift from Jackson grocery store magnate Henry Holman. Its presence dominated the dining hall and the story behind it provided terrific conversation-openers. "Henry had it in his office at Jitney Jungle and when the family sold the company, he called and said, 'My wife won't let me bring Bozo home. Can you take him?' and I said sure," said Hoffman, who bought WorldCom stock as it tanked. "Bernie was a good friend and I wanted to support a Mississippi company. Fortunately, I don't have enough money to piss away like that, so it didn't hurt me too bad."

After Ebbers' divorce in 1997, he taught a 9:15 A.M. Sunday school class for young married couples and participated in the subsequent hour-and-a-half worship service at Easthaven Baptist Church in Brookhaven. Soon after his forced resignation, he confided to *Clarion-Ledger* business editor Scott Waller in a rare interview: "People ask me how I'm doing. You know what, I am a child of the King, and the King is still King Jesus, and I am absolutely content and happy."

In his persona as a hard-working, passionate cowboy, Ebbers occasionally got into scuffles like the one that stunted his basketball career. Stories buzzed around town about Ebbers getting into a fist fight at The Dock, a rowdy boathouse bar on the Ross Barnett Reservoir in Ridgeland, located across the harbor from Sullivan's condominium. However, the stories were never confirmed. "For some reason, people wanted to protect Bernie," said the owner of a boathouse on a pier across from the bar, "and for the most part, they stayed out of his business."

Regardless of his flaws, everybody wanted to be an FOB (Friend of Bernie).

Pink Slipped

Business is doing extremely well. We're not revising guidance.
Bernie Ebbers, Chief Executive Officer, March 2001

Rumors were rampant that WorldCom would lay off about 15 percent of its global workforce, or roughly 11,550 employees, by March 2001. Even though the numbers were not as high as anticipated, WorldCom gave nearly 7 percent of its workforce, or approximately 6,000 employees, the pink slip on February 28, as the company continued streamlining operations.

Employees were not surprised. "Even though there was no official announcement, we knew through the rumor mill the layoffs were coming," said Alicia Connor, an account relations manager for WorldCom. "We checked the internal WorldCom message board online and saw where the layoffs were coming at 10 o'clock in the morning, down the pipe at the same time in all time zones. I was sitting in my cubicle waiting, and at 10 o'clock on the dot, my boss, who was based in Louisiana and was rarely in Jackson, poked her head around my cubicle and gave me the news. I felt a little duped because I'd been hired in November."

Connor was pleased, however, when she received a lump sum minimum severance package—three months' salary. "I thought that was rather generous, since I'd only been there three months." Another WorldCom employee, who was laid off in another round, later thanked his director "for laying me off in April. At least I got my severance pay for 20 years. His last words to me were, 'You are lucky. It's going to get worse.'"

Even though WorldCom reported a 38 percent drop in earnings for the first quarter of 2001, analysts praised the company's cost-cutting performance. "Business is doing extremely well," an upbeat Ebbers told investors in March. "We're not revising guidance. We stick by our guidance. We are not going to miss. But we're not revising upward at this point." Grubman raised his first-quarter revenue growth expectations for WorldCom's data unit to 12.5 percent, from 12 percent, and increased the full-year target to 14 percent, from 13.2 percent. When asked if WorldCom was for sale, company spokesperson Charlie Sutlive dodged answering the question directly. Instead, he said that the company's goal was to increase shareholder value: "We believe that executing our 2001 business plan is the best way to drive value at this time."

Ebbers insisted the company's strength would come from its sales force. "In this business, we tend to talk a lot about technology and strategy," Ebbers told *Internetweek*. "All that makes me sick. The only statistic that matters—because everything else is derived from this one statistic—is how much new revenue your sales rep sells every month."

Inside WorldCom, selling new accounts was not that simple. Multiple sales teams offering the same products competed against each other for accounts, and salespeople had no incentive to play by the rules in the cutthroat environment. If they were not creative, they risked missing quotas or losing commissions. When WorldCom fired several salespeople in early 2002 for improperly booking accounts to boost their commissions by $3 million, the company claimed to have rooted out "a few bad apples." The company said that revenue from the accounts had been counted twice in the company's revenues, and the practice would not be tolerated.

Records reflected that the practice had been tolerated for quite a while. On June 6, 2001, internal auditor Cynthia Cooper told the WorldCom board: "Accounts that moved from one billing system to another resulted in commission overpayments . . . 292 accounts had been moved over a year's period . . . overpayments of 28 of those accounts resulted in overpayments of commissions of $930,000."

Billing disputes were another problem for WorldCom salespeople. "I interviewed some of their reps and they told me that when there was a billing dispute, they were required to handle it," said Gerard Gibert, president and CEO of Venture Technologies, Inc., a technology solutions firm in Ridgeland, Mississippi. "The billing department would turn over disputes to them and it was their responsibility to resolve them, so the reps' commissions would be reversed until the dispute was settled. Every rep I interviewed from WorldCom, the first question they'd ask was, 'Who does the billing and who's responsible for reconciling any disputes?' "

"I'd always wanted to work for WorldCom and was finally hired in 2001," said a former WorldCom sales representative. "But the entire time I was there—all nine months—I stayed confused. I thought telecom was telecom, but it wasn't. That's why I returned to BellSouth. How would I describe work life at WorldCom? Kinda like *Dilbert*."

Jack Goeken, founder of MCI, said salespeople who stayed with MCI after the company merged with WorldCom, felt stymied. "I bumped into one guy a few years back who told me, 'Aw Jack, this company's not like it was. I just brought in a $20 million order and they want to analyze it to see if they want to accept it. When you were there, I'd bring in a $500 order and you'd take me out and buy me a hot dog."

In May 2001, an employee faxed an anonymous note to WorldCom COO Ronald R. "Ron" Beaumont, pointing out several examples of improper billing by a manager to inflate commissions. The employee ended with an ominous tone about WorldCom's Boca Raton offices, where Sullivan sometimes worked: "There are lot more instances of things like this going on . . . just ask around and you will find out." Beaumont, who has a master's degree in electrical engineering from Stanford University and was notoriously strict about documentation, was not amused. "Ron was a stickler for details," said a former coworker. "He liked his position and used it to get things done for his people—he wasn't going to worry about penny-ante coffee, for example—and he really got slapped in the face with all this."

In June 2001, former WorldCom employees joined a shareholder lawsuit against the company in federal court in Jackson, Mississippi, with allegations representing a scandalous laundry list of accounting errors, including double bookings. By all accounts, the WorldCom board of directors never bothered to look into it and was taken off the hook before it became a pressing issue. In the spring of 2002, after learning of the SEC inquiry into WorldCom's accounting practices, U.S. District court Judge William H. Barbour Jr. of the Southern District of Mississippi tossed out the 113-page lawsuit, dismissing it with prejudice, meaning that he would not consider an amended filing.

The complaint, which should have raised red flags everywhere and prompted a thorough internal investigation, was backed by 100 interviews with more than a dozen former WorldCom employees and related parties. It included detailed allegations of various accounting tactics and misdeeds—double bookings, uncollectible accounts receivables, delayed payments to vendors, hiding of bad debt, backdating of contracts, and deliberate understatement of costs—all designed to boost profits. Kenneth Vianale of Milberg Weiss Bershad, Hynes & Lerach, the lead attorney in the shareholder lawsuit, said the complaint "was even more specific than pleading laws require . . . (and) laid out the who, what, when, why and where of WorldCom's fraud."

Delinquent accounts could be easily manipulated to make the books look better. Like most corporations, WorldCom recorded revenue from an account when it became due. But unlike other companies, if the account fell in arrears, World-Com continued to book the revenue as if the customer had paid the debt. By 1999, WorldCom had accumulated more than $600 million in uncollectible receivables on its books, the lawsuit said.

The lawsuit also claimed other billing tactics were used to boost revenue. Two years after completing the MCI merger, WorldCom still had not combined the companies' billing systems. Option One of Tulsa, Oklahoma, handled WorldCom's billing system. Option Two of Richardson, Texas, operated MCI's billing system. By having two choices, the company could bill the same customer at different rates and record the revenue from both. For example, when Aubrey G. Lanston & Co., an economic forecasting firm, renegotiated its $30,000 Internet service contract on Option Two for $15,000, WorldCom booked $45,000 in revenue.

Instead of addressing the issue, Ebbers focused on deal making. He planned to continue aggressive growth initiatives to capture significant market share in global Internet Protocol-Virtual Private Networks (IP-VPNs), Web-hosting, and other emerging growth markets by offering a full complement of ebusiness-enabling communications services for enterprises worldwide. He also planned to expand the company's global Internet and high-speed data networks deeper into Europe and Asia-Pacific Rim to provide the reliability, performance, and scale that business customers in those rapidly growing regions needed to expand their operations and communications.

Ebbers also unveiled his blueprint for dividing the company's primary entities—WorldCom and MCI—into separate tracking stocks beginning June 8, 2001. Ebbers revealed the restructuring only days after AT&T announced plans to splinter its corporation and approximately 163,000 employees into four distinct entities operating under the AT&T brand name. It was AT&T's third breakup since 1984.

Ebbers explained that WorldCom Group (Nasdaq: WCOM), which opened with a stock price of $17.85, would own and operate "the industry's most extensive, state-of-the-art global facilities-based communications networks, providing unmatched reach and scale." He pointed out that—with its networks, integrated sales efforts, and capital investments—the WorldCom Group reported revenues of $22.8 billion in 2000. Data, Internet, and international operations represented a $16 billion high-growth revenue stream. Its international business consisted of revenue streams generated outside the United States, with revenues approximating $6 billion in 2000, operations in more than 65 countries, and local networks in more than 20 cities across Europe, Latin America, and Asia-Pacific Rim. Additionally, business voice generated revenues of more than $7 billion in 2000.

The MCI Group stock (Nasdaq: MCIT) opened with a stock price of $18.06. It provided investors with dividend income and tracked the company's high-cash flow businesses. With revenues of more than $16.3 billion in 2000, MCI Group's focus was to continue providing shareholders with an income-oriented investment opportunity linked to some of the company's most established enterprises. As one of the largest providers of consumer long-distance services, MCI planned to leverage its globally recognized brand, marketing channels, and broad consumer product offerings.

"Realigning WorldCom's structure in this way will enable the respective businesses to achieve greater management and resource focus to execute business strategies that work most effectively for each," Ebbers explained to a happy crowd of shareholders at WorldCom's annual meeting in June 2001. "At the same time, the new structure is designed to create greater shareholder value by providing two distinct, clear and compelling investment opportunities, while serving customer needs with a more efficient operation."

Shareholders were convinced it was a good idea. "Tracking stocks . . . allow the parent company to have their cake and eat it too," wrote Nancy Lottridge Anderson, CFA, a financial columnist for *Mississippi Business Journal.* "The fast grower, the World-Com Group, needs cash to build out networks and continue to grow. While the WorldCom Group is, in a sense, a cash hog, MCI is a cash cow. The consumer long-distance business has limited growth opportunities, but it is still making money. How do you get the cash to leap from one set of financials to another? First, when you pull apart the balance sheet of the parent, you give most of the cash balances to the more needy child, WorldCom Group. Next, you give the bulk of the assets to WorldCom Group and charge MCI for the use of them. In fact, WorldCom Group actually owns the trademark, 'MCI,' and MCI must pay them for use of it. Is this brilliant or what?"

On paper, the plan seemed terrific. To shareholders, it was a great deal. If they owned 100 shares of WorldCom stock before the tracking stock began, they ended up with 100 WCOM shares and four MCIT shares. But the tracking stock plan failed for a multitude of reasons, and having two distinct companies opened up a world of opportunity for artificially inflating earnings.

"SkyTel was put into the MCI Group and that turned out to be an extremely poor fit," said a former SkyTel product manager. "The management team of MCI was probably not far from running the business entirely into the ground. They ruled it by the same principles they ruled MCI, which was consumer-oriented with principles that really didn't apply to our business. That's when things turned real bitter inside WorldCom and MCI. Inside SkyTel, we had differentiated between the two entities. I mean, everyone disliked WorldCom, but there wasn't the hatred like there was for MCI."

Ebbers' mistakes began piling up. He was criticized for paying too much—$6 billion—for Intermedia Communications, a nearly bankrupt telecom company with some CLEC (competitive local exchange carrier) assets of questionable value, to gain control of Digex, a leading management Web-hosting provider. In February, WorldCom settled a lawsuit with Digex shareholders to make the deal work. When the merger closed in July—the twelfth major acquisition in as many years—WorldCom expanded its presence in the highly fragmented hosting market by controlling a 54 percent interest in Digex. Several months later, WorldCom sold Intermedia's Business Internet (IBI) assets to Allegiance Telecom for an undisclosed sum.

In December, WorldCom finalized its acquisition of Rhythms DSL assets for $31 million, a purchase price 20 percent less than when it had been announced three months earlier. Brian Brewer, WorldCom's chief marketing officer, said the acquisition left the company "better positioned to leverage DSL as an important component of WorldCom's strategy to deliver a wide range of business-class access services that enables our data and Internet customers to grow their business."

The year 2001 ended with WorldCom reporting more than $35 billion in revenue. However, WorldCom's place in the long-distance voice and data markets had declined to fourth, behind Verizon, SBC, and AT&T. For the company loan, the WorldCom board forced Ebbers to put up as collateral: Joshua Holdings, LLC; BC Yacht Sales; Douglas Lake Land & Timber Company; Douglas Lake Properties; and BCT Holdings.

The stunning reversal of fortune was unquestionable by early 2002. In January, WorldCom shares were hit hard by the fallout from Global Crossing's bankruptcy filing. On March 7, few people were surprised when the SEC questioned WorldCom on a sweeping list of topics. The agenda included the loan to Ebbers, then valued at $366.5 million, disputed customer bills and sales commissions, organizational charts and personnel records for former employees, integration of WorldCom and MCI's computer systems, and goodwill accounting practices for at least 60 acquisitions. WorldCom's goodwill—the purchase price that exceeds the value of an acquired company's tangible assets—had swelled to approximately $50.8 billion by the end of September 2002, with $28.2 billion of that attributed to the MCI acquisition. To write down the goodwill, the company would incur a cash crunch. The SEC gave WorldCom until July 1 to respond. The company would later agree to write off up to $50 billion by the end of the year.

By month-end, WorldCom's books reflected assets totaling approximately $107 billion—nearly double what Enron claimed when it filed the nation's largest bankruptcy in December 2001—and liabilities totaling approximately $41 billion. Around this time, Ebbers proposed cutting by half the budget of the company's internal audit unit while doling out performance bonuses that exceeded base salaries for favored WorldCom executives. In 1999, performance bonuses ranged from $15,113 to $628,174. The U.S. Bankruptcy Court would later investigate whether the bonuses were based on quantitative performance factors or used for improper purposes. By the end of the month, WorldCom stock had plummeted from an all-time high of $64.50 to $9.80, the first close below $10 since August 1995, and Ebbers was again forced to sell shares to cover margin calls. Concerned that if Ebbers sold significant shares, the already delicate market for WorldCom would be flooded, the board loaned Ebbers more money, for a total of $408.2 million at a charitable interest rate of little more than 2 percent. According to SEC documents, interviews with members of the WorldCom compensation committee, and Ebbers' personal records, he spent nearly $28 million of that loan on personal business ventures that had nothing to do with the stock. In addition to spending $1.8 million on his Brookhaven home, Ebbers gave $2 million to a family member for personal expenses, $1 million to a WorldCom officer and other friends, and $22.8 million on other personal business interests for a total of $27.6 million.

In April, WorldCom won a 10-year, $450-million contract with the Defense Information Systems Agency to build the Defense Research and Engineering Network. The company entered an agreement with DIRECTV Broadband, Inc. to expand DIRECTV DSL service across the western and midwestern United States, launched "d street," an online marketplace for U.S. small businesses, and The Neighborhood Plan to compete with AT&T's new calling plan, AT&T Unlimited. The company also fired 3,700 employees.

To sell The Neighborhood Plan, WorldCom contracted with telemarketers to sell the all-in-one unlimited local and long-distance calling plan for a flat rate of less than 50 dollars a month. A sample conversation: "I was just calling you, ma'am, to let you know we're going to extend your local calling area over the entire United States, so what that means is that all your calls you make in the future will now be unlimited and local calls, okay? So you're not going to have to worry about paying long distance or anything like that." When asked what company she represented, the telemarketer replied, "The Neighborhood, billed by MCI, a new local phone company." *Is it new?* "Yes." *The company or the plan?* "Uh, the plan."

By the second week in April, WorldCom stock had plunged to $5.41, the lowest level in nearly eight years. At the same time, WorldCom was urging the Federal Communications Commission to renew its competition contract as part of its "triennial review" of the 1996 Telecommunications Act requirements and to resist pressure from the Bell companies to limit the range of unbundled network elements (UNEs) that must be made available to competitors under federal law. "The FCC must not reward the Bells for six years of litigation and other stonewalling by relieving them of the obligations that could finally lead to making their markets competitive," said Michael H. Salsbury, WorldCom's general counsel. Industry watchers had pretty much agreed that the landmark law was a failure anyway, especially since the Bells retained a 95 percent market share of the $50 billion local market.

On April 22, the stock price dropped again to $4.03. The vultures were circling. Ebbers had sold his beloved yacht, but he was still holding on to 27 million shares of WorldCom stock. A top WorldCom executive told *Time:* "Tying up so much of your financial life in one single investment like that was really dumb."

With mounting pressure from investors and analysts angry about Ebbers' loan, the SEC inquiries into the company's accounting practices, and WorldCom's poor stock performance, the unthinkable happened: Ebbers was given the pink slip. "(Bernie) seemed paralyzed," said a former WorldCom associate. "He didn't have a vision." The last straw came when the board directors learned that Ebbers was in violation of an agreement to put up collateral for loans made by the company to cover margin calls. Ebbers still held on to choice assets even after the loans topped $400 million.

Thanks to his buddy Stiles A. Kellett Jr., head of World-Com's compensation and stock option committee since 1991, Ebbers walked away a richer man when he was unofficially ousted but officially resigned as CEO on April 29, 2002. During the three-year period from January 1, 1999, through December 31, 2001, when Bobbitt, Gordon Macklin, and Lawrence C. Tucker were members of the compensation committee, Ebbers earned more than $77 million, or roughly $25.7 million a year, including a $10 million retention bonus that Sullivan also received. The severance package agreement, which WorldCom included with documents filed with the SEC in May, called for Ebbers to receive a guaranteed $1.5 million a year for life as long as a payment on the company loan was never missed. If Ebbers' thirtysomething wife, Kristie, outlived him, she was to collect $750,000 a year for life. Other perks included paid medical and life insurance, a company-issued computer, and the use of the company's plane for 30 hours a year. He also gained several million stock options, which were essentially worthless. He was banished from the corporate empire he had built in Clinton and relegated to an office in downtown Jackson, where he agreed to consult on request until 2007. His longtime secretary, Debra Blackwell, the only person with access to Ebbers' e-mail account (which he rarely used), moved with him to the downtown office. "It'll be interesting to see if any lawsuits happen to Debra in this whole thing," said a financial analyst. "She's a nice woman, but she basically controlled his schedule."

The five-year payout plan for his personal loan, amended the day he resigned, called for the first payment of $25 million plus interest due April 29, 2003, $25 million in 2004, $75 million in 2005, $100 million in 2006, and $183 million, or all remaining principal, in 2007. In a pledge agreement dated April

18, 2002, Ebbers granted WorldCom an interest in BC Yacht Sales, Douglas Lake Land & Timber Company, Douglas Lake Properties, and BCT Holdings, and a 35 percent security interest in his 86.25 percent share of Joshua Holdings LLC, also owned by James Truett Bourne Jr. and W. Mark Lewis. About his resignation, Ebbers told a Jackson TV station: "I feel like crying. But I am 1,000 percent convinced in my heart that this is a temporary thing."

Others weren't convinced. "Bernie was out of his league," said a local telecom executive. "He wasn't qualified to be the CEO of a global telecom company. You can try to spin it any way you want, but the bottom line is that he's a peddler. He likes to peddle and make deals. But when it came to actually organizing, operating, and managing a major corporation, he didn't do very well.

"He didn't surround himself with good people to run the company. He personally couldn't do it. He was more intrigued with more mergers, more acquisitions, and more deals than he was with actually making money. They're just fortunate they experienced a period that we all did in our industry of 'crazy money,' that 1995 to 2000 time frame where even idiots could make money. You didn't have to outsmart the other guys. You didn't have to be that good. When that counted and mattered, people started failing left and right. WorldCom was no exception."

Ebbers' pal Alan Mott said the problem with Ebbers was that he wouldn't sell unnecessary assets. "He could only buy," he said. "The Sprint deal showed he didn't know how to get his ego out of the way."

Despite the bad press surrounding his ousting, Ebbers retained many admirers. "Bernie did a phenomenal job and I'm proud to say that I worked for him," said Chris Eddy, who worked directly for Ebbers for 11 years. "He was a great man who achieved what most people could only dream of doing in their lifetime. People misunderstood him. He did a lot more for them than many will ever realize."

Whatever the public opinion, life was good for Ebbers for a while. *Clarion-Ledger* columnist Orley Hood wrote about Ebbers: "Success was so sweet one whiff of it could make you fall-down dizzy . . . you were Midas . . . when you sneezed, America grabbed a Kleenex."

The Worst Job in Corporate America

When I first took this job, my wife said I was a moron.
John W. Sidgmore, Chief Executive Officer, WorldCom

On April 30, 2002, John Sidgmore took control of the company. Earlier in the month, on April 9, he had celebrated his 51st birthday with his wife and adolescent son. With WorldCom collapsing around him, Sidgmore fully realized he had inherited the worst job in corporate America. He barely slept. Even then, he had a cell phone glued to his ear. He stayed alert by downing a dozen cups of black coffee (without cream, but with countless packets of Sweet'n Low) and consuming a half dozen cans of Diet Coke daily, mostly in his office. He had an eclectic mix of furnishings there, including a lava lamp and a guitar autographed by members of U2.

When the brouhaha began, which insiders say Sidgmore instigated, the choice of Ebbers' replacement had not been a unanimous decision. Max E. Bobbitt and Stiles A. Kellett Jr., two of Ebber's closest pals and the longest serving board members, opposed the idea. At a hastily organized board meeting held in a Washington, DC, law firm on the last weekend of April, with Ebbers' resignation in hand, the board hastily approved Kellett's nomination of Bobbitt as CEO. A seasoned senior executive at Alltel Corporation, Bobbitt planned to serve as interim chief executive only long enough to sell WorldCom, perhaps to a Baby Bell or Verizon Communications. But his CEO tenure lasted but a few hours, just long enough for WorldCom chairman Bert C. Roberts Jr. to catch a whiff of the plan. Roberts adamantly opposed selling WorldCom.

When Bobbitt stepped back, two volunteers came forward to take Bobbitt's place: Roberts and Sidgmore. Both had been largely inactive for more than a year, and the board was in a gridlock. After vacillating for two days, board members gravitated toward Sidgmore, who pointed out that he had spent nearly his entire career successfully running companies and promised to restore faith in WorldCom. Roberts pledged more active participation in running the company, for which he was paid more than a million annually; and Sidgmore, who earned $700,000 a year as vice chairman, was unanimously voted in.

In May, Sidgmore devised a turnaround plan for WorldCom. He knew that competition was continuing to drive down data-service fees, and had watched WorldCom Group's revenue growth shift from 19 percent in 2000 to zero in 2002. He focused on the international market, where revenue growth was more than 20 percent, and on new products like Web hosting. He realized fat profits were history, so he cut capital spending in half and announced another round of layoffs while mulling a plan to replace key executives. He exited the wireless resale business, deeming the $1 billion division unprofitable and "not a core asset" and immediately began dissipating the division's nearly two million customers.

Because Sullivan was handling the SEC inquiry, Sidgmore focused on debt and competition. To prepare for the Baby Bells gaining nationwide access to the nation's long-distance market, WorldCom beefed up efforts to tout The Neighborhood Plan. Despite Sidgmore's best efforts, May was shaping up to be a terrible month and June would mark only the beginning of WorldCom's darkest hours.

Red flags began popping up en masse. On May 1, as part of standard procedure, a clerk e-mailed a March 2002 capital expense report to finance managers. Appalled to see the numbers distributed, Buford "Buddy" Yates Jr., WorldCom's former director of general accounting, slipped Myers a note that said, "Where do I sign my confession?" Myers demanded to know why the report was distributed. "I thought we were never again distributing this," he said, scolding the clerk's supervisors.

On May 9, WorldCom's bond rating was lowered to junk status. Four days later, WorldCom was removed from the S&P 500. On May 14, a world-record 670 million shares of WorldCom stock were traded and AXA Financial of France ended up with nearly 11 percent of the company.

On May 16, the *Fort Worth Weekly* published the findings of former WorldCom financial analyst Kim Emigh, who was laid off in March 2001 after challenging a directive to reclassify expenses. "For years, he'd seen the limos provided by vendors arrive at the WorldCom's Richardson offices to whisk a manager nicknamed Mr. Free Lunch away to dine at The Mansion or other exclusive restaurants, week after week," reported Gayle Reaves. "He'd witnessed first-hand the anger of executives when he questioned statements from their favorite subcontractors who were asking payment for, say, 10 workers who somehow had only five Social Security numbers among them. He'd had other managers ask him for advice on how to carry out corporate directives that he thought were unscrupulous. But up until that day in December 2000, nobody had asked him to do anything that he believed would break the law. This time, he believed, what the company wanted him to do could be construed as tax fraud. He sent word of his concerns up the corporate chain, and the reply came back down: Do it anyway." He didn't.

Emigh conveyed the message to a woman he knew who worked for WorldCom COO Ron Beaumont. "I said, 'Sue, I'll get fired over this,' (and) she said, 'Oh, nobody would do that,'" he told Reaves. He was, and immediately filed a $35 million lawsuit against the company, which was dismissed. Emigh's laundry list detailed a bartender who was contracted at a $120,000-a-year rate to do data entry work, improper billing of payroll expenses to capital projects, and the scam by some managers to take advantage of the situation (rising capital costs justified bigger operating budgets) by spending money on parties, limousines, and other goodies. A capital expense audit for 2001 showed an outside contractor was paid for working 3,053 hours during the first nine months of the year, or nearly 16 hours a day, five days a week without a break for three straight quarters. "Before, no one wanted to listen to the story," said Emigh. MCI founder Jack Goeken said he wasn't surprised. "I know of one fellow who worked one day a month and (WorldCom) was paying him $1.5 million a year," he said.

The strong balance sheet, as everyone eventually found out, was a myth. Since Sullivan was the only person who fully knew the company books, Sidgmore promoted him to executive vice president and counted on him to persuade bankers to refinance the company's bloated debt burden. In mid-May, Sidgmore hired KPMG to replace Arthur Andersen, the company's independent auditors since 1989.

However, a former Andersen accountant said the same auditors continued to come and go at WorldCom corporate headquarters under a new employer: KPMG. On May 15, KPMG announced that two former partners and nine staff members of

Arthur Andersen LLP in Jackson had joined the local firm, but the names were not listed in the press release. Both accounting firms were housed in One Jackson Place in downtown Jackson. KPMG is located in Suite 1100. Arthur Andersen was located in Suite 1300. "For eons, auditors have moved around from one firm to another, so it's not unusual," said Dr. Rick Elam, an accounting professor at the University of Mississippi. "It's also not unusual when a corporation changes auditors for some of the auditors from the predecessor firm to join the new firm." On July 11, a KPMG spokesperson said that no former Andersen staff members or partners identified with the WorldCom case were currently working on it at KPMG.

Around the same time, Sidgmore ordered a sweeping assessment of WorldCom's myriad divisions and subsidiaries and a thorough examination of the company's books as part of a 30-day plan to reboot WorldCom and reassure investors and analysts.

On May 21, the board of directors announced it had unanimously voted to eliminate the tracking stocks structure, effective July 12. Coincidentally, WorldCom entered the volatile Middle Eastern fray when the company closed a deal on June 6 with Telephone Systems International, a New York-based privately held communications company. It was to provide long distance transport services via satellite links to TSI's affiliate in Afghanistan, Afghan Wireless Communications Company, in Kabul and other city networks under construction in Afghanistan. WorldCom was making strategic moves, but they were not pretty.

Seasoned internal audit team leader Cynthia Cooper led the internal investigation ordered by Sidgmore. A hometown girl and a top student at Clinton High School, Cooper earned an undergraduate accounting degree from the University of Alabama and a master's degree in accounting from the University of Southern Mississippi in 1987. She was a respected neighbor and friend who faithfully attended Pinelake Baptist Church in Brandon, Mississippi. She lived in the Windward Oaks subdivision on Ross Barnett Reservoir, within spitting distance of Sullivan's lair, with her stay-at-home husband and two young daughters. Judy O'Neal Gressett, who taught Cooper senior English at Clinton High School, described Cooper as "totally honest," with a character trait "this country needs more of, and that's integrity."

But schooling hadn't prepared her for the crossroads she soon faced. After realizing she had unearthed evidence that showed possible criminal fraud involving billions of dollars, Cooper had to make a choice. Should she pursue the investigation and risk being fired like Arthur Andersen and other internal accountants who had questioned the accounting methods of WorldCom's inner sanctum? Even the unflappable Ebbers had resigned under pressure. Undaunted, Cooper forged ahead.

Instead of finding leverage for new financing options, Cooper found that some of WorldCom's businesses were holding debt that hadn't been consolidated on the company's balance sheet. Cooper also noticed that ordinary expenses had been booked as capital investments, a calculation that enabled Sullivan to spread those outlays over many quarters, making the company appear profitable. And there was a mysterious $1.4 billion line item that had been added to the company's capital expenses. On March 6, Cooper raised some of these issues with the audit committee, the day before the SEC request came down the pike. Nothing happened.

Earlier, in March, John Stupka, former SkyTel CEO and the director of WorldCom's wireless division, had dropped by Cooper's office with a beef. He was upset because he was about to lose $400 million in set-aside money for the third quarter of 2001 to cover losses for customers that didn't pay their bills. It was a legitimate accounting practice that was common in the wireless business and didn't affect the company's bottom line. Stupka found out that Sullivan planned to use that money elsewhere. Andersen auditors Melvin Dick and Kenny Avery had backed Sullivan's decision when Stupka's team complained. They did so again when Cooper raised questions about it. She added the information to her growing list of suspicious accounting tactics. In August, Stupka would resign, saying his position was no longer needed at the company.

On May 28, internal auditor Gene Morse discovered $500 million in fraudulent computer expenses. When he approached Cooper, she told him to "keep going." To avoid arousing suspicion, internal auditors combed through millions of entries at night when Sullivan was nowhere on the radar screen. Cooper's dad often brought midnight snacks to the close-knit team. By day, Morse often retreated to the company's cramped and windowless audit library to work unnoticed. He had tapped into the heart of the company's accounting records, off limits to anyone but those approved by Sullivan, and when he tried to print thousands of journal entries to match up with receipts, the server had nearly crashed. The episode drew unwanted attention and soon after, Sullivan approached Morse in the company cafeteria and asked him what he was working on. Because Sullivan had only talked to Morse twice in five years, the confrontation was unusual. When Morse muttered, "international capital expenditures," Sullivan turned on his heel and briskly walked away.

When questioned by Cooper on June 11 about the company's record keeping of assets and expenses, Sullivan was dismissive. He asked Cooper to postpone the investigation until the third quarter. Sullivan and Myers pressured Cooper to drop the issue entirely. Myers sent Cooper a personal note appealing for the reassignment of one of her deputies, saying, "[I'm] not trying to get in your business so please don't take it that way." When that did not work, Myers sent a terse note the next day directing her to reprioritize the deputy's assignment. That did not work, either.

According to internal audit reports, Sullivan began justifying the journal entries by saying that items related to "prepaid capacity" represented costs associated with underutilized or unused leased lines, which had been capitalized. While revenues declined, the costs associated with these leases were fixed, creating a "matching problem." Sullivan claimed the practice of capitalizing line costs began in third-quarter 2001, and prior to that reporting period, the costs had been recorded as current expenses. He said the costs were directly related to the amounts paid for line leases and that WorldCom fully expected to take a restructuring charge in second-quarter 2002 concerning prepaid capacity entries, a practice he claimed would end.

Myers explained that beginning about 2001, WorldCom's management determined that the company's cost structure had become too high and that the "field" had been asked to lower the cost structure of the network. Myers also stated that the line items were booked based on what the margins, such as ratio of line costs to revenues, had been historically and that no accounting principles supported the entries. Cooper knew it was smoke and mirrors.

While the internal audit investigation was heating up, Sidgmore held a month-overdue annual company meeting. The mostly Mississippi audience cheered when Sidgmore told them on June 14 that WorldCom's home office would remain in Clinton. Besides, it would have cost the company tens of thousands of dollars to relocate corporate headquarters during a time when unnecessary expenses were being scrutinized. Then the bad news: He confirmed that as many as 16,000 jobs were in jeopardy. An accounting fraud involving billions of dollars and WorldCom's highest ranking accountants was unthinkable.

By then, Cooper had discovered that accounting executive Betty L. Vinson, who reported to Yates, recorded the questionable transfers. On June 17, the same day Standard & Poor's downgraded WorldCom's debt once again, Vinson told Cooper that even though she made the entries, she "did not know what they were for and did not have support for them."

Despite conversations to the contrary two years earlier, Yates told internal auditors that he did not know what prepaid capacity was. When Cooper confronted Myers that afternoon, he admitted there was no accounting support for the expense changes and that he had been uneasy with the practice. He also confided in Cooper that if cost reductions were not forthcoming, WorldCom "might as well shut its doors." When asked how the company would explain the adjustments to the SEC, Myers "stated he had hoped it would not have to be explained," according to an internal audit memorandum. "David also stated that they probably shouldn't have capitalized the line costs, but once it was done the first time (2Q01), it was difficult to stop. David indicated that he has felt uncomfortable with these entries since the first time they were booked."

Myers, another hometown executive, had grown up in Jackson, Mississippi, attended Woodland Hills Academy, and was known as a nice, all-American, and solid Christian guy. E-mails reflecting a change in Myers would later surface during the House Financial Services Committee investigation. In January 2002, he issued a stern warning via e-mail to Steven Brabbs, manager of WorldCom's European and Asian accounts, who noticed in March 2000 that an accountant at company headquarters had inflated the profit margin figures he had compiled for the international division. Brabbs had contacted Arthur Andersen. According to documents released by the House Financial Services Committee, Myers was allegedly furious and advised Brabbs not to "have any more meetings with AA (Arthur Andersen) for any reason." The January 22 e-mail read: "I do not want to hear an excuse, just stop . . . don't make me ask you again." Myers zapped an e-mail to another employee, referring to Brabbs' contact with Andersen: "Not that I was looking for another reason to have him executed." Brabbs said he was told that Sullivan had boosted the numbers by making a $33.6 million reduction in line cost adjustment. "Despite repeated requests, we were given no support or explanation for the entry," Brabbs wrote in a memorandum.

During the frenzied days before the accounting disclosure, the mood was ominous in Myers' second-floor office suite, where federal investigators milled around constantly. "David was always in a conference or his secretary was snippy," said a former clerical worker. "I remember thinking, 'What's the deal?' He used to be so friendly and accessible. Then all of a sudden he was not."

Dissatisfied with Sullivan's explanations for the whole ordeal, Cooper, along with internal auditor and childhood pal Glyn Smith, reported the findings to Max Bobbitt, head of the board's audit committee. On June 13, the day before a scheduled committee meeting, they met Bobbitt at a Hampton Inn near corporate headquarters. Cooper and Smith showed him where they had stumbled on evidence that Sullivan and Myers were overseeing two sets of books, one of them fraudulent. After hearing the evidence, Bobbitt asked Cooper not to disclose the problem at the committee's meeting the next day until they had a chance to interview Sullivan again. "Max agreed he would discuss the issue with Scott on the return flight and that IA (internal audit) could carry on with their audit as planned Monday morning (6/17)," according to internal audit correspondence.

On June 19, Sullivan was asked to submit a written explanation overnight. At the June 20 board meeting, with Andersen and KPMG auditors present, Sullivan's "White Paper" rationalizing his accounting practices failed to persuade the

WorldCom board that they were legitimate. According to the first interim report of bankruptcy court examiner Dick Thornburgh, Sullivan explained in the White Paper that, after WorldCom's merger with MCI in September 1998 was complete, WorldCom sold MCI's SHL Systemhouse for $1.4 billion. The proceeds were used to expand WorldCom's network because of the expected continued rapid development in the telecommunications industry.

During this time, WorldCom entered into long-term, fixed-rate line leases to connect its network with ILEC (incumbent local exchange carriers) networks and entered into network leases to expand its data, Internet, and local services assuming that revenue would follow. When that did not happen, Sullivan referenced Staff Accounting Bulletin No. 101 and Financial Accounting Standards Board No. 91 to support his conclusion that the lease costs incurred should not be expensed until WorldCom recorded matching revenue. He reasoned that "the cost of deferrals for the unutilized portion" of line leases was "an appropriate inventory of this capacity" and ultimately would be amortized before the contracts expired.

In support, Sullivan defined an asset as "probable future economic benefits obtained or controlled by a particular entity as a result of past transactions or events." In addition, he gave a description of the characteristics of an asset, according to the Statement of Financial Accounting Concepts No. 6. The second quarter of 2002, Sullivan wrote, marked the first time in company history that revenue had decreased for two consecutive quarters. He blamed the decrease on a weak economy, customer downsizings and bankruptcies, foreign exchange losses, and "product migrations."

Sullivan offered further explanation for the timing of writing off previously capitalized expenses: Ebbers' resignation, the company's junk-status debt rating and liquidity concerns, and because line leases could not ultimately be realized. Sullivan concluded by explaining that the preparation of WorldCom's financial statements "requires the company to make estimates and assumptions that affect the reported amount of assets and liabilities as well as the reported amount of expenses, including line costs . . . significant management judgments and estimates must be made and used in connection with establishing these amounts." At the meeting, Andersen auditors denied knowing about the line cost transfers and refused to explain why their audit failed to uncover them. Later, the manipulation of reserve accounts would play a prominent role in the story of the irregularities in WorldCom's financial statements.

"When we knew there was a problem, really and for sure, was on the 20th of June," Sidgmore told the SEC. "All that we knew then was that the accountants were nervous, very nervous, about the accounts. Even KPMG, who had all of this information, did not determine it was a problem until the 20th." Sullivan and Myers were asked to resign. Sullivan refused and was fired on June 24. Sullivan immediately contacted Al London, a board member of the Le Lac Homeowners Association, and assured him the Boca Raton mansion being built would be completed by the end of the year. Myers stepped down voluntarily. Grubman issued a sell report. WorldCom stock dropped below $1 and closed at 91 cents.

"When I first learned of a potential accounting problem on June 20, 2002, I was stunned," Bert C. Roberts, chairman of the board of WorldCom, told the House Financial Services Committee on July 7. "My emotions ran the gamut, from disbelief to concern to anger. When the problem was confirmed and brought to the board's attention, action on the part of the company was swift and decisive."

That's bunk, said a former MCI employee who started working for MCI in 1981 and was laid off from WorldCom in April 2002. "Old Bill McGowan (longtime MCI executive who died of a heart attack in June 1992) must be spinning in his grave to see all he has built come to this," he said. "Bill would have . . . shut the doors before he would have let anyone take this company from his control. Makes me wonder why Bert Roberts hasn't been kicked off the board. He is just as responsible . . . but then again, Bert wasn't much of a CEO. I could never understand what Bill saw in him."

Many WorldCom employees, even longtime middle managers, were unaware of the dark clouds looming over the accounting department. "I knew something was wrong with the telecom industry after the fall of the dot-coms, which escalated in 2001, but I didn't know anything was wrong with our company," said a WorldCom marketing director. "The industry, the economy . . . I knew it was going to eventually catch up with our revenue opportunity, and everyone knows the market is very demanding and unforgiving. There was obviously a significant amount of pressure for us to make our earnings, and that became more difficult as our economy slowed down, but I thought we were infallible. Did I know in January? No. I didn't know there was a problem until they announced that Scott Sullivan and David Myers had left."

Kate Lee, a WorldCom internal communications manager who was laid off in 2002, said she frequently worked with Myers and was shocked by the revelation of the accounting fraud. "David was always such a nice, polite person, very quick to respond," she said. "I never would have conceived of him doing this. It doesn't make any sense."

The fraud troubled Lee. "With any company, there's a little bit of massaging earnings that always goes on at the end of the quarter to make the numbers work, and I thought, well, a few million here, postpone some expenses, push some stuff forward, but you never think of it in terms of billions. That's not managing your money, that's fraud. I felt betrayed."

Sidgmore remained front and center of perhaps the most expensive scandal in the world when he publicly disclosed the accounting misdeeds on June 25. "When I agreed to take over as CEO, it was clear that the company faced significant challenges," Sidgmore said. "But I never imagined what was in store for us." By the close of business that day, WorldCom stock dropped to 83 cents and then plunged to 20 cents in after-hours trading. When the stock fell to nine cents in premarket activity on June 26, the Nasdaq halted trading.

On news of the latest corporate accounting scandal, European equities crumbled. Mexico's peso closed at its weakest level since February 10, 1999, and stocks hit new lows for the year on fears that investors would liquidate Mexican assets to raise cash. Donald Rumsfeld, U.S. Secretary of Defense, dismissed concerns that WorldCom's mounting woes posed a threat to the U.S. military, one of WorldCom's largest customers.

The accounting scandal pummeled WorldCom bondholders. The next day, its bonds plummeted 73 percent, trading between 12 and 15 cents on the dollar. The desecration of WorldCom shares cost investors nearly $175 billion—almost three times the loss in the Enron implosion—and the SEC filed fraud charges against the most feared telecom company in the world. WorldCom became "WorldCon."

"When we first started using the 'WorldCon' graphics, we got some backlash, absolutely," said Stuart Kellogg, president and general manager of WAPT-TV, the ABC affiliate in Jackson. "Ninety-five percent of the viewers that wrote or called the station to comment were unhappy. Some said we were editorializing, but once we pointed out that WorldCom admitted the fraud, the response was, 'Well, okay then.' The other sense was 'You're kicking a Mississippi institution while it's down,' and we responded that we understood, but it was an accurate portrayal of what happened."

The initial reaction in the local business community was shock, said Kellogg. "Then it was, 'Circle the wagons, because

Bernie's a local guy.' Now it isn't weighing as heavily," Kellogg said in November 2002. "If we didn't have a Nissan manufacturing plant coming in and other ongoing economic developments, it might be different, but the other good news helped vindicate us. Unlike suburban Washington and other big WorldCom centers, the impact wasn't as great on us."

Amid a rush of lawsuits and investigations filed the day after the accounting disclosure, the SEC led the charge by launching an investigation and filing a civil fraud lawsuit against the company. Because he owned WorldCom stock, one official who wouldn't handle the probe was U.S. Attorney Dunn Lampton, the lead Justice Department attorney in Jackson, near WorldCom's corporate headquarters in Clinton. In Mississippi, it was difficult to find anyone with a little extra money who did not own WorldCom stock. "I have been supremely disappointed in the stock's performance," said Mark Pollock of Jackson, a WorldCom stockholder who had sold his shares earlier in the year. "I went from a $55,000 profit to a $3,500 loss. I rode it like the *Titanic.*"

Sidgmore's June 26 e-mail, meant to reassure employees, said the accounting scandal was no cause for concern. "There is absolutely no impact to our company's cash position for 2001 and 2002," he wrote. "We continue to have significant cash on hand." Meanwhile, Sidgmore was being investigated for his role in the debacle. SEC Chairman Harvey Pitt remarked on NBC's *Today* morning news show, "Criminal charges may be too good for the people who brought about this mess." After a series of political missteps that embarrassed the Bush White House, Pitt resigned under pressure November 5, in the middle of investigations into the WorldCom case.

Even WorldCom employees were cynical. When one of Sidgmore's memos included the line, "Our customers can count on WorldCom to meet their communications needs today and tomorrow," circulated around the office, one wit wrote: "Friday is sort of doubtful." After Sidgmore wrote, "I know I can count on you to be with me," the jokester added: "Don't bother with a resume; no other telecoms are hiring." Some employees bailed, even if only temporarily. WorldCom spokesperson Claire Hassett, who was often quoted in national print publications, began maternity leave on June 26. "I'm sure she was ready to take a break," said a business reporter who contacted her frequently. "She was getting zinged with questions all the time."

Though many outsiders hailed the internal auditors as heroes, a few workers wished the accounting issues had been left alone. Some employees hinted that the accounting fraud might have been avoided if internal auditors had been doing their jobs. They did not realize the roadblocks internal auditors had encountered, such as financial limitations and lack of support from senior management, the board of directors, and the auditing committee. Because the internal audit department reported both to the CFO and the WorldCom audit committee, getting around Sullivan was risky. The internal audit department's lack of a comprehensive audit plan would be addressed later. By the end of the month, 5,100 WorldCom employees nationwide would be laid off.

WorldCom workers forwarded e-mails containing revised lyrics to a parody of Don McLean's "American Pie" (EMI Records): "We were singing/Bye Bye WorldCom MCI/My portfolio was heavy when the stock was still high/Now Wall Street boys just got a poke in the eye/Saying this is what you get when you buy/This could make the company die."

While forensic accountants were explaining the highly creative accounting tricks used by Sullivan to cook the books— treating expenses as capital expenditures and thus inflating EBITDA (earnings before interest, taxes, depreciation, and amortization)—billions more dollars were being uncovered in the investigation. In corporate America, EBITDA was becoming the default measure for cash flow and would later be discovered as an accounting tactic for WorldCom's additional $3.3 billion in improperly reported earnings. Patrick McGurn, vice president of Institutional Shareholder Services, joked on a talk show: "We've heard redefinitions for EPS and EBITDA. They now mean 'eventual prison sentence' and 'earnings before I trick the dumb auditor.'"

Speculation swirled about Sullivan's intentions. Did he believe he was simply pushing the envelope within the legal realms, or did he deliberately doctor the books? "I have a hard time believing Scott did this maliciously," said a former Tier 1 executive of the company. "Maybe he felt like he had a good basis in his accounting argument and convinced himself it made sense. If he was trying to do something underhanded, he could have come up with a better scheme."

Mississippi Business Journal publisher Joe Jones, CPA, said the basic premise was elementary: "There are only two ways to overstate income. One is to overstate income and the other is to understate expenses. Other than outright lying with no attempt to develop a plausible position, overstating income would be difficult. Understating expenses is easy and apparently this is the route chosen by WorldCom's senior accountants."

Jones explained that understating expenses could be calculated by using an unjustifiably long useful life for computing depreciation on buildings and equipment, which would understate depreciation expense. They could also be calculated by classifying regular operating expenses as a cost of production, with those expenses remaining on the balance sheet as an asset until the inventory is sold. Or the company could classify regular operating expenses as prepaid expenses by implying that they will benefit a future period and should therefore be reflected as an asset on the balance sheet.

"It appears that WorldCom's accountants chose number three," said Jones. "Though it works in the short run, it is a temporary fix. At some point these 'prepaid expenses' must be considered as having outlived their utility and they are then reclassified back to an operating expense. My guess is that they thought the economic recession would be short-lived and they could flow the expense through the financial statements as an expense within the next year or so and their indiscretion would not be detected. Meanwhile, the bonuses calculated on net profit would line the pockets of senior management and no one would be the wiser."

MCI founder Jack Goeken called it "plain old greed." "I never took a salary, so it really bothers me to see CEOs and CFOs taking big salaries and bonuses. It shows me their intent is not necessarily to make money for shareholders, but for themselves."

At the same time that the company laid off the first wave of 17,000 employees, WorldCom was treating its top salespeople to a paid vacation at a posh resort in Maui. "Talk about bad timing," said Frank Cho, business writer for the *Honolulu Advertiser.* "They were living it up. Of course, they were not too interested in appearing in the paper here having a good time while thousands were being laid off. I don't know if any of the ones who were here got pink slipped. They did have a nice private fireworks show, which lasted about 25 minutes and must have cost a lot of money."

12

That Dog Don't Hunt

We think Bernie Ebbers is up to his eyeballs in this.

U.S. House Energy and Commerce
Spokesman Ken Johnson

Fireworks of another sort were emanating from WorldCom headquarters. On July 1, WorldCom filed a key events summary with the Securities and Exchange Commission, and along with the SEC, the Justice Department and Mississippi Attorney General's office immediately launched investigations into possible corporate criminal misdeeds. The House Financial Services Committee, chaired by Ohio Republican Mike Oxley, served subpoenas for a July 8 hearing to Ebbers, Sidgmore, Sullivan, Grubman, Roberts, and former Arthur Andersen senior partner Melvin Dick, who signed off on World-Com audits.

On June 30, Sidgmore announced that WorldCom Group represented nearly three billion shares of stock; MCI Group had a little more than 118 million shares. According to the company's 2002 annual shareholder meeting proxy statements, all WorldCom directors and executive officers as a group owned 40.37 million shares of WorldCom Group and 947,678 shares of MCI Group stock. "We said from the outset of our new management team that we would take the bold steps necessary to build on our strong balance sheet and strengthen operational efficiencies that will better position the company for future growth," he said. "This is one of those steps." But few people were paying attention. All eyes were focused on the July 8 hearing. A record number of viewers worldwide tuned in to watch the drama unfold on Capitol Hill, which DotCom Scoop coined "As The WorldCom Turns."

Before the House hearing, photographers snapped Ebbers chumming with Sullivan. Both were dressed appropriately in dark suits—Sullivan wore a blue tie and Ebbers had a red one, which led to jokes about Sullivan being Democrat and Ebbers showing his Republican colors—but Ebbers was wearing an inappropriate smile. During a break, however, he stood alone with one hand covering his watch as if to stop time. Close up, his eyes appeared red and he looked gaunt. He was no longer smiling.

Ebbers hired high-priced defense attorney Reid H. Weingarten, a partner in the Washington, DC-based law firm Steptoe & Johnson, and one of the nation's top defenders of fallen corporate executives. A 1971 graduate of Cornell University and 1975 graduate of the Dickinson School of Law at Penn State University, the $600-an-hour lawyer had helped out a fellow Mississippian in 1998 when he won an acquittal for Agriculture Secretary Mike Espy, even after Espy pleaded guilty to accepting illegal contributions.

Weingarten was at Ebbers' side during the hearing and when he gave a self-gratifying opening statement followed by invoking his Fifth Amendment rights—Sullivan also pleaded the fifth—

on a litany of questions fired by congressmen. "When all of the activities at WorldCom are fully aired and when I get the opportunity—and I'm very much looking forward to it—to explain my actions in a setting that will not compromise my ability to defend myself in the legal proceedings arising out of the recent events, I believe that no one will conclude that I engaged in any criminal or fraudulent conduct during my tenure at World-Com," a stone-faced Ebbers told congressmen.

Ebbers was threatened with contempt when Texas Democrat Max Sandlin argued that Ebbers should have been forced to testify after making his statement. "I am not aware of this new concept of selective Fifth Amendment protection," he told the committee. Ebbers took the Fifth even when Sandlin asked if he was a U.S. citizen. Weingarten said that if Ebbers ever were put on trial, his dream jury would include "12 Martians."

Congressman Billy Tauzin, a Republican from Louisiana, told CNN's *Moneyline* that Sullivan admitted to lawyers that Ebbers was aware of the improprieties. "The fired CFO of the company, the guy in charge of financial affairs of the company, admitted to those lawyers that the chairman of the company, Bernie Ebbers, did in fact know that millions of dollars, hundreds of millions of dollars, had been moved into capital debt rather than expensing it as ordinary debt of the corporation," he said. "This is the first evidence that we've seen that the muddy little footprints may lead back to Bernie Ebbers' doorstep," added House Energy and Commerce spokesman Ken Johnson. "We think Bernie Ebbers is up to his eyeballs in this."

The House Financial Service Committee mercilessly grilled the two men who would talk: Dick and Grubman. After Dick graduated from the University of South Dakota with an accounting degree in 1975, he joined Arthur Andersen as a staff auditor, eventually working his way to partner, and beginning with WorldCom's fiscal year ended December 31, 2001, was in charge of WorldCom's books. Andersen had labeled WorldCom a maximum-risk client, having noted in a 1999 memorandum that "in the past, we have noted situations where management has taken aggressive accounting positions, particularly in the area of purchase accounting." Also, Andersen was still reeling from the public bashing it received when Enron collapsed in December 2001 as a result of a complex scheme that masked losses.

Accounting experts disagreed over whether WorldCom's improperly logged entries would have been easy for Andersen auditors to spot. Andersen claimed to have been shut out of the process, but during the internal audit, the accounting firm refused to respond to some of Cooper's inquiries. Andersen auditor Kenny Avery told her he only took orders from Sullivan. "If the reports are true that Mr. Sullivan and others at WorldCom improperly transferred line cost expenses to capital accounts so as to misstate the company's actual performance, I am deeply troubled by this conduct," Dick, now CFO of catalog clothier Coldwater Creek, told the committee.

"It's a black eye to the industry and we didn't need another one," said Dr. James R. "Jimmy" Crockett, an accounting professor at the University of Southern Mississippi. "There's no excuse for missing $3.8 billion. I'm very disappointed."

Grubman, the Salomon analyst and friend of Ebbers who came under fire for recommending WorldCom stock as it tanked, told the committee, "In hindsight, I regret that I was wrong in rating WorldCom highly for too long, though in this regard I note that I surely would have downgraded the company much earlier had I known the truth about its financial performance." When Grubman resigned as managing director in the U.S. Equity Research Division shortly after the hearing, Salomon Smith Barney CEO Michael Carpenter told *USA Today:* "The reason he left the firm is very simple. You can't do your job when your photo is on the front page of *BusinessWeek,* and the *Wall Street Journal* and the *New York Times* just have to have a story about you every day, and CNBC chases you down the street."

Salomon's parent company, Citigroup, which had been pelted by potential losses and liabilities, might have also had something to do with Grubman's abrupt resignation.

With Saudi Arabian Prince Alwaleed bin Talal Alsaud as the bank's largest shareholder and CEO Sanford "Sandy" Weill at the helm, Citigroup was feeling the heat of investigations by New York Attorney General Eliot Spitzer and the National Association of Securities Dealers. Grubman's pet companies (he had recommended all 10 telecommunications companies that were among the 25 largest bankruptcy filings in the United States) were undergoing or facing intense scrutiny from investigators. On August 13, the House Financial Services Committee issued a subpoena to Salomon seeking details of the firm's allocation of shares in initial public offerings to WorldCom executives during the technology stock boom days. On September 23, Salomon agreed to pay a $5 million fine to settle charges that it issued misleading research reports from Grubman. In an attempt to reform itself, Citigroup announced October 30 that it would separate research from investment banking.

Despite the backlash from his actions, Grubman left the firm with fatter pockets, which included the balance of earnings from a lucrative five-year contract he signed in 1998, paid legal bills, and approximately $12 million of stock in Citigroup. A $19 million company loan to Grubman was reportedly forgiven.

Meanwhile, Sidgmore had become the tar baby. "About two months ago, when I agreed to take over as CEO, it was clear that the company faced significant challenges, but I never imagined what was in store for us," Sidgmore told the House Financial Services Committee. When he fielded questions for *Washington Post*'s Live Online on July 11, he stated that Digex and UUNET were not for sale and emphatically denied that Bill Gates and Warren E. Buffett were possible suitors. Industry watchers speculated that Sidgmore's response was pat only because there was no offer on the table. *Business-Week* speculated that James Q. Crowe, Ebbers' nemesis and former WorldCom chairman, was considered a possible buyer of WorldCom's network units even though Buffett and others had propped up his company, Level 3 Communications Inc., with a half-billion-dollar investment.

Speculation swirled that selling the MCI long-distance division would unload an increasingly unprofitable albatross. "We have laid out our strategic plan for the business and have announced which pieces of the business we don't feel are core assets for the future," Sidgmore told *Live Online*. "These include our wireless resale business, certain other wireless technologies, Latin American assets and some real estate. We believe that our large corporate customers will be unaffected by our strategy."

But other corporate lenders were unhappy with World-Com's financial state. On July 12, twenty-five banks filed suit against WorldCom, claiming the company had bilked them out of nearly $2.5 billion only six weeks before disclosing its suicidal accounting fraud. The day before, the WorldCom board had nixed plans to pay a final 60 cents per share dividend on MCI tracking stock, a move that made investors nervous. Hoping to buy time and stave off creditors, Sidgmore warned that if WorldCom had to file for bankruptcy protection, "shareholders would come out very badly" and would be the last debtors repaid in a long line of debt holders. Across the Atlantic, the International Accounting Standards Board (IASB) in London announced on July 16 that it would propose new rules by the end of 2002 to require all European Union corporations to expense stock options within five years, a move spurred by the WorldCom debacle.

Sniffing disaster and citing "regrettable, but necessary" reasons, the Heritage Classic Foundation, host organization of the Heritage Classic PGA Tour event, terminated its contract with WorldCom on July 19 as title sponsor of the prestigious nationally televised event. The announcement was quietly issued July 22, a day after WorldCom filed for bankruptcy protection, because "we didn't want to add salt to the wound," said tournament director Steve Wilmot.

At the last WorldCom Heritage Classic, which ended April 21, 2002, pro golfer Justin Leonard set a 54-hole scoring record on the recently renovated golf links and closed with a 14-under 270 total to win the title and $720,000. "Our golf tournament represents an enormous economic impact for our entire community, which we are not willing to jeopardize," said foundation chairman Joseph B. Fraser. "It has become obvious that we must find a new title sponsor in order to maintain the tournament's forward momentum."

To help fill in the $2.3 million gap to cover the 2003 event's estimated $8.2 million cost, Hilton Head Island Mayor Tom Peeples and the town council unanimously adopted a one-year, one percent hospitality tax increase on September 17. The temporary increase was estimated to bring in roughly $1.8 million while tournament officials sought major sponsors. "That's assurance for us to move forward," said Wilmot, with a deep sigh. "We regretted the need to make the decision to terminate our contract with WorldCom. I'd had a great 16-year relationship with the same folks—Cindy Palmer in the DC office had worked with me the entire time—so it was tough because there were emotional ties. But the relationship needed to be severed."

In July, Ebbers appealed to the people whom he considered to be his closest allies: church members at Easthaven Baptist Church in Brookhaven, Mississippi. At the Sunday morning worship service, Ebbers, who appeared lankier than usual, warmed up to the crowd: "I just want you to know you aren't going to church with a crook. I don't know what all is going to happen or what mistakes have been made. [But] no one will find me to have knowingly committed fraud." A dour Ebbers teared up, paused, and then added, "More than anything else, I hope that my witness for Jesus Christ will not be jeopardized." The congregation erupted in a standing ovation.

Journalists pounced on Ebbers' use of the term "crook," with one editor pointing out that it was "not a good sign. Such denials just don't ring true since [former U.S. president] Richard Nixon immortalized the term." Two ex-WorldCom employees jumped on Ebbers' use of the word crook and wrote the song, "Telecom Cowboy," that ended with a sound bite of Nixon proclaiming that he was "not a crook." Academics were cynical, too. "Most people who take the Fifth Amendment do so because they have something to hide," said Jack Wade Nowlin, an assistant professor of constitutional law and criminal procedure at the University of Mississippi. "We all know that O.J. Simpson didn't take the stand, for instance."

On the church grounds two months later, Ebbers was not so warm and fuzzy. When Canadian Broadcasting Corporation (CBC) host/anchor Dianne Buckner approached him as he was coming out of church, Ebbers said that she should be ashamed of herself and "get out of his way," related Susan Gittins, a producer for *Venture,* the national business show of the CBC, which aired a profile on Ebbers on October 6, 2002. As he climbed into his big pickup truck, Buckner asked him how he could not have known about the WorldCom accounting errors. "Really, who should be ashamed here?" said Gittins. "When Dianne asked a laid-off WorldCom employee if he wanted to see Bernie Ebbers go to jail, he shouted, 'Not only do I want to see Bernie Ebbers go to jail, I want to *pick* the jail.'"

Edmonton Journal staff writer David Staples best described the unfettered swell of support for Ebbers in his adopted state:

"Here in sweltering Mississippi, here in the land of believers, where the Bible belt is cinched up tight, Edmonton boy Ebbers found his home, his faith and his WorldCom fortune. In the 1990s, Ebbers turned WorldCom into the second-largest telecommunications company in America and became a Mississippi hero and icon. The entire state stood up and gave him a decade-long standing ovation. Ebbers succeeded because he's a man of a certain faith. It's a modern Mississippi faith, a strange mix of differing creeds . . . made up of family values, state pride, American patriotism, God, Jesus, markets, mergers and money . . . values that often contradicted one another, which is why Bernie Ebbers is also a man of contradiction and contrast."

Even though Ebbers was under intense scrutiny outside the safe haven of Lincoln County, with at least a half dozen investigations in the works by state and federal lawyers, forensic accountants and politicians, he acted like nothing had happened. He continued feasting on lobster at Tico's with a circle of friends that included an odd mix of politicos, trial lawyers, and businesspeople. He continued swigging beer at the Dixie Springs Café in Summit, where he sought refuge the night he resigned as CEO and the day after his congressional appearance. He jokingly asked co-owner Joe Kimmel for a job. He often called former colleagues, usually middle managers, to gossip about the latest WorldCom news. And he continued to drive to Easthaven Baptist Church in a luxury Lexus SUV to teach Sunday school. In August, he was spotted lounging at his Canadian ranch.

For every Ebbers foe, there was a friend quick to defend him. "He would never knowingly do anything unethical in terms of the books," said retired WorldCom executive Chris Eddy. "Not to place blame on anyone else, but he believed in what people told him from an accounting perspective. If Sullivan did something wrong, why the hell didn't Arthur Andersen catch it? Bernie would have put a stop to it. His philosophy was to conduct business in such an ethical and professional manner so that it never gave anyone reason to sue the company."

Mississippi publishing magnate Wyatt Emmerich, who owns more than a dozen weekly newspapers around the state, gave his view on the debate over who was at fault—Ebbers or Sullivan?—when he wrote: "Ebbers was our financial savior. He could do no wrong. We had total faith in him. He could, we thought, walk on water . . . (but) Jesus had his Judas too."

"People that have problems admitting what they don't know are people who get in a world of trouble," Ebbers told the *New York Times* in 1998. "I'm not an engineer by training; I'm not an accountant by training. My job is to bring in people who do have those specific skills and then rely on them. I'm the coach. I'm not the point guard who shoots the ball."

Ebbers was a mouthpiece, said a financial analyst. "People like Sullivan would tell him what could be done, not necessarily how it could be done, and he would make a decision," said the analyst. "They would tell him what to say and he would say it. On one occasion when a projection wasn't met, Bernie was furious because his ass was out on a limb. Believe me, there were consequences. He never liked being put in that position."

Susan Kalla, an analyst at Friedman, Billings & Ramsey, said, "WorldCom wasn't operated at all, it was just on auto pilot, using bubble gum and Band-Aids as solutions to its problems . . . Bernie was endearing, but he didn't even have a working knowledge of the business."

"Bernie was not the driving force in the company, so maybe that's why he's walking around Jackson like he did nothing wrong," said a Jackson businessperson. "When expectations run way up from where they ought to be and you don't recognize it in time, it builds on itself. Then ultimately, instead of admitting it, you resort to manipulation. Maybe now we'll find out who was the driving force."

Because the head of one of the world's most technically advanced companies did not use newfangled technological gadgets, Ebbers left no paper trail. His well-known private meetings behind closed doors did not merit taking minutes or recording notes. Ebbers always covered his tracks. So with WorldCom on the brink of bankruptcy, and nearly $4 billion unaccounted for, the burning question on everyone's mind, including those closest to Ebbers, who remained coy even as his 26.9 remaining million shares of WorldCom stock dwindled in value to roughly $4 million, was: "What did Bernie know?"

Hoodwinked

Business was much worse than we knew for years and (Scott Sullivan) had us all hoodwinked.

Robert Gensler, portfolio manager of the $425 million
T. Rowe Price Media & Telecommunications
fund, August 1, 2002

On July 21, 2002, a warm and sunny Sunday afternoon in Manhattan, WorldCom and its approximately 300 domestic subsidiaries and 200 foreign affiliates filed the nation's largest bankruptcy. WorldCom's petition for Chapter 11 bankruptcy protection in the U.S. District Court for the Southern District of New York allowed the company to continue functioning while it reorganized its debts. "When you file Chapter 11, time really slows down," Sidgmore said. "Your bills aren't due right away, so you have time to figure out your next move."

The day after the filing, it was back to business as usual at WorldCom. The company completed the sale of Advanced

Building Networks division (a business unit it acquired when it bought Intermedia in 2000) to Atlanta-based Cypress Communications for $32 million. WorldCom had been in the process of selling off Intermedia's assets since it bought the company to claim rights on Digex. WorldCom now had a more pressing mission: to submit a reorganization plan by Christmas to restructure its $32.8 billion in debt, sell off noncore assets, and focus on key businesses so it could emerge from bankruptcy protection as a viable corporation.

Even though Sidgmore unveiled a one-year timetable to bring WorldCom out of bankruptcy, analysts predicted that because of the filing's size and complexity, it could take years to complete. Signaling the complexity of the deal, U.S. Bankruptcy Court Judge Arthur J. Gonzalez, assigned to oversee the WorldCom case, allowed WorldCom 90 days to file required financial statements instead of the traditional 15 days granted to most companies filing bankruptcy protection. In October 2002, he granted WorldCom an extension to submit the reorganization plan by March 2003.

In a move that increased scrutiny of WorldCom's business practices, Gonzalez approved a request from the Justice Department to appoint an independent examiner, former U.S. Attorney General Richard Thornburgh, to investigate the company. "WorldCom put extraordinary pressure on itself to meet the expectations of securities analysts," Thornburgh would write in his initial report. "This pressure created an environment in which reporting numbers that met these expectations, no matter how these numbers were derived, apparently became more important than accurate financial reporting."

At the time of the filing, WorldCom had only $200 million in cash, and Gonzalez quickly approved a $2 billion financing package to supplement the company's cash flow during the Chapter 11 proceedings. "Chapter 11 enables us to create the greatest possible value for our creditors, preserve jobs for our employees, continue to deliver top-quality service to our customers and maintain our role in America's national security," Sidgmore said. "We will use this time under reorganization to regain our financial health and focus while operating with the highest integrity. We will emerge from Chapter 11 as quickly as possible and with our competitive spirit intact. Our total focus will be to take this company forward in the best way possible and with the highest ethics so that WorldCom can continue to be an important part of our economy. To that we are totally committed." Uh-huh, mumbled the rest of the world. "Let's see that neat trick," said an industry watcher. One consolation for scorned shareholders: When WorldCom filed for bankruptcy protection, Ebbers effectively lost the generous annual payment of $1.5 million that WorldCom board member Stiles Kellett had arranged.

It was not business as usual for everyone else. Even though it had been expected for several weeks—WorldCom missed $74 million in payments July 15 on its $30 billion in debt—the reality of the filing sent chills around the globe. Scott Cleland, CEO of Precursor Group, a telecom research firm, called it "a case of lose-lose." He said: "It's like a virus that gets spread to everyone. Suppliers get shortchanged. People who do business with them get shortchanged. A lot of bad debt will get absorbed."

Many people wondered how the bankruptcy would affect WorldCom Group's 70,000 route miles of network connections that linked metropolitan centers and regions across North America, Europe, the Middle East, Africa, Latin America, Australia, and Asia to provide customers with integrated data, Internet, and commercial voice communications services. When measured by revenues and traffic carried, it was the world's leading global data, Internet, and network services provider.

What would become of the WorldCom Group, which provided network services for the U.S. government's critical applications? These included communications services for customer service support to 80 million Social Security beneficiaries, air traffic control applications for the Federal Aviation Administration, network management for the Department of Defense, and critical data network services for the United States Postal Service. WorldCom Group also provided long-distance voice and data communications services for the U.S. House of Representatives, Senate, General Accounting Office, and other government agencies.

How would the bankruptcy affect MCI Group, the second largest telecommunications company for consumer and small business long distance in the United States? It serviced approximately 20 million residential and small business customers and more than 470 carriers and other resellers. "It's a damn shame," said MCI founder John D. "Jack" Goeken, who lost several million dollars on WorldCom stock. "Up until this happened, MCI was an example for college kids, what they could do if they had a dream and were dedicated to making it a reality. If someone like me with absolutely nothing could make MCI into the nation's second-largest telecommunications company doing $35 million a year, anyone could do it. The MCI story gave those kids the encouragement to express ideas they might like to try, not to see how dedicated people can take a dream and make it a reality only to have some other people to come in and tear it apart out of greed."

Industry watchers predicted two possible outcomes: World-Com would either negotiate with creditors for friendlier terms and emerge with lower operating costs and the ability to charge less for its services and nab customers from its rivals, or sell itself to the highest bidder. Before the bankruptcy filing, the company's $30 billion in long-term debt—J.P. Morgan Trust Company had the lion's share, with WorldCom's bond debt of $17.2 billion—had stopped rival telecommunications firms from buying it.

When some of that debt was wiped out, industry executives huddled in boardrooms to devise game plans that would weather FCC scrutiny. "It is more appropriate to liquidate WorldCom through Chapter 7 rather than to reorganize it in Chapter 11," said J. Gregory Sidak, CEO of Criterion Economics, an economic consulting firm based in Washington, DC. "Regulators should not resist the natural workings of the capital markets to bring WorldCom's existence to an end." Telcos feared the idea of a leaner, meaner WorldCom. "That would be a disaster," said telecom analyst Drake Johnstone. The 700,000-member Communications Workers of America, which WorldCom considers "the Bells' lapdog," called for WorldCom's head, plus rights on its federal government contracts totaling an estimated $2 billion. When WorldCom reported on October 22 a two-month loss of $429 million despite an $80 million daily income, industry watchers speculated whether a new company would emerge at all.

"Nobody's sure how it will play out," said Ram Kasargod, a senior analyst at Morgan Keegan, who continues to use MCI long-distance service at his Memphis residence. "The creditors want WorldCom to emerge out of bankruptcy because they want to get value for their investment, but it won't be the same company. It will be an interesting independent company and the creditors will call the shots when this whole thing shakes out. The other telecom companies would like to see WorldCom liquidated because they say it's not fair for WorldCom to come out of bankruptcy with no debt and to put more pressure on telecom companies that have debt. There are mixed feelings on whether they should be allowed to keep the contracts. It's something we're keeping an eye out for."

Another financial analyst asked: "Who's got the money to buy telecom assets? The Bells have too much debt. If there is a buyer, what would creditors get for the company? WorldCom's best bet is to downsize and create value and then a year down the line we'll hopefully be looking at an improved scenario."

WorldCom's bankruptcy lawyers and consultants became part of the feeding frenzy, with bankruptcy fees setting new record highs. Bill McLucas of Wilmer, Cutler & Pickering raked in an unheard of $715 an hour, and lobbyists' lobbyist Tommy Boggs, son of Louisiana legend Hale Boggs and brother of ABC News political pundit Cokie Roberts, racked up $700 an hour for congressional inquiry damage control. Investment bank Lazard Freres Company lobbied for a $15 million "success" fee to restructure the company. Turnaround specialist AlixPartners offered a cure. Everyone wanted to gather around the trough.

The WorldCom board, which had signed off on financial statements that had overstated profits by more than $7 billion since 2000, was shaken up. Among other concerns, board members knew that an indictment could pave the way for breaking major contracts. Moody's Investors Service chairman Clifford Alexander Jr. had exited the board in January 2002 after missing half the meetings the year before. His company did not downgrade WorldCom until April 2002. "Bernie's Boys"—Carl J. Aycock, Stiles A. Kellett Jr., Max E. Bobbitt, and Francesco Galesi—were losing power without Ebbers at the helm.

"Prior to his resignation . . . Mr. Ebbers exercised substantial influence over the board's decision-marking process and actions," said bankruptcy court examiner Dick Thornburgh. "It appears from interviews of board members that his sway was attributable to the board's perception of the company's success and growth under his direction, the high esteem in the Wall Street financial community in which he seemingly was held, his apparently forceful personality, and the loyalty of board members whose companies had been acquired by WorldCom and whose personal fortunes through ownership of the company's stock had, for a long period of time, been greatly enhanced during his leadership at WorldCom. Critical questioning was discouraged and the board did not appear to evaluate proposed transactions in appropriate depth, even though several members of the board had a significant percentage of their personal wealth tied to the value of the company's stock."

When Danny Dunnaway, an original board member from Brookhaven, Mississippi, who had sold all his WorldCom stock and severed ties with the company in the mid-1990s, checked on Aycock in late spring, he did not look good. While on a mission trip to Latin America, Aycock had gotten sick and lost a lot of weight. "Carl's going through the wringer right now," said Dunnaway. "He's a great guy. He'll be okay."

Bobbitt, who had revealed the accounting fraud to the board after his meeting with Cooper, was holding his own. In the spring of 2001, Bobbitt had betrayed Ebbers by attempting to take over the company. He had allegedly offered Beaumont, Sidgmore, and Sullivan hefty incentive packages of about $1 million a year for life if they supported his coup for CEO. The plan failed when Roberts found out about it. The move was unusual because at every formal open board meeting from at least as far back as 1999 to May 2, 2002, all matters that required board approval received it unanimously. No dissenting votes were reflected in the minutes.

Kellett, an Atlanta millionaire whose investors in a private stable of businesses included Ebbers, was coming under intense scrutiny for drafting a lender-friendly agreement on Ebbers' $408.2 million company loan. It included the leasing of a Falcon 20F-5 corporate jet for $1 a month, plus a $400-per-hour usage fee, and participation in Salomon hot initial stock offerings. Between 1996 and 2000, he received 31,500 Grubman-endorsed IPO shares. Yielding to pressure just days before Halloween, Kellett resigned from the WorldCom board and was asked to repay $1.4 million for the use of the corporate jet. His term would have ended March 13, 2003, the same date as the rest of the board.

Three directors who were members of the former MCI board remained in place: Roberts, Judith Areen, and Gordon S. Macklin. "When the reorganization plan is in place, they all may go," said a financial analyst familiar with the situation. "There are mixed schools of thought on whether anyone associated with the company in the past should be identified with the company in the future. I'm sure the creditor's committee will look for a clean management team. It would be in their best interest."

Nicholas deB. Katzenbach and Dennis R. Beresford were elected as new members to WorldCom's board of directors and appointed to the board's special investigative committee to conduct an independent review of the company's accounting practices and financial statement preparation. A private attorney, Katzenbach served as the U.S. attorney general from 1965 to 1966 and under secretary of state from 1966 to 1969, and was senior vice president and general counsel for IBM Corporation from 1969 to 1986. An accounting professor at the University of Georgia, Beresford served as chairman of the Financial Accounting Standards Board from 1987 to 1997. Neither had previously been involved with the company. Former Equifax CEO C. B. Roger Jr. was also added as a director. "The additional board members of this caliber demonstrate our seriousness in attracting independent board members and establishing a quality governance structure for our corporation," Sidgmore said. "Their willingness to serve is also an indication of the importance of our company's future." Wall Street's response was lukewarm.

Despite Sidgmore's swift appointment of turnaround specialists Gregory F. Rayburn as chief restructuring officer and John S. Dubel as CFO, and other strategic moves to push the company forward, WorldCom's woes intensified. At least five investigations by federal agencies, two congressional probes, two state inquiries, several reviews called by stockholders' attorneys, and a couple of internal examinations were underway. On July 29, citing WorldCom's recent bankruptcy filing and the pending restatement of its financial statements for 2001 and the first quarter of 2002, the Nasdaq delisted its securities and began trading over the counter (OTC) on Pink Sheets.

Early on August 1, a clear, bright morning in New York City, Sullivan, sporting a dark business suit, blue starched shirt, conservative tie, tasseled loafers, and a frown, and David F. Myers, 44, of Madison, Mississippi, equally sharply dressed, were arrested and strolled before a bevy of television cameras in handcuffs. "Corporate executives who cheat investors, steal savings and squander pensions will meet the judgment they fear and the punishment they deserve," said U.S. Attorney General John Ashcroft. The public applauded. The same day, the New York Stock Exchange revised its listing standards to require all NYSE-listed companies to have an internal audit function.

The seven-count indictment filed August 28 in federal court in Manhattan charged Sullivan with a long-running conspiracy to artificially boost earnings reports by hiding operating expenses. Myers, who was named in an earlier criminal complaint, was not indicted, but the Securities and Exchange Commission (SEC) filed a civil enforcement action against him on September 26. It charged participation in a major fraud that inflated the company's earnings, after he pleaded guilty to one count each of securities fraud, conspiracy to commit securities fraud, and filing false statements with the SEC.

The U.S. Justice Department charged that Sullivan gave Myers orders to transfer five quarterly line costs from operating expenses in a conspiracy to commit securities fraud. The costs ranged from $560 million to $941 million from April 2001 to April 2002 and were placed into the PPE (property, plant, and equipment) category on WorldCom's ledgers. Other charges included securities fraud and filing false SEC reports.

Soon after he was arrested, Sullivan tapped into the value of his unfinished estate in Boca Raton, Florida, for half of his $10 million bond. Myers' $2 million bond was secured by two Mississippi properties. The WorldCom board had already sued Sullivan for the return of a $10 million retention bonus and Myers for the return of a $795,000 bonus. When they were released, Sullivan left in a limousine; Myers took a cab.

Prosecutors also signaled that three of Sullivan's subordinates—accounting executives Betty L. Vinson and Troy M. Normand, who were fired in late August, and Yates—would plead guilty and cooperate with investigators in the criminal probe of the nation's largest accounting scandal. The indictment claimed the trio participated in shifting expenses between accounts. Yates was indicted; Vinson and Normand were charged as unindicted co-conspirators. A pretrial hearing on criminal charges was postponed until January 14, 2003 at 4 P.M., and the stage was set for snaring Ebbers, who had eluded frustrated prosecutors with his tiresome "don't-know-nothin'" routine. Jacob Frenkel, a former senior counsel in the SEC's enforcement division and former federal prosecutor in private practice at Smith Gambrell & Russell in Atlanta, said, "It's like when you see a batter warming up and getting ready to hit."

Yates, 46, a stocky man with quizzical eyebrows that framed round eyeglasses and a neatly trimmed beard, supervised the closing of WorldCom's books at the end of each financial reporting period as director of general accounting from 1997 to August 2002. "Buddy was extremely arrogant and a lot of people didn't like him," said a WorldCom employee who worked on the same floor as Yates but did not report to him. "I don't know if he was arrogant because he thought he was great looking, which he wasn't, or because he was a Tier 3, which is on up there." On October 7, Yates entered a guilty plea to two counts of securities fraud and conspiracy and faced 10 years in prison and a $1 million fine unless he cooperated with authorities, which he would. On the same day, the SEC filed a civil enforcement action against Yates for securities fraud, which is still pending. Yates told U.S. Magistrate Judge Andrew Peck he raised "serious concerns" about the entries, but was overruled by superiors.

Three days later, the SEC filed a civil enforcement action for securities fraud against Vinson and Normand, who pleaded guilty to two criminal counts of conspiracy and securities fraud. Coworkers described Vinson, 47, as friendly but reserved. They considered Normand, 35, uptight. "I used to ride the elevator with him and couldn't help but notice how he buttoned up his shirts real tight," said a former coworker. "It was the body language, too."

On the morning of August 8, WorldCom announced in seemingly nonchalant fashion that another $3.3 billion in earnings dating back to 1999 had been improperly reported and appeared to be a mix of similar irregularities related to the $3.8 billion error disclosed June 25. With other disclosures, the total to date: approximately $7.68 billion. Thornburgh would report on November 4 that another $3 billion could be added to the wake. "A picture is clearly emerging of a company that had a number of troubling and serious issues," he said. "These issues relate to the culture, internal control, management, integrity, disclosures and financial statements of the company."

The shockwaves from WorldCom's demise sparked a domino effect worldwide. "This isn't going to be a ripple on a pond. It's a tidal wave from a boulder," said Atlanta telecom analyst Jeff Kagan. Because technology represents about 20 percent of the U.S. economy, and WorldCom represented a chunk of that sector, investor confidence on Wall Street was shaken. European media outlets publicly criticized America's free enterprise system, calling it a breeding ground for corporate criminals. Even though trading was up in the Asian markets on the day that WorldCom filed bankruptcy, investors were cynical. "I have no confidence about what's going to happen tomorrow," Masanori Hoshina, a trader at BNP Paribas Securities in Tokyo, told the Associated Press. "The buying here today is happening because people expected things to be worse."

Politically, it spurred a wave of reform in Congress to appease angry voters, who were among the millions of shareholders worldwide that lost roughly $179.3 billion on WorldCom stock. Legislation passed at such lightning speed that Senator Mike Enzi, a Republican from Wyoming, called it "earthshaking." On July 30, President George W. Bush signed into law the Sarbanes-Oxley Act of 2002, a sweeping reform bill meant to wake up the accounting industry and corporate boards and to lay the foundation for restoring public trust and confidence in corporate America and its markets. "Many Mississippians, including myself, were disappointed and saddened about the financial problems at Mississippi-based WorldCom," said Senate Minority Leader Trent Lott. "WorldCom's misfortunes were an economic problem, not a political one, and I'm glad Congress supported President Bush's plan for tougher laws and stiffer penalties for those who violated the trust of employees, shareholders and the public." Pension reform would be tackled next by Congress.

Politicians who received campaign contributions from WorldCom also scrambled for damage control. In July, Senate Majority Leader Tom Daschle said he would donate the $10,000 he received in political contributions from WorldCom to its recently laid-off workers. That action spurred Kate Lee of Atlanta, a laid-off WorldCom executive, to make sure he kept his promise. After a bankruptcy court capped severance packages at $4,650 for each of the recently laid-off 17,000 workers, Lee and three other former employees faxed letters to Daschle and 91 other politicians nationwide who had received contributions from WorldCom urging them to funnel the money into their

private relief fund, the Ex-WorldCom Employee Assistance
Fund. By Election Day 2002, the committee had raised $141,000
of the $740,000 WorldCom had given politicians during the
election cycle. Politicians sent $63,000 back to PACs (political
action committees) and $29,000 to local charities. After hear-
ing that WorldCom executives wanted to help, the committee
sent them letters "asking very nicely for them to make a donation," said Lee. "Not a single one ever responded, not even to
say, 'No, I won't do that.'"

Mississippi Third Congressional District Representative
Chip Pickering, a political protégé of Senator Lott, and
whose dad, Judge Charles W. Pickering Sr., was denied a
seat on the 5th U.S. Circuit Court of Appeals by Congress earlier in the year, received the most money from WorldCom—
nearly $83,000 in donations. He also caught the most flak,
even though he sits on the House Commerce Committee and
Telecommunications Subcommittee and the contributions
were justifiable. Pickering's opponent, former Mississippi
Fourth District Congressional Representative Ronnie Shows,
attempted to use WorldCom's political favoritism of Pickering
against him in a hotly contested congressional race. When the
lines were redrawn because Mississippi's population growth
didn't keep pace with the national average and a district was
lost, Pickering and Shows, both well-liked incumbents, essentially ran for an open seat. "Shows tried to make corporate
wrongdoing stick with Pickering, but it didn't," said Joe Parker,
a professor of political science at the University of Southern
Mississippi, Shows' alma mater. In the November 5, 2002, pri-
maries, Pickering emerged the undisputed winner.

WorldCom had stepped in with $1 million in May 1999 to
underwrite a star-studded fund-raising gala hosted by Mississippian Morgan Freeman and featuring singer Marilyn
McCoo, when the University of Mississippi, Lott's alma
mater, wanted to establish a political science center, the Lott

Leadership Institute. The gala raised more than $10 million. Little was said about the connection, probably because WorldCom had doled out money to Republicans and Democrats alike, and this political contribution made sense. Ole Miss graduates with WorldCom connections included Diana Day-Cartee, who worked closely with Ebbers during the early years and to whom board members gave much of the credit for the company's early successes; Charles Cannada, who preceded Sullivan as CFO; Cannada's wife, who roomed with Day in college; and Myers. Ebbers had been good to the school for years. Still, everyone dodged for cover.

14

Infectious Greed

[WorldCom's troubles are] creating a suction that pulls others into the abyss.

Scott Cleland, CEO, Precursor Group

The WorldCom debacle demolished what was left of Arthur Andersen's reputation, which had become tainted with malfeasance following the Enron book-cooking scandal. Cofounded in 1913 by Northwestern University accounting professor Arthur Edward Andersen, the Chicago-based firm would bear his name and become one of the Big Five, specializing in corporate audits, before it took a nosedive in respectability.

"The turn of the century was a time of snake oil and scandal," said Sean Coffey of BBC's *The Money Program*, who profiled Andersen. "Investors didn't know who to trust. What they needed were auditors . . . Arthur Andersen set up a firm they could rely on . . . (and) built on his reputation as a stickler. Clients soon found out that he was even prepared to lose their business than sign off misleading accounts."

In January 1947, Andersen died of a heart attack at the age of 61. His unexpected death left the accounting firm and Andersen's family mired in turmoil. Leonard Spacek, a partner in the firm, arranged a secret midnight visit from Andersen's estranged younger brother at his Chicago wake. Andersen's widow, Emma, never forgave him. The incident perhaps foreshadowed what was to be Andersen's legacy. George Catlett, who had worked with Andersen since 1940, told the *Wall Street Journal*'s Rick Wartzman: "There were different factions. It was really an argument about who was going to run the firm." Andersen had never signed a partnership agreement and his son, Arthur Jr., believed he had inherited the firm. Senior partners thought they should run it. After "vociferous arguments," as Spacek described them, Andersen's 25 partners voted to liquidate the firm but retain the name.

Andersen's first misstep in a string of scandals was signing on John DeLorean, an obscure automaker who planned to build a futuristic sports car. "DeLorean came to Northern Ireland to build his dream car," reported Coffey. "The British government, desperate to create jobs, gave him 80 million pounds. It was Andersen's job to see the money was safe . . . DeLorean asked for 17 million dollars to be paid into a Swiss bank account of a company called GPD. Nobody quite knew who controlled it. Even Walter Stryker, DeLorean's good friend and chief financial officer, was worried."

"All of a sudden, John had a lot of money and he was spending it in the United States, and that to me was highly suspicious," said Stryker. When he voiced concerns, Andersen ignored them. After DeLorean filed bankruptcy and 2,000 workers lost their jobs, the British government and investors sued Andersen, who ponied up $60 million to settle the issue.

"The Prime Minister (Margaret Thatcher) was furious," said Coffey. "Maggie was so angry, she banned Andersen from doing any more public sector work in Britain."

With Waste Management, the world's largest waste disposal company headquartered across town from Andersen in Chicago, the accounting firm turned a blind eye when corporate accountants depreciated their rubbish trucks much longer than they lasted to falsely pump up profits. The Securities and Exchange Commission fined Andersen $7 million and banned some audit partners from practicing. "By now, the world's biggest accountancy firm had wrought havoc in cars and dustbins," reported Coffey. "In Florida, the next deception would strike at the heart of the American kitchen."

Sunbeam CEO "Chainsaw" Al Dunlap inflated the company's earnings by 16 percent to raise the stock price and make the company more attractive to potential buyers. Among other accounting tricks used to achieve that goal, barbecue grills were falsely booked in winter. Diedra Dendanto, an ex-Andersen employee, was among those who blew the whistle. "In my mind, Andersen clearly knew," she told Coffey. By the time Dunlap was fired in 1998 and new management exposed the fraud, investors had lost nearly $4 billion. Andersen was forced to pay $110 million, and the SEC sued Andersen audit partner Philip Harlow.

While Andersen was embroiled in the book cooking at Houston, Texas-based Enron, the accounting firm was simultaneously auditing the books for the fraudulent company Baptist Foundation of Arizona, which bilked nearly $600 million from elderly Christians in the Grand Canyon State. An unidentified whistle-blower contacted Andersen staffers—audit partner Jay Ozer and manager Ann McGrath—with elaborate diagrams of the scam, but Ozer, whose compensation depended on productivity, and McGrath, who yearned to be a partner, did nothing.

A second whistle-blower, financial adviser Dee Anne Griebel of Phoenix, Arizona, facilitated a state investigation and the Baptist Foundation collapsed in the largest nonprofit bankruptcy in the United States. "Enron was just the Baptist Foundation with more zeros," Griebel told Coffey.

On June 15, 2002, just 10 days before WorldCom's fraudulent accounting practices became public, a jury convicted Andersen of obstruction of justice—not of accounting fraud—for shredding documents in the Enron case. To keep the books for the 4,300 companies created by the energy-trading giant, Andersen had earned roughly a million dollars a week. The $500,000 fine was insignificant. The five years' probation sentence was simply annoying. Ironically, a simple accounting mistake over an obscure accounting rule caused Enron's house of cards to collapse. "Andersen became a firm that couldn't say no to a client, and in fact said, how can we help you do it?" reported Coffey.

The only survivors of the Andersen debacle were members of its consulting group, a $9.4 billion division that smartly paid a $1 billion fee set by an arbitrator in 2000 to break free and create a new company, Accenture.

Andersen's collapse also ruined the career of a seasoned professional, Andersen CEO Joseph Berardino, a New York native who coincidentally resigned a month before Ebbers. When he was elected CEO in 2001, Andersen was a $9.3 billion global accounting giant with 85,000 employees in 84 countries. The disgraced executive said: "I paid the price. I lost my job. I lost my firm. I've got less money today than I had as the newly elected CEO. I lost my partner capital. I lost my retirement. I don't have any stock options. I may never work again."

While Arthur Andersen executives were licking their wounds, WorldCom was under a magnifying glass. After an initial evaluation of the company, bankruptcy court examiner

Dick Thornburgh remarked: "Few companies in the annals of American business have grown so large and so fast in such an intensely competitive marketplace. WorldCom did not achieve its growth by following a predefined strategic plan, but rather by opportunistic and rapid acquisitions of other companies. The unrelenting pace of these acquisitions caused the company constantly to redefine itself and its focus. The company's unceasing growth and metamorphosis made integration of its newly acquired operations, systems and personnel much more difficult. This dramatic growth and related changes also made it difficult for investors to compare the company's operations to historical benchmarks."

WorldCom's management, systems, internal controls, and other personnel did not keep pace with that growth, said Thornburgh. "Its stock was the fuel that kept WorldCom's acquisition engine running at a very high speed," he wrote. "WorldCom needed to keep its stock price at high levels to continue its phenomenal growth."

Telecom players, some already troubled financially and others that counted WorldCom as a customer, took a beating following WorldCom's collapse; Nortel, Baby Bells such as Qwest Communications, Level 3 Communications, Sprint, and AT&T were among them. WorldCom owed Israel-based Gilat Satellite System, a maker of equipment that links telephone networks by satellite, about $12 million. Bankruptcies littered the marketplace, and several of the industry's top firms were being investigated for their accounting practices.

When second-quarter 2002 earnings were released, overall corporate profits were down 30 percent over the previous year. AT&T and Lucent Technologies Inc. accounted for 16 percent alone—or $20.6 billion in losses. On July 1, EDS shares dropped 18 percent to $30.45, after an announcement that WorldCom owed it $150 million for unpaid services. The bankruptcy was a blow to already unsteady AOL Time Warner when Gonzalez ruled that WorldCom could walk away from a contract worth about $182 million with the media giant, a deal that had been made in June 2001. Scott Cleland told *BusinessWeek* that 24 of the 29 telecom firms he tracked were on the edge of bankruptcy, adding that WorldCom's troubles are "creating a suction that pulls others into the abyss."

Disconnected

As a manager, I've been laying off people for about 10 years.
Now I know how it feels.

Mike Pallatino, laid-off WorldCom executive,
August 2002

ormer WorldCom employees struggling to make ends meet organized websites to vent frustrations, share news stories, post job leads, provide helpful hints on benefits, and compare bankruptcy information. "For many WorldCom workers, being laid off was devastating," said Kate Lee of Atlanta, a laid-off WorldCom executive who helped organize the website. "I'm married so the financial pressure wasn't as great, and I have a young son who started school in the fall and I was able to spend some time with him, but I wanted to help, not only by making phone calls to track down severance checks, but also for moral support. One guy thought he was getting two weeks' pay (including vacation pay) and he got a severance check for $26. If the company had communicated with us, there would have been a lot less disgruntled unhappiness, but when WorldCom said we were a moot issue, it really pissed people off."

Mike Pallatino, a 19-year MCI company veteran who was laid off in June and was unable to make house payments on the $300,000-plus home he had purchased in Loudoun County, Virginia, when WorldCom transferred him from Colorado earlier that month, helped organize www.exworldcom5100.com. "You move to a new area, lose your job, but you figure, 'Hey, at least I got a big severance.' I like this area and want to stay in Washington, but I've already tapped into my savings," said Pallatino. Through networking, Pallatino landed a job with a Washington, DC, firm that was founded by former WorldCom managers and was able to remain in his new home.

Nest eggs were wiped out overnight. California Public Employees Retirement System, the nation's largest pension fund, estimated a $565 million loss on WorldCom earnings. New York's state retirement system watched approximately $300 million evaporate. Amid the plethora of lawsuits, David G. Bronner, CEO of Alabama's pension system, sued former WorldCom executives and accounting and executive firms for $1.1 billion in damages over its losses. The lawsuits were filed in state court in Montgomery instead of federal court, hoping the case would be expedited in state court, which also allows punitive damages.

Some investors were able to recoup their money in other ways. Mark S. Bounds, CCIM, president of Mark S. Bounds Realty Partners, Inc., in Madison, Mississippi, became the sole local representative for WorldCom property when New America International (NAI), an international real estate firm based in Hightstown, New Jersey, with Hilco Real Estate LLC, won the WorldCom liquidation account. "We've evaluated all their leases and we have buyers for both buildings (in downtown Jackson and in Clinton), if it comes to that," said Bounds. "We're just waiting for the final decision by the bankruptcy judge to determine the size of the company. This may be a way to get back some of what I lost when WorldCom went belly up."

Others recovered their WorldCom losses by getting naked. Nearly a dozen current and former WorldCom employees posed for *Playboy*'s "Women of WorldCom" December 2002 issue and made $10,000 each. Shellie Sloan, a financial analyst at company headquarters in Clinton, whose husband is also a WorldCom employee, was the Mississippi model. To make extra money on the venture, the Sloans created a website featuring her signed photograph for $7 and autographed issues of the magazine for $10. "It was an opportunity of a lifetime," said Sloan. "There aren't too many avenues for getting into *Playboy*."

Despite Sidgmore's cheerleading to boost team morale, the chasm between WorldCom divisions deepened. "It was not just MCI or UUNET versus WorldCom," said Allan Liska, a former UUNET worker who lost his job in June. "It was also UUNET versus Digex, UUNET versus MCI." Nepotism added to the chaos. "I was with WorldCom from 1995 to 1997 and left for another job at Intermedia," said a current WorldCom employee whose husband was laid off in June. "We [at Intermedia] were encouraged to buy the company stock in our 401(k). At the time it was a good idea. Then WorldCom came in and bought our company, the whole sector and market went down and then the bankruptcy and my 401(k) is virtually gone."

In a peppy e-mail to employees, Sidgmore wrote: "Your continued dedication is critical to maintaining customer confidence." Nevertheless, countless WorldCom resumes landed at rival companies, with Sprint, Southwestern Bell, and AT&T as major recipients of talent and, as a bonus, many of World-Com's customers. By the time WorldCom received permission from a bankruptcy court October 29 to spend $25 million to retain 325 senior employees, excluding the company's four top posts, morale among the rank-and-file had already plummeted. Employees knew the company was making a list of 20,700 workers to lay off by the end of the year and the roulette wheel was spinning.

Sidgmore's support began slipping in mid-August when board members Bobbitt and Kellett called for his replacement, saying he did not keep them informed of new developments. They insisted that a new leader with no ties to the company's sordid past would accelerate WorldCom's fiscal recovery. Some analysts agreed. "From the get-go, I thought WorldCom would be better off having an outsider in there instead of Sidgmore," said Drake Johnstone, an analyst with Davenport & Co. in Richmond, Virginia. "If he knew what was going on (with the accounting fraud), that's bad. If he was on the board and didn't know, that's equally as bad." Sidgmore's reminder that "we audited our external auditors and we found what they missed" and "we turned ourselves in" didn't appease many people.

Even though Sidgmore had the support of the majority of the board, on September 11, bowing to pressure and hoping to slip under the glaring media radar screen on the day that Americans commemorated the one-year anniversary of the lives lost in the first successful foreign terrorist attack on the continental United States, Sidgmore resigned. "I have concluded that having moved WorldCom through the initial phase of the bankruptcy process now is the appropriate time for the company to initiate a search for a long-term CEO," he said. "By returning to my vice chairman role, after the search is complete, I, along, with Bert Roberts, will be able to remain active in a strategic capacity while our new CEO manages the day-to-day operations of the company and the overall bankruptcy process." Soon after, rumors began circulating that WorldCom might change its name.

By the time autumnal winds turned chilly at WorldCom headquarters in Clinton, where the city was celebrating its sesquicentennial, there was very little talk about Ebbers. "People were more focused on survival," said a member of WorldCom's product marketing group. "So many executives had left in the last six or eight months. Bernie was just one of them."

Sidgmore continued to mold WorldCom into a viable company. Just before Halloween, in an effort to quickly introduce a much-needed new revenue stream product, WorldCom unveiled The WorldCom Connection, an IP-based service that operates across any WorldCom-provided network architecture. Analysts praised the new product, saying WorldCom was taking a lead role in merged data and voice systems.

"It solves what we call the last mile problem," said a WorldCom marketing manager. "AT&T can get you to the pole at your house, but it can't get from the pole to your house because that's where BellSouth has the fiber. Our product avoids the Bell companies' current structure, which changes the cost model. We believe this will be our watershed product going out of bankruptcy. It's extremely profitable . . . and pretty cool stuff."

Sidgmore put in motion a plan to hire a new corporate controller and four line controllers to oversee revenue accounting, operational accounting, financial accounting, and financial controls and procedures. He would double the internal audit department staff and develop a new reporting relationship between departments: The audit committee would report directly to the WorldCom board. Two new operational CFO positions would be created, one for the company's Asia-Pacific Rim business and another for its European business, each with dotted line authority to the WorldCom CFO.

Despite the improvements, Dick Thornburgh, the court-appointed bankruptcy examiner, reported on November 4,

"Our preliminary observations reflect cause for substantial concern regarding the company's past practices, particularly with respect to the reasonableness and integrity of its accounting and financial reporting functions and related oversight by persons within the company, the board of directors and the independent auditors of WorldCom.

"Our investigation strongly suggests that WorldCom personnel responded to changing business conditions and earnings pressures by taking extraordinary and illegal steps to mask the discrepancy between the financial reality at the company and Wall Street's expectations," Thornburgh wrote in his first interim report. "It appears clear that some of these steps involved various manipulations of periodic revenue and income figures. It also appears clear that these efforts culminated in the brazen and fraudulent capitalization of line costs. We still are investigating to determine which of the company's revenue, income or other adjustments, were improper, but we believe our investigation will reveal that there were improper and unsupported adjustments that go beyond the more than $7 billion in adjustments already restated by the company."

Despite its troubles, WorldCom remained the second-largest telecommunications company in the United States; and its tag line, "the preeminent global communications company for the digital generation," reminded customers of its place in the world. "This is a terrific company with outstanding employees and loyal customers," said Sidgmore. "WorldCom is not the handful of people you have read about in the newspaper. I wish I could wave a magic wand and make the events that put the company where it is today go away. Unfortunately, I can't."

*God Almighty, WorldCom was such a great company to have in
the South. What a nightmare.*

A financial analyst, October 2002

Regardless of Sullivan's intent and whether or not Ebbers
knew about the accounting fraud, WorldCom as it had
been known for nearly two decades was disconnected
after the summer of 2002. WorldCom shareholders had been
deceived and betrayed.

The analysis of WorldCom's demise continued. "World-
Com was a big rollup company, one that was created through
acquisitions, and when it ran out of companies to buy, there
wasn't much left," said Bill Brame, a financial adviser from
Jackson, Mississippi. "The Sprint deal fell through. The revenue growth stopped but their expenses didn't. Market forces
changed when cell phones revolutionized the whole concept of
long distance. And with the Internet, even though WorldCom

owned a lot of capacity, it's like owning all the highways. Unless you're charging a toll for every person that gets on it, what's the use? WorldCom was unable to tap into profitable areas and the company imploded. More than likely, WorldCom will sell off noncore assets and the company will reemerge owned by someone else or a smaller version of its former self."

Another native Mississippian philosophized: "The world has been stunned to realize that because of technology and telecommunications, the actions of one terrorist, with a handful of followers, can influence and destroy the lives of billions of people around the planet. Equally as stunning is the realization that the investment of billions of dollars by millions of people, the commercial and military telecommunications infrastructure, and the jobs of tens of thousands of people, can be at such risk by one man, with the acquiescence of a few, by making the decision to simply violate the rules of generally accepted accounting practices in the drive to show a profit."

In the Magnolia State, as Mississippi is known, where the Confederate flag still flies despite troubling racial overtones, life went on. During rosier times, the Mississippi Development Authority, the state's lead economic development arm, had referred to WorldCom, one of the state's 30 public companies, as a "homegrown Mississippi company" that "packs a potent global punch," but business was still progressing in the state of nearly three million people.

Nissan North America continued building its $1.4 billion automotive plant in Canton, located 35 miles away from WorldCom corporate headquarters. In August 2002, Lockheed Martin Aeronautics opened a world-class facility at the Stennis Space Center, on the Mississippi Gulf Coast, to design and produce propulsion systems for satellites and thermal blankets and control systems for space vehicles. Ashley Furniture Industries continued its record-breaking expansion—$38 million since 1994—in northeast Mississippi, considered the uphol-stered furniture capital of the world.

"I've been in Mississippi for a year now, and what I've found is a real commitment to attracting companies to this state, and helping existing companies to grow their business," said Robert J. "Bob" Rohrlack Jr., who moved from Tampa Bay, Florida, where he was senior vice president of the Greater Tampa Chamber of Commerce's Committee of 100 and Tampa Bay International Trade Council, to take over as head of the Mississippi Development Authority in October 2001. "Mississippi leaders make decisions about where they want to be and who they want to attract to this state and then they work hard to compete for the jobs. Mississippi is on the radar screen now because people know that we cannot only make commitments, but we also live up to them."

The world waited and watched for progress on the World-Com case. Would billions more in fraudulent accounting practices be discovered? What would happen to the four World-Com accountants—Myers, Yates, Vinson, and Normand—who pleaded guilty to securities fraud and a variety of other charges? Would Sullivan plea bargain and turn in Ebbers? Or would Sullivan be convicted, sentenced, and fined? Would WorldCom emerge as a viable telecom competitor or would hungry creditors sell it? Where would Sidgmore fit in? Would Grubman remain a rich retiree? And what would happen to the people who lost their fortunes—$179.3 billion—to WorldCom?

"In all my years of practice, I never would have dreamed we'd be asking ourselves these questions," said J. Martin Mooney, a retired lawyer from Seminary, Mississippi. "It will be very interesting to see where all the roads lead."

It's been an unusual ride.

David Singleton, November 2002

At press time, WorldCom accountants David F. Myers, Buford Yates Jr., Betty L. Vinson, and Troy M. Normand, had plea-bargained with prosecutors in the criminal probe of the nation's largest accounting scandal. The Securities and Exchange Commission (SEC) had filed additional fraud charges against WorldCom, saying that the company inflated earnings by almost $2 million more than it had previously disclosed. The SEC permanently banned Myers and Yates from acting as officers or directors of a public company. Scott Sullivan had not yet gone to trial. No action had been taken against Bernie Ebbers, who remained close to his Brookhaven home.

In mid-November, WorldCom hired former Hewlitt-Packard president and Compaq Computer turnaround wizard Michael D. Capellas, as chairman, CEO, and president, effective December 2. He passed up the No. 3 job at Microsoft to join the beleaguered telecommunications giant. Soon after, WorldCom struck a deal with the SEC to settle the civil fraud suit against the company.

In his first full month on the job, Capellas, who lacks telecom experience but is a seasoned information technology executive with international management experience and credibility, justified his $50 million pay package, laid off 3,000 workers, and made known his intent to conduct corporate business from WorldCom offices in Ashburn, Virginia, where he made his first stop after being hired. For the time being, he said, the official company headquarters would remain in Clinton, Mississippi. He also began working on a reorganization plan, delayed until April 2003.

By mid-December, most of the WorldCom board had resigned. Judith Areen relinquished her seat on the board a week before Carl Aycock, Max Bobbitt, Francesco Galesi, Gordon Macklin, Bert Roberts, and John Sidgmore departed. Nicholas Katzenbach, Dennis Beresford, and C. B. Rogers were the only remaining board members. Bernie's Boys were gone. The company that was formed in a Hattiesburg coffeehouse nearly two decades earlier was almost unrecognizable.

Time magazine selected WorldCom's Cynthia Cooper, along with Enron's Sherron Watkins and the FBI's Coleen Rowley—women who took huge risks to blow the whistle at their respective organizations—as Persons of the Year for 2002.

President George W. Bush selected investment banker William H. Donaldson, former chairman of the New York Stock Exchange, as the new SEC chairman. The U.S. District Court of the Southern District of New York had nearly two dozen civil and criminal cases pending for action in 2003 against Sullivan. The SEC had yet to indict Sullivan. "Timing is everything," said a SEC spokesperson. "We don't like to lose." And the WorldCom investigations continued.

Even though I did not realize it at the time, I began reporting on WorldCom when I was a senior marketing student at the University of Southern Mississippi in 1983. Following the company's progress became more game than work. In the hallways and around campus, professors buzzed about changes to come from the Ma Bell fallout and debated the potential role of computers. The late Dr. Richard C. Vreeland was perhaps the most radical and unconventional professor of the bunch. He gathered his apprentices in a circle and espoused marketing gems while picking apart case studies—and he was dead-on with his predictions of how the telecommunications industry would take over the world.

When LDDS was formed late that summer, not many people noticed. Yet news of a novice local long-distance phone company began cropping up in conversations, with most people wondering how long it would last. "Nobody can go up against AT&T," was the common consensus. We were all wrong.

After a phenomenal run, WorldCom evolved from upstart underdog to the world's most feared telecom company and then the world's largest failure. The former took seventeen years; the latter took two. The journey was fascinating to observe. As LDDS cofounder Danny Dunnaway once said, "You couldn't write this script and have somebody believe you."

In researching this book, very few people agreed to talk on the record. WorldCom employees were threatened with immediate termination of employment if they were caught talking to the press. Former employees were often reluctant to chat because many had friends who remained at the company. After working closely with a source for several days on a particular section, she asked me not to use her name after all: "I don't want to get in trouble down the road." Mississippi is a small state, where people seem to have three degrees of separation, not six. In many good ways, it is like a big cohesive family.

Unnamed sources, many of whom I have known and respected all my life, and have proven to be reliable and accurate on countless occasions, were invaluable during the research phase. I was very careful to reflect the consensus opinion and to verify facts if a source could not be disclosed. I relied heavily on hundreds of hours of transcripts and thousands, maybe millions, of pages of court documents and company records. I interviewed countless sources from local, state, national, and international levels representing nearly every walk of life. WorldCom remains one of the most fascinating corporate stories in history.

Prologue

Page xvii: "On a cool, sunny morning . . ." The associate is a composite character, sketched by countless interviews with people privy to events that took place during this time period at WorldCom headquarters in Clinton, Mississippi. Any resemblance to a particular person is purely coincidental.

Page xxiii: "The seedlings of WorldCom were planted . . ." John C. Wohlstetter, "The Rise and Fall of the Ebbers Empire," *National Review Online,* June 28, 2002.

CHAPTER 1 Migrating South

Page 1: "The WorldCom sales executive . . ." The executive is a composite character. Any resemblance to a particular person is purely coincidental.

Page 3: " 'Our work ethic came . . .' " Reed Branson, "WorldCom's Ebbers Builds Mississippi Muscle," *Commercial-Appeal,* November 9, 1997.

Page 3: " 'We didn't have much . . .' " Thomas J. Neff and James M. Citrin, *Lessons from the Top: The Search for America's Best Business Leaders* (New York: Doubleday, 1999).

Page 7: "Ebbers once told an acquaintance . . ." David Staples, "A Telecom Prophet's Fall from Grace," *Edmonton Journal,* July 28, 2002.

Page 8: " '[Bernie] almost played . . .' " Reed Branson, "WorldCom's Ebbers Builds Mississippi Muscle," *Commercial-Appeal,* November 9, 1997.

Page 8: " 'Allen told him . . .' "Reed Branson, "WorldCom's Ebbers Builds Mississippi Muscle," *Commercial-Appeal,* November 9, 1997.

Page 11: " 'He enjoyed being in charge . . .' " Reed Branson, "World-Com's Ebbers Builds Mississippi Muscle," *Commercial-Appeal,* November 9, 1997.

Page 12: " 'We lived like a band of gypsies . . .' " Kevin D. Jones, "LDDS," *Mississippi Business Journal,* November 1989.

CHAPTER 2 Information, Please

Page 18: " 'A lot of WATS . . .' " The brother of longtime Mississippi Senator Thad Cochran, Mississippi Public Service Commissioner Nielsen Cochran of Raymond was initially elected in November 1983 and has served continuously since then. The divestiture of AT&T officially began two days after he was sworn into office.

Page 22: " '. . . unique ability to get along with others.' . . ." "Scott Sullivan: Master of the Mega Merger," *Oswego,* Spring/Summer 1999.

Page 22: " 'Even back in 1983 . . .' " "Scott Sullivan: Master of the Mega Merger," *Oswego,* Spring/Summer 1999.

Page 22: " 'It's funny talking . . .' " Jeremy M. Brosowsky, "Is Less More for Sidgmore?" *Business Forward,* December 2000.

Page 24: " '. . . we knew nothing . . .' " Kelli Langlois, "LDDS Phones Home," *Daily Leader,* April 27, 1995.

Page 27: " '. . . the meanest SOB . . .' " Kevin D. Jones, "LDDS," *Mississippi Business Journal,* November 1989.

Page 27: "Ebbers, Thornhill, Aycock, and Dunnaway . . ." According to David Wilson of the Mississippi State Tax Commission, U.S. citizenship was a requirement for Mississippi Alcohol & Beverage Control (ABC) licensees in the early 1980s. Since then, the rules have changed and licensees are not required to be U.S. citizens. They must, however, be legal residents of the United States.

CHAPTER 3   The Spending Spree

Page 29: " 'I'm not a technology dude . . .' " Stephanie Mehta, "Can Bernie Bounce Back?" *Fortune,* January 2001.

Page 31: " 'Brookhaven mafia.' . . ." Kelli Langlois, "LDDS Phones Home," *Daily Leader,* April 27, 1995.

Page 31: " 'We did have very humble beginnings . . .' " Kelli Langlois, "LDDS Phones Home," *Daily Leader,* April 27, 1995.

Page 37: "Rumors circulated widely . . ." Nearly everyone interviewed for this time period of the company history made some mention of a possible romantic link between Ebbers and Day.

Page 42: " 'We were proud of our company . . .' " Kevin D. Jones, "LDDS," *Mississippi Business Journal,* November 1989.

Page 43: " 'One of the things I do that's effective . . .' " Kevin D. Jones, "LDDS," *Mississippi Business Journal,* November 1989.

CHAPTER 4   The Power Surge

Page 45: "You couldn't write this script . . ." Kelli Langlois, "LDDS Phones Home," *Daily Leader,* April 27, 1995.

Page 47: "Technology guru George Gilder . . ." George Gilder, *Telecosm: How Infinite Bandwidth Will Revolutionize Our World* (Free Press, 2000).

Page 47: "Are jeans normal dress . . ." Kevin D. Jones, "LDDS," *Mississippi Business Journal,* November 1989.

Page 48: " 'They learn not to come to Bernie . . .' " Kevin D. Jones, "LDDS," *Mississippi Business Journal,* November 1989.

Page 48: " 'The room was an afterthought . . .' " Kevin D. Jones, "LDDS," *Mississippi Business Journal,* November 1989.

Page 53: " 'We only have 5 percent of the market . . .' " 1995. Annual Report, p. 4. Reprinted by permission of *Forbes* magazine, Forbes, Inc., 1995.

Page 55: " 'We'd send in one set of numbers . . .' " Charles Haddad, "WorldCom's Sorry Legacy," *BusinessWeek,* June 28, 2002.

Page 56: " 'Michael Jordan came . . .' " Kelly Russell, "WorldCom Chief Quells Rumors of Relocation," *Mississippi Business Journal,* April 29, 1996.

Page 57: " 'You build a team carefully . . .' " 1995. Annual Report, p. 6. Reprinted by permission of *Forbes* magazine, Forbes, Inc., 1995.

Page 57: " 'Two years ago . . .' " 1995. Annual Report, cover page. Reprinted by permission of *Forbes* magazine, Forbes, Inc., 1995.

CHAPTER 5　The Ultimate Drug

Page 60: "Mississippi College President Howell Todd followed . . ." "A New Dawn," *The Beacon,* Spring 1997.

Page 62: "High-powered CEOs of pet companies . . ." Charles Haddad, "Inside the Telecom Game," *BusinessWeek,* August 5, 2002.

Page 63: " 'He was very snide . . .' " Seth Schiesel and Gretchen Morgenson, "Analyst Probe Escalates Its Scope," *New York Times,* August 24, 2002.

Page 64: " 'No one has ever seen this kind of growth . . .' " Alan Spoon, "In the Digital Age," *Netpreneur Exchange,* November 12, 1997.

Page 64: " 'We're getting to the point . . .' " Peter Elstrom, "The New World Order," *BusinessWeek,* October 13, 1997.

Page 64: " 'How many times . . .' " Charles Haddad, "Saving World-Com: An Impossible Dream?" *BusinessWeek,* May 13, 2002.

Page 65: " 'With the Telecommunications Act . . .' " Saroja Girishankar, "WorldCom Grabs for the Telecom Spotlight," *CommunicationsWeek,* June 30, 1997.

Page 65: "Six months after the MFS acquisition . . ." Saroja Girishankar, "WorldCom Grabs for the Telecom Spotlight," *CommunicationsWeek,* June 30, 1997.

Page 65: "Sidgmore, who headed WorldCom's Internet division . . ." Jeremy M. Brosowsky, "Is Less More for Sidgmore?" *Business Forward,* December 2000.

Page 66: "Andy Zmolek, manager of network architecture . . ." Andy Zmolek, "Don't Skimp on Your Customer Service," *InternetWeek,* August 28, 2000.

Page 66: " 'It was clear . . .' " Jeremy M. Brosowsky, "Is Less More for Sidgmore?" *Business Forward,* December 2000.

Page 68: "The first duel took place . . ." *Down Brick Streets: A Guide to Historical Sites in Clinton, Mississippi* (American Association of University Women, 1976).

Page 69: "During the duel . . ." *Down Brick Streets: A Guide to Historical Sites in Clinton, Mississippi* (American Association of University Women, 1976).

Page 72: " 'Everybody knew Kristie . . .' " Though not confirmed, many people discussed the strong possibility of an intimate relationship between Ebbers and Webb before they divorced their respective spouses.

Page 72: " 'We will not be forming international alliances . . .' " Saroja Girishankar, "WorldCom Grabs for the Telecom Spotlight," *CommunicationsWeek,* June 30, 1997.

Page 73: " 'We do not see a need for more acquisitions . . .' " Saroja Girishankar, "WorldCom Grabs for the Telecom Spotlight," *CommunicationsWeek,* June 30, 1997.

Page 73: " 'The U.S. establishment telcos . . .' " George Gilder, *Telecosm: How Infinite Bandwidth Will Revolutionize Our World* (Free Press, 2000).

Page 74: " 'Who was this Ebbers man . . .' " David Usborne, "Paper Tiger," *The Independent-London,* February 21, 2001.

CHAPTER 6   Masterstroke

Page 75: "On a whim I said . . ." Joseph McCafferty, "Scott Sullivan," *CFO,* September 1998.

Page 75: " 'On a whim, [Sullivan] said . . .' " Joseph McCafferty, "Scott Sullivan," *CFO,* September 1998.

Page 76: " 'I was convinced . . .' " "Scott Sullivan: Master of the Mega Merger," *Oswego,* Spring/Summer 1999.

Page 79: "Even though Roberts returned . . ." Peter Elstrom, "The New World Order," *BusinessWeek,* October 13, 1997.

Page 80: "So Ebbers was triumphant . . ." Michael Meyer, "Who Is This Guy?" *BusinessWeek,* October 13, 1997.

Page 80: "'We were exuberant ...'" Joseph McCafferty, "Scott Sullivan," *CFO*, September 1998.

Page 81: "'WorldCom is here to stay. It's a smart addition to any portfolio.' ..." "Digital Cyber Elite Top 50," *Time*, 1998.

Page 81: "'Ten years ago, WorldCom ...'" Peter Elstrom, "The New World Order," *BusinessWeek*, October 13, 1997.

Page 81: "Ebbers became known ..." Reed Branson, "WorldCom's Ebbers Builds Mississippi Muscle," *Commercial-Appeal*, November 9, 1997.

Page 81: "Dave Neil, vice president ..." Lynn Haber, "Fifteen Events that Changed Networking," *Network World*, March 26, 2001.

Page 81: "Tom Aust, a telecom analyst ..." Peter Elstrom, "The New World Order," *BusinessWeek*, October 13, 1997.

Page 81: "Many Europeans considered the merger ..." "WorldCom-MCI Merger: A Bad Omen for European Carriers?" *Information Society Trends*, November 10, 1997.

Page 81: "Ebbers insisted the merger was vital ..." Saroja Girishankar, "WorldCom Grabs for the Telecom Spotlight," *CommunicationsWeek*, June 30, 1997.

Page 82: "'It was truly the case ...'" Nancy Lottridge Anderson, CFA, "WorldCom and MCI: A Moral Merger?" *Mississippi Business Journal*, March 30, 1998.

Page 83: "'Hmmm ... Rev. Jackson ...'" Nancy Lottridge Anderson, CFA, "WorldCom and MCI: A Moral Merger?" *Mississippi Business Journal*, March 30, 1998.

Page 84: "'(Ebbers) had no interest ...'" George Gilder, *Telecosm: How Infinite Bandwidth Will Revolutionize Our World* (Free Press, 2000).

Page 85: "'I think the world changed today ...'" Peter Elstrom, "The New World Order," *BusinessWeek*, October 13, 1997.

Page 87: "'It became apparent ...'" Joseph McCafferty, "Scott Sullivan," *CFO*, September 1998.

Page 88: "'[CompuServe and AOL] had a mixture ...'" Linda Corman, "As Good as It Gets," *CFO*, November 1998.

Page 89: "He told *CFO* magazine ..." Linda Corman, "As Good as It Gets," *CFO*, November 1998.

Page 91: "'In this part of the country ...'" David Staples, "A Telecom Prophet's Fall from Grace," *Edmonton Journal*, July 28, 2002.

CHAPTER 7   The Honeymoon Is Over

Page 93: "Sidgmore was so pissed off . . ." Charles Haddad, "WorldCom Laying It on the Line," *BusinessWeek,* November 20, 2000.

Page 97: "Another rumor circulating . . ." People around town talked about both musical performances, but neither was confirmed. One or both could be urban legend.

Page 99: " 'We have a head start . . .' " Joseph Mccafferty, "Scott Sullivan," *CFO,* September 1998.

Page 99: " 'I liked Bernie . . .' " Jeremy M. Brosowsky, "Is Less More for Sidgmore?" *Business Forward,* December 2000.

Page 100: " 'Bernie has never liked Sidgmore . . .' " Charles Haddad, "WorldCom Laying It on the Line," *BusinessWeek,* November 20, 2000.

Page 100: " 'He's the brains . . .' " Charles Haddad, "WorldCom Laying It on the Line," *BusinessWeek,* November 20, 2000.

Page 101: " 'I think that was the beginning . . .' " Kevin Maney, "WorldCom Unraveled as Top Execs' Bond Crumbled," *USA Today,* June 28, 2002.

Page 102: " 'They were a great tag team . . .' " Jerry Mitchell, "Merger King Sullivan was Wall Street Darling before Collapse," *Clarion-Ledger,* June 28, 2002.

Page 102: "Ebbers invariably deferred . . ." Charles Haddad and Dean Faust, "WorldCom's Sorry Legacy," *BusinessWeek,* June 28, 2002.

Page 102: " 'They often seemed to be . . .' " Renae Merle, "Sullivan Rose by the Numbers," *Washington Post,* August 2, 2002.

Page 103: "When questioned by Philip L. Spartis . . ." Gretchen Morgenson, "IPO Plums for Telecom Execs Like WorldCom," *New York Times,* August 4, 2002.

Page 103: " 'If you were at headquarters . . .' " Gretchen Morgenson, "IPO Plums for Telecom Execs Like WorldCom," *New York Times,* August 4, 2002.

Page 104: " 'Scott said if we can do it . . .' " Gretchen Morgenson, "In a Broker's Notes, Trouble for Salomon," *New York Times,* September 22, 2002.

Page 104: " 'We spend so much dang time . . .' " Michael Meyer, "Bernie's Dream of WorldComination," *BusinessWeek,* October 18, 1999.

Page 105: " 'This damaged my standing . . .' " Brad Stone, "MCI: Meltdown and Misconnection," *Newsweek,* August 30, 1999.

Page 105: "'After the AT&T frame-relay ...'" www.cctec.com/maillists/nanog/historical/0005/msg00500.html.

Page 107: "WorldCom spokeswoman Barbara Gibson ..." Robert Schoenberger, "Registration Fuels Merger Buzz," *Clarion-Ledger,* May 26, 1999.

Page 110: "'Ebbers may in fact ...'" Buddy Bynum, "Spotlight of Public Scrutiny Falls on Ebbers," *Mississippi Business Journal,* November 17, 1997.

CHAPTER 8   The Courting of Sprint

Page 113: "In October 1999, Ebbers really sent ..." David Usborne, "Paper Tiger," *The Independent-London,* February 21, 2001.

Page 114: "'(Bernie) is the Ted Turner ...'" Reed Branson, "WorldCom's Ebbers Builds Mississippi Muscle," *Commercial-Appeal,* November 9, 1997.

Page 116: "'Bernie does a wonderful job ...'" Robert Schoenberger, "WorldCom: Downfall in 2000," *Clarion-Ledger,* August 10, 2002.

Page 117: "To retain Kmart as a customer ..." David Usborne, "Paper Tiger," *The Independent-London,* February 21, 2001.

Page 117: "Kinks in the regulatory system ..." Allan Sloan, "Behind the Phone Frenzy," *BusinessWeek,* October 18, 1999.

Page 117: "Analysts began criticizing ..." Dana Blankenhorn, "Familiar Lessons from WorldCom's Fall," *ClickZ,* June 23, 2000.

Page 117: "'(He) apologized for the lack of chairs. ...'" Nancy Lottridge Anderson, CFA, "WorldCom Wireless-ing Its Future with Deal," *Mississippi Business Journal,* May 8, 2000.

Page 119: "When the U.S. Department ..." Jade Boyd, "WorldCom, Sprint Call Off Merger," *InternetWeek,* July 13, 2000.

Page 120: "'The kiboshing of the Sprint merger was ...'" Kurt Eichenwald, "For WorldCom, Acquisitions Were behind ehind Its Rise and Fall," *New York Times,* August 8, 2002.

Page 120: "'That was not a smart thing to do ...'" Jade Boyd, "WorldCom, Sprint Call Off Merger," *InternetWeek,* July 13, 2000.

Page 120: "'We recognize that we ...'" *Financial Times,* October 26, 2000.

Page 121: "Andy Zmolek, manager of network architecture ..." Andy Zmolek, "Don't Skimp on Your Customer Service," *InternetWeek,* August 28, 2000.

Page 123: "'We dropped the ball.' . . ." Stephanie Mehta, "Can Bernie Bounce Back?" *Fortune,* January 2001.

Page 123: "'(Ebbers) disappointed me . . .'" Robert Schoenberger, "WorldCom: Downfall in 2000," *Clarion-Ledger,* August 10, 2002.

Page 124: "'Don't think of WorldCom . . .'" Kurt Eichenwald, "For WorldCom, Acquisitions Were behind Its Rise and Fall," *New York Times,* August 8, 2002.

Page 127: "'Bernie is running a $40 billion company . . .'" Charles Haddad, "Woe Is WorldCom," *BusinessWeek,* May 6, 2002.

Page 128: "'How could this place stay . . .'" Kevin Maney, "WorldCom Unraveled as Top Execs' Bond Crumbled," *USA Today,* June 28, 2002.

Page 128: "'There seems to be no regard . . .'" Jonathan Krim, "Fast and Loose at WorldCom," *Washington Post,* August 29, 2002.

Page 130: "In reply, company spokesperson Ginger Fitzgerald . . ." Steve Allen's MCI Shareholders Address, 1999.

Page 130: "'There was a time when . . .'" Fritz Capp, "Wrestling Fans against Censorship," *Straight Shooting,* June 16, 2000.

Page 130: "'I am much more a stockholder . . .'" Bernie Ebbers, "I May Have to Fire Myself," *Fortune,* January 22, 2001.

Page 131: "'We came up with the idea . . .'" Jeremy M. Brosowsky, "Is Less More for Sidgmore?" *Business Forward,* December 2000.

Page 131: "'My role at WorldCom has changed . . .'" Jeremy M. Brosowsky, "Is Less More for Sidgmore?" *Business Forward,* December 2000.

Page 132: "'Wow! I had no idea . . .'" Jonathan Krim, "Fast and Loose at WorldCom," *Washington Post,* August 29, 2002.

Page 133: "'My positions at WorldCom were reflective . . .'" Keith Epstein, "Washington Techway Live," *Washington Post,* July 11, 2002.

CHAPTER 9   Hockey, Pals, and the Farm

Page 138: "Holloway welcomed Byrd . . ." Elizabeth Kirkland, "Jackson's Bandits Staying in the Capital City," *Mississippi Business Journal,* September 30, 2002.

Page 141: "In November 2002 . . ." Jessica Sommar, "Not Chicken Feed," *New York Post,* November 13, 2002.

Page 142: "'New layout, carefully landscaped . . .'" www.golfreview .com.

Page 145: "'He was very down-to-earth . . .'" Karen Kaplan, "Unlikely Pair at Center of Tempest," *Los Angeles Times,* June 27, 2002.

CHAPTER 10   Pink Slipped

Page 150: "'All that makes me sick.' . . ." Kate Gerwig, "No Worrying over Dress Code," *InternetWeek,* December 7, 1998.

Page 153: "Kenneth Vianale of Milberg Weiss Bershad . . ." Neil Weinberg, "Asleep at the Switch," *Forbes,* July 22, 2002.

Page 155: "'Tracking stocks . . . allow the parent company . . .'" "Having It All with WCOM and MCIT," *Mississippi Business Journal,* June 18, 2001.

Page 156: "However, WorldCom's place . . ." Table: "How World-Com Stacks Up," *BusinessWeek,* May 6, 2002.

Page 159: "'Tying up so much of your financial life . . .'" Tim Padgett, "The Rise and Fall of Bernie Ebbers, *Time,* May 13, 2002.

Page 159: "'(Bernie) seemed paralyzed . . .'" Christopher Stern, "Shake-Up Sought at WorldCom," *Washington Post,* August 17, 2002.

Page 161: "'He could only buy . . .'" Oliver Burkeman, "South Rallies to Wall Street's Enemy No. 1," *The Guardian,* June 28, 2002.

Page 162: "'Success was so sweet . . .'" Orley Hood, "You are Bernie Ebbers . . . Now What?" *Clarion-Ledger,* June 28, 2002.

CHAPTER 11   The Worst Job in Corporate America

Page 163: "When I first took this job . . ." Kevin Maney, "WorldCom Unraveled as Top Execs' Bond Crumbled," *USA Today,* June 28, 2002.

Page 165: "'Where do I sign . . .'" Jonathan Krim, "Fast and Loose at WorldCom," *Washington Post,* August 29, 2002.

Page 166: "A capital expense audit . . ." Gayle Reaves, "Accounting for Anguish," *Fort Worth Weekly,* May 16, 2002.

Page 166: "'Before, no one wanted to listen . . .'" Dan Malone, "Well-Blown Whistle," *Fort Worth Weekly,* September 5, 2002.

Page 168: "Judy O'Neal Gressett . . ." Clay Harden, "Auditor Who Blew the Whistle Praised," *Clarion-Ledger,* July 6, 2002.

Page 169: "She added the information . . ." Susan Pulliam and Deborah Solomon, "How Three Unlikely Sleuths Discovered Fraud at WorldCom," *Wall Street Journal,* October 30, 2002.

Page 169: "When Morse muttered . . ." Susan Pulliam and Deborah Solomon, "How Three Unlikely Sleuths Discovered Fraud at World-Com," *Wall Street Journal,* October 30, 2002.

Page 169: "Myers sent Cooper a personal note . . ." Jonathan Krim, "Fast and Loose at WorldCom," *Washington Post,* August 29, 2002.

Page 177: "Even WorldCom employees . . ." Daniel Kadlec, "World-Com," *Time,* July 8, 2002.

CHAPTER 12 That Dog Don't Hunt

Page 181: "We think Bernie Ebbers . . ." Charles Haddad, "What Did Bernie Know?" *BusinessWeek,* September 23, 2002.

Page 183: "Ebbers was threatened with contempt . . ." Dan Carney, "His Heart Bleeds for Fat Cats," *BusinessWeek,* September 23, 2002.

Page 183: " 'We think Bernie Ebbers . . .' " Charles Haddad, "What Did Bernie Know?" *BusinessWeek,* September 23, 2002.

Page 184: " 'The reason he left the firm . . .' " Noelle Knox, "CEO of Salomon Defends Grubman," *USA Today,* August 21, 2002.

Page 185: " 'About two months ago . . .' " Keith Epstein, "Washington Techway Live," *Washington Post,* July 11, 2002.

Page 186: "*BusinessWeek* speculated that James Q. Crowe . . ." Joseph Weber, "Going Fishing," *BusinessWeek,* August 26, 2002.

Page 186: " 'We have laid out our strategic plan . . .' " Keith Epstein, "Washington Techway Live," *Washington Post,* July 11, 2002.

Page 188: " 'I just want you to know . . .' " Nicole Harris, "World-Com Deals Mental Blow to Business-Needy Mississippi," *Wall Street Journal,* July 1, 2002.

Page 188: "Journalists pounced on Ebbers' use . . ." "Somebody Has to Pay," *Cape Cod Times,* July 3, 2002.

Page 188: " 'Most people who take the Fifth Amendment . . .' " Arnold Lindsay, "Tactic Raises Questions," *Clarion-Ledger,* July 9, 2002.

Page 189: " 'Here in sweltering Mississippi . . .' " David Staples, "A Telecom Prophet's Fall from Grace," *Edmonton Journal,* July 28, 2002.

Page 189: "Even though Ebbers was under intense scrutiny . . ." Jayne O'Donnell, "Ebbers Acts as if Nothing Is Amiss," *USA Today,* September 19, 2002.

Page 190: " 'Ebbers was our financial savior.' . . ." Wyatt Emmerich, "Let's Look at the Truth," *Delta Business Journal,* August 2002.

Page 190: " 'People that have problems admitting . . .' " Seth Schiesel, "The Re-engineering of Bernie Ebbers," *New York Times,* April 27, 1998.

Page 190: " 'WorldCom wasn't operated at all . . .' " Kurt Eichenwald, "For WorldCom, Acquisitions Were behind Its Rise and Fall," *New York Times,* August 8, 2002.

CHAPTER 13 Hoodwinked

Page 193: "Business was much worse than we knew . . ." Renae Merle, "Sullivan Rose by the Numbers," *Washington Post,* August 2, 2002.

Page 193: " 'When you file Chapter 11 . . .' " Robert Schoenberger, "Where Will the Road Lead?" *Clarion-Ledger,* September 15, 2002.

Page 195: " 'It's like a virus that gets spread . . .' " Jim Krane, "Industry Awaits WorldCom Collapse," *Washington Post,* July 21, 2002.

Page 197: " 'It is more appropriate to liquidate WorldCom . . .' " J. Gregory Sidak, "The Failure of Good Intentions: The Collapse of American Telecommunications after Six Years of Deregulation," 2002; Beesley Lecture on Regulation, The Royal Society of Arts, London, October 1, 2002.

Page 197: " 'That would be a disaster . . .' " Jim Krane, "Industry Awaits WorldCom Collapse," *Washington Post,* July 21, 2002.

Page 199: "Bobbitt, who had revealed . . ." Charles Haddad, "How Ebbers Kept the Board in His Pocket," *BusinessWeek,* October 14, 2002.

Page 202: "Jacob Frenkel, a former senior counsel . . ." Kevin Maney, "Latest Charges Leave WorldCom in Limbo," *USA Today,* August 2, 2002.

Page 203: "Yates told U.S. Magistrate Judge Andrew Peck . . ." Sentencing hearing is January 9, 2003.

Page 203: " 'This isn't going to be a ripple . . .' " Jim Krane, "Industry Awaits WorldCom Collapse," *Washington Post,* July 21, 2002.

Page 204: " 'I have no confidence . . .' " John Porretto, "Some Question Sidgmore's Suitability in Bankruptcy," Associated Press, July 22, 2002.

Page 204: "Politically, it spurred a wave of reform . . ." The loss in total market value was calculated from the peak stock price— $64.50 on June 21, 1999—to the date of the bankruptcy filing.

CHAPTER 14   Infectious Greed

Page 207: "[WorldCom's troubles are] creating . . ." Charles Haddad, "WorldCom's Sorry Legacy," *BusinessWeek,* June 28, 2002.

Page 207: "'The turn of the century . . .'" June 23, 2002.

Page 208: "'There were different factions.' . . ." Rick Wartzman, "Déjà vu," *Wall Street Journal,* May 1, 2002.

Page 210: "'Andersen became a firm . . .'" David Strahan, producer, "No Accounting for Greed," BBC, *The Money Program,* 2002.

Page 210: "'I paid the price.' . . ." John A. Byrne, "Learning from Mistakes," *BusinessWeek,* August 12, 2002.

Page 211: "When second-quarter 2002 . . ." Charles Haddad, "WorldCom's Sorry Legacy," *BusinessWeek,* June 28, 2002.

CHAPTER 15   Disconnected

Page 213: "As a manager, I've been laying off people . . ." Martin Kady II, "Ex-WorldCom Workers Unite, Fight Back," *Washington Business Journal,* August 12, 2002.

Page 214: "'You move to a new area . . .'" Martin Kady II, "Ex-WorldCom Workers Unite, Fight Back," *Washington Business Journal,* August 12, 2002.

Page 215: "'It was an opportunity of a lifetime . . .'" Robert Schoenberger, "Telecom Workers Pose for *Playboy,*" *Clarion-Ledger,* October 25, 2002.

Page 215: "'It was not just MCI or UUNET versus WorldCom . . .'" Andrew Backover and Michelle Kessler, "WorldCom Sees Divisions Deeper," *USA Today,* August 28, 2002.

Page 216: "'From the get-go, I thought WorldCom . . .'" John Porretto, "Some Question Sidgmore's Suitability in Bankruptcy," Associated Press, July 22, 2002.

ACKNOWLEDGMENTS

D isconnected: Deceit and Betrayal at WorldCom would not have been possible without the help of my husband, Pepper Jeter, who slept very little during the research phase of this book. When he wasn't making countless phone calls, scouring the Internet, tracking down elusive information, poring over documents, proofreading, and acting as IT guru, he was running the errands required of a family of six so I could work uninterrupted. During challenging times, my dad Martin Mooney's advice, "Keep moving," along with the support of my mother, Dimple, brother, John, and children, Stephanie, Betsy, Matthew, and Josh, kept us on the right track.

This book would never have happened without the blessings of *Mississippi Business Journal* publisher Joe Jones and editor Jim Laird, who gave me free rein on writing about WorldCom. Their unconditional support and continued involvement were invaluable. So was the hospitality of Joe and Debra Jones, whose country home is a wonderful haven.

Thanks to Ken Stribling, Stacey Wall, and Bill Brame, who planted the seeds of writing a book about WorldCom, and to Martin Hegwood, Jimmy Vines, and Debra Englander, for making it happen. Thanks to those who were not directly involved with WorldCom—Paul and Barbara Michaelove, Evelynn Stewart, and Carley Davis—but made life easier for us in a significant way.

I have been careful to tell the story only as an observer and not to make judgments. Did Bernie do it? I don't know. Short of a confession, an unknown paper trail, or a betrayal by those close to him, we may never know the truth about his involvement.

And no, I never had enough spare money to purchase WorldCom stock. When the stock was rising, it was a regret. When it tanked, it was a blessing.

L. J.

Lynne Jeter is an award-winning journalist who has written for some of the nation's top magazines and newspapers and international publications. She began her writing career in high school as a newspaper and yearbook editor in Seminary, Mississippi, a Mayberry-type village located approximately 30 miles from Hattiesburg, where WorldCom was birthed. In 1984, Jeter graduated from the University of Southern Mississippi, located in the heart of Hattiesburg. Many of her classmates later became intertwined with the WorldCom culture.

Jeter has been a regular contributing writer and the primary WorldCom reporter for the *Mississippi Business Journal,* the only statewide business publication, and a regular contributing reporter for the *Clarion-Ledger,* the state's largest daily newspaper. She has written about business and industry for various regional and national business publications, magazines, journals, and news organizations, including Clear Channel Communications and Reuters/Bridge News Service. Jeter has won awards for news reporting, feature writing, series planning, and editing, and was named SBA Small Business Journalist of the Year for Mississippi in 1999. In 2002, she participated in the prestigious Fellowship Program for Professional Journalists at the University of Mississippi. She lives in Asheville, North Carolina, with her husband and children.